NĀGĀRJUNA'S

REFUTATION OF LOGIC (NYĀYA)

VAIDALYAPRAKARAṆA

BUDDHIST TRADITION SERIES

Edited by
ALEX WAYMAN

VOLUME 24

NĀGĀRJUNA'S REFUTATION OF LOGIC (NYĀYA)

VAIDALYAPRAKARAṆA

ŹIB MO RNAM PAR ḤTHAG PA
ŹES BYA BAḤI RAB TU BYED PA

Edition of the Tibetan Text, English Translation and Commentary, with Introduction and Notes

FERNANDO TOLA
CARMEN DRAGONETTI

MOTILAL BANARSIDASS PUBLISHERS
PRIVATE LIMITED • DELHI

First Edition: Delhi, 1995
Reprint: Delhi, 2004

ISBN: 81-208-0920-3

MOTILAL BANARSIDASS
41 U.A. Bungalow Road, Jawahar Nagar, Delhi 110 007
8 Mahalaxmi Chamber, 22 Bhulabhai Desai Road, Mumbai 400 026
236, 9th Main III Block, Jayanagar, Bangalore 560 011
120 Royapettah High Road, Mylapore, Chennai 600 004
Sanas Plaza, 1302 Baji Rao Road, Pune 411 002
8 Camac Street, Kolkata 700 017
Ashok Rajpath, Patna 800 004
Chowk, Varanasi 221 001

Printed in India
BY JAINENDRA PRAKASH JAIN AT SHRI JAINENDRA PRESS,
A-45 NARAINA, PHASE-I, NEW DELHI 110 028
AND PUBLISHED BY NARENDRA PRAKASH JAIN FOR
MOTILAL BANARSIDASS PUBLISHERS PRIVATE LIMITED,
BUNGALOW ROAD, DELHI 110 007

To
Dr. Richard A. Gard
Pioneer of the Mādhyamika Studies in America,
President of The Institute for Advanced Studies of World Religions,
with our gratitude.

F.T. and C.D.

FOREWORD

The *Vaidalyaprakaraṇa* is certainly an important work, whether or not Nāgārjuna is its actual author. One should concede that the *Vaidalya's* refutation of Nyāya logical categories is consistent with Nāgārjuna's own debunking style. The edition, translation, and explanation of this work by Fernando Tola and Carmen Dragonetti critically examine the authorship attribution. The undersigned has always had doubts about Nāgārjuna's authorship of this treatise. This is not just because the known Mādhyamika commentators do not cite it, but, also because Nāgārjuna in his other authentic works deals with Buddhist categories: he appears to have Buddhist Abhidharma realism as his adversary.

But, doubts do not amount to certitude. After reading this book by Tola and Dragonetti, the reader should have a solid basis to decide on the authorship. And whether or not Nāgārjuna is the author, it is wonderful to have this important work in the present exacting form for its own content.

Alex Wayman

ACKNOWLEDGEMENTS

We thank the Lawrence Research Foundation for having granted both of us a fellowship to complete our work on *V* in The Institute for Advanced Studies of World Religions (IASWR), State University of New York at Stony Brook; Dr. Chia Theng Shen, Chairman of the Board of Trustees; Dr. Richard A. Gard, President of the Institute; the Staff of the Institute: Estelle Auerbach, Margaret Chen, James Fowler, Lorraine Frey, Ugen Gombo, Geeta Shrestha, Carol Simensen, Michele Wang and Lena Yang, for their friendliness and collaboration during our stay at Stony Brook, U.S.A. And, last but not least, we thank our daughters Eleonora and Florencia who with their love and cleverness during our absence from home allowed us to have the necessary peace of mind to carry out our work.

Stony Brook, U.S.A.
April 1989

F. Tola
C. Dragonetti

ACKNOWLEDGEMENTS

CONTENTS

INTRODUCTION

INTRODUCTION

The Text

In the Tibetan Buddhist Canon is found the translation of a treatise attributed to Klu sgrub = Nāgārjuna, which bears the following title:

In Tibetan: *Źib mo rnam par ḥthag pa źes bya baḥi rab tu byed pa* (D, P, C, N)

In Sanskrit: *Vaidalyanāmaprakaraṇa* (D, P, C, N)

This treatise comprises 73 Sūtras and their commentary.

In the Tibetan Canon is found likewise a separate translation of only the Sūtras (73) attributed also to Klu sgrub = Nāgārjuna, under the title:
In Tibetan: *Źib mo rnam par ḥthag pa źes bya baḥi mdo* (D, P, C, N)
In Sanskrit: *Vaidalyasūtranāma* (D, P, C, N)

The bibliographical references, in the four principal editions of the Tibetan Canon, are for the Treatise (*Prakaraṇa*)

D: Dbu ma, tsa ff. 99 b 1-110 a 4 (*Tōhoku* 3830)

C: Dbu ma, tsa ff. 99 a 7-109 a 7 (*Microfiche ed. IASWR*, LMpj 020, 018 4/10)

P: Dbu ma, tsa ff. 114 a 8-126 a 5 (Vol. 95, *Catalogue* 5230)

N: Dbu ma, tsa ff. 104 b 7-116 b 5 (*Comparative List* 3221)

and for the *Sūtras*:

D: Dbu ma, tsa ff. 22 b 6-24 a 6 (*Tōhoku* 3826)

C. Dbu ma, tsa ff. 22 b 6-24 a 6 (*Microfiche ed. IASWR*, LMpj 020, 018 1/10)

P: Dbu ma, tsa ff. 25 a 7-27 a 4 (Vol. 95, *Catalogue* 5226)

N: Dbu ma, tsa ff. 22 b-24 a (*Comparative List* 3217)

The translators of the *Prakaraṇa* were, according to D and C: the *paṇḍita* Jayānanda of Kashmir (P and N have Jayāntata which probably is a mistake for Jayānanda) and the *lotsāba* Mdo-sde ḥbar from Khu.[1] These translators lived in the second half of the eleventh century and beginning of the twelfth century.[2] The translators of the *Sūtras* were, according to D, P, C and N, the *paṇḍita* Ananta from Kashmir and the *lotsāba* Grags-ḥbyor śes-rab. Probably Ananta = Ānanda, which could be an abbreviation of Jayānanda. Grags-ḥbyor śes-rab lived also in the second half of the eleventh century and beginning of the twelfth century.[3]

The differences among the four editions (D P C N) and between D and DD in relation to both texts are in general slight, with the exception of some cases, as for instance, in Sections XLI and XLVIII, where D and C have omitted part of the text which is present in P and N.

The Sanskrit originals of both texts have not come to us. There is not a Chinese translation of them.

The Title of V

We think that the word *vaidalya*, which serves as title for the Treatise of Nāgārjuna, comes from *vi-DAL*.[4] *Vi-DAL*, according to Böhtlingk and Roth, *Sanskrit-Wörterbuch* III, p. 543 *sub* DAL, has as one of its meanings: 'aufreissen', 'zerreissen', *i.e.* 'to tear to pieces', 'to dismember'. So *vaidalya* may mean 'tearing'. This title agrees with the contents of the Treatise whose aim is to destroy the Nyāya's categories. This interpretation is corroborated by the title given by the Tibetan translation to the Treatise: *Źib mo rnam par ḥthag pa źes bya baḥi rab tu byed pa. Źib mo rnam par ḥthag pa* means 'the minutely grinding'. Asaṅga's *Abhidharmasamuccaya*, p. 79 (ed. Pradhan) explains why *vaipulyam* is called *vaidalyam* saying: *sarvāvaraṇavidalanataḥ*: 'because the tearing (or rending asunder or splitting) of all the obstacles'. In Japan this Treatise is known under the names of *Kōharon* and *Saiharon*, which mean 'to crush', 'to pulverize'.[5]

Aim and Contents of V

This treatise is a polemical one, directed against the Naiyāyikas. Its aim is to demonstrate the logical impossibility of the existence of all the Nyāya categories or *padārthas* as enumerated and dealt with in Gautama's *Nyāyasūtras* and Vātsyāyana's *Bhāṣya* thereof.

The scheme of the work is the following one:

Section	*I*	:	Introductory stanza.
Sections	*II-XX*	:	Rejection of the *Pramāṇa* and *Prameya*.
Sections	*XXI-XXIII*	:	Rejection of *Saṃśaya*.
Section	*XXIV*	:	Rejection of *Prayojana*.
Sections	*XXV-XXXI*	:	Rejection of *Dṛṣṭānta*.
Section	*XXXII*	:	Rejection of *Siddhānta*.
Sections	*XXXIII-XLIX*	:	Rejection of *Avayavas*.
Section	*L*	:	Rejection of *Tarka*.
Section	*LI*	:	Rejection of *Nirṇaya*.
Sections	*LII-LVI*	:	Rejection of *Vāda*.
Section	*LVII*	:	Rejection of *Jalpa* and *Vitaṇḍā*.
Sections	*LVIII-LXVII*	:	Rejection of *Hetvābhāsa*.
Section	*LXVIII*	:	Rejection of *Chala*.
Section	*LXIX*	:	Rejection of *Jāti*.
Sections	*LXX-LXXII*	:	Rejection of *Nigrahasthānas*.
Section	*LXXIII*	:	Conclusion.

The Position of V in the History of Indian Philosophy

The *V* dedicates Sections II-XX to the refutation of the *pramāṇas* as means of knowledge. Therefore it belongs to the Indian philosophical tradition which did not admit the *pramāṇas* as valid means of knowledge and which thereby could be called the 'agnostic tradition'. The Mādhyamika school belonged to this tradition. The thesis of the non-validity of the *pramāṇas* is developed in *VV*,[6] attributed to Nāgārjuna, appears in several passages of Nāgārjuna's works and very probably the polemic found in *NS* 2, 1, 8-20 against the non-acceptance of the *pramāṇas* is directed against the Mādhyamikas.[7] To this same tradition belong also the Materialists[8] (*bārhaspatyas, cārvakas, lokāyatas*), among whom some admitted as means of valid knowledge only the perception and some not even the perception; Jayarāśi Bhaṭṭa (eighth century A.D.), the author of *Tattvopaplavasiṃha*,[9] who rejected all the means of valid knowledge; Śrīharṣa (twelfth century A.D.), the author of *Khaṇḍana-khaṇḍakhādya*[10] who adopts the same position as Jayarāśi, although starting from different philosophical ground.

The V and the Vāda Tradition

The *V* is also connected with the Indian *Vāda* tradition. As Oberhammer says, 'Ein Beitrag zu den Vāda-Traditionen Indiens', p. 63, the Indian Logic began with the reflexion on the rules to which a scientific debate is submitted and this stage of development of Indian Logic presents itself in the handbooks of *Vāda*, in which these rules are collected for practical uses and very few of which have come to us. Among these *Vāda* manuals there are the *Vāda* sections of the *Carakasaṃhitā*,[11] the *Fang pien hsin lun* = *Upāyahṛdaya* = *Prayogasāra* (*U*),[12] the *Ju shih lun* = *Tarkaśāstra* (*TŚ*),[13] the *Vāda* texts contained in the works of Asaṅga.[14] The Books I and V of Gautama's *Nyāyasūtras* (*NS*) incorporated much material taken from the *Vāda* tradition.[15] Together with these handbooks should be mentioned the *Tantrayuktis*,[16] the lists of technical terms of Logic found in the *Carakasaṃhitā*,[17] the *Suśrutasaṃhitā*[18] and Kauṭilya's *Arthaśāstra*.[19]

The *V* attacks the *padārthas*, which were admitted by the *Vāda* tradition and constituted its conceptual framework, utilizes the arguments (many times of a sophistical nature) that the *Vāda* tradition analyzes and handles, and in a general way is immersed in the dialectical atmosphere that characterizes that tradition, although its aim is to show the groundlessness of the dialectic.

The V as a Buddhist Work

The *V* in the form it presents itself now can be considered as a Buddhist work. This Buddhist origin can be affirmed taking into consideration some parts of it, as for instance (1) the commentary of the introductory stanza which refers to the *śūnyatāvādins* in a way that indicates that the treatise's author is one of them, (2) the form it mentions the Hindu gods and authors in Section IX, (3) the non-acceptance of the whole (*avayavin*) which is characteristic of Buddhist thought (Sections XXXIII-XL), (4) the denial of the existence of names, (5) the identification of *nirvāṇa* and liberation in the last Section, and (6) the many points of contact the treatise presents with other Buddhist texts or texts considered by tradition as Buddhist, such as *ŚŚ* attributed to Āryadeva,[20] *U* attributed to Nāgārjuna, the *TŚ* attributed to Vasubandhu,[21] the *VV* attributed to Nāgārjuna, the *MMK*[22] of Nāgārjuna.

The reasons adduced under points 1, 4, 5 and 6, together with the facts that the agnostic position was a characteristic of the Mādhyamika school, and that the *V* has been traditionally attributed to Nāgārjuna—all this allows us to maintain that *V* is a *Mādhyamika* treatise.

In Relation to the Authorship of V

A most important problem in regard to *V* is that of its authorship, because the solution of this problem can throw some light in relation to the date of its composition. And on the date of composition of *V* depends the idea we can have of the relation of *V* and the Nyāya school. We have some doubts concerning the attribution of *V* to Nāgārjuna grounded on the facts and remarks that follow:

1. The colophons of the Tibetan translations (eleventh-twelfth centuries) of the *VSūtra* and of the *VPrakaraṇa* put them under the name of *Klu sgrub* (= Nāgārjuna).

2. The *Madhyamakaśāstrastuti*[23] stanza 10, attributed to Candrakīrti (*c.* 600-650 A.D.), enumerates the *Vidalā* among the works written by Nāgārjuna.

3. Bhavya (?),[24] *Madhyamakaratnapradīpa* 264, *b*, 5-6 (*Sde-dge* edition) mentions the *V* together with other works of Nāgārjuna: *MMK*, *VV*, *Y*, *Śū*.

4. Buston (fourteenth century), *History of Buddhism* (*Chos ḥbyung*) I, pp. 50-51 (Obermiller's translation) includes the *V* among the six main treatises of Nāgārjuna.

5. Tāranātha (end of sixteenth century–beginning of seventeenth), in his *History of Buddhism in India*, p. 57, ll.3-4, Schiefner's edition (= p. 71 Schiefner's translation) refers to the 'five treatises on Nyāya' (rigs paḥi tshogs lṅa, yukti corpus, Ruegg, *The Literature of the Madhyamaka School*, p. 8). According to Schiefner, p. 302 of his translation of Tāranātha, with that Tibetan expression, the following works are referred to: *MMK*, *Y*, *Śū*, *VV* and *V*.

Remarks to points 1-5. The works under 2-5 do not indicate if they refer to the *VSūtra* or *VPrakaraṇa* or to both. In relation to the *Madhyamakaśāstrastuti* Ruegg, *op. cit.*, p. 8, thinks it refers to both.

We think that the problem of authenticity must be solved separately for each of both works.

All the testimonies (1-5) in favour of the authenticity of *V* are separated from Nāgārjuna (second century) by a good number of centuries. This fact weakens the credibility of these testimonies.

6. Another argument is based on the style and tenets of *V*, which, as Lindtner (*Nagarjuniana*, p. 87) thinks, 'would indicate the same author as for *Vigrahavyāvartanī*', generally considered a work by Nāgārjuna.

An argument in favour of the authenticity based on the style and tenets of the work is not decisive by itself as any person belonging to the Mādhyamika school could have written in the style of the Master and expressed and defended his same tenets. We indicate, under points 26 and 27, two characteristics of the style of the treatise that do not seem to belong to the works that can undoubtedly be attributed to Nāgārjuna.

7. Lindtner, *Nagarjuniana*, p. 87, expresses that he has 'never noticed any quotation of the *Vaidalyaprakaraṇa*'. It would be strange that, if the *V* were really a work of Nāgārjuna, it has not been quoted by any of his disciples and followers.

8. The commentary *ad* 7, 8, 9, 12, 16, 18, 33, 35, 37, 38, 39, 51, 55, 65 and 69 presents points of contact with the *ŚŚ*; *ad* 7, 9, 12, 30, 48 and 67 with the *TŚ*; and *ad* 7 and 12 with the *U*. See our notes to the translation.

The *ŚŚ* is commonly attributed to Āryadeva, but this attribution is not very sure.[25] As for the *TŚ* and the *U*, they are sometimes attributed to Vasubandhu and Nāgārjuna respectively, but, in neither case, there are definite arguments to support any of these views.[26] Likewise the date of composition of these three works cannot be fixed with certainty.

9. There are also points of contact between the commentary *ad* 2, 4, 5, 6, 7, 8, 11, 12, 13, and 14 and the *VV*,[27] and between the commentary *ad* 4, 6, 7, 8, 11, 65, 67, and 69 and the *MMK*. See our notes to the translation.

Remarks on points 8-9. In relation to the points of contact between, on one side, the *V* commentary and, on the other side, *ŚŚ*, *TŚ*, *U*, we cannot decide whether the commentary draws ideas from the other three texts (*i.e.* depends on them) or *vice versa*: they draw ideas from the commentary (*i.e.* depend on it) or all the four texts draw ideas from the *Vāda* tradition (*i.e.* depend on this tradition), since, we have no other elements to help us to take a decision regarding this dependence.

Something similar is to be said in relation to the dependence among the *V* commentary, *VV* and *MMK*.

10. It cannot be doubted that *V* has in view, in order to criticize them, some tenets and passages of *NS*:

V	*NS*
I	1, 1, 1
IX	1, 1, 25
XVII	reference to Nyāya criterion of validity of knowledge
XVIII	1, 1, 5
XX	1, 1, 9
XXII	1, 1, 23
XXIV	1, 1, 24
XXVIII-XXX	1, 1, 25 and 1, 1, 34-35
XXXIII	1, 1, 32
XXXVIII	1, 2, 8
XL	1, 1, 33
XLI	1, 1, 34-35
XLVII	3, 1, 1-30
L	1, 1, 40
LI	1, 1, 41
LII	1, 2, 1
LIII	2, 1, 53 (?)
LIII	1, 1, 1
LIII	reference to Nyāya realism
LIV	2, 1, 56 (?)
LVII	1, 2, 1
LVIII	1, 2, 4-9
LIV-LVI	1, 2, 5
LXIII	1, 1, 34
LXV	1, 2, 9
LXVIII	1, 2, 10-17
LXIX	1, 2, 18 and 20
LXX	5, 2, 14-16

See our notes to the translation.

11. We can also be sure that, at its turn, *NS* criticizes some thesis and arguments that are found in *V*:

NS	*V*
2, 1, 16-19	II-VI
5, 1, 7-8	VII-VIII
2, 1, 8-11 and 5, 1, 18	XII
2, 1, 44	XXIII-XXXI
4, 2, 8	XXXIII
2, 1, 53 (?)	LII
2, 1, 55	LIII
2, 1, 56	LIV

See our notes to the translation.

Remarks on points 10-11. This mutual criticism between the *NS* and the *V* must not surprise us. Owing to the compilatory nature of *NS*, it is possible that some tenets of the oldest parts of the *NS* (*adhyāyas* I and V of predominantly *Vāda* inspiration) were criticized by *V* and, at its turn, *V* was criticized by the earliest parts of *NS* (*adhyāyas* II-IV of predominantly polemical inspiration).

If the dates of the oldest parts (*adhyāyas* I and V) and of the latest parts (*adhyāyas* II-IV) could be fixed with certainty, the first date would give us a *terminus post quem* and the second date, a *terminus ante quem* for *V*. The *V* would have to be located between both dates. But unfortunately the dates of these different parts and of the compilation, and therefore of the *NS* as a whole have not, yet, been established in a sure way.[28]

But, we must also take into account that it is possible that some similar ideas in *V* and in *NS* are common stock ideas of the *Vāda* tradition from which both *V* and *NS* could have taken them.

12. *V* seems to have in mind also Vātsyāyana's *Bh ad NS*:

V	*NSBh*
V	Introduction
XXII	*ad* 1, 1, 23
XXIII	Introduction
L	*ad* 1, 1, 40
LI-LXI	*ad* 1, 2, 5
LIX	*ad* 1, 2, 18

See our notes to the translation.

13. Vātsyāyana in his *Bh ad NS* refutes some tenets and arguments that appear in V:

NSBh	*V*
ad 2, 1, 16-20	II-VI
ad 5, 1, 7-8	VII-VIII
ad 2, 1, 8-18 and 5, 1, 18	XII
ad 2, 1, 44-45	XXVIII-XXXI
ad 4, 2, 8	XXXIII

See our notes to the translation.

Remarks on points 12-13. But, we cannot say with certainty that Vātsyāyana had in mind the *V*, since the tenets and arguments he refutes were common heritage of the Madhyamaka school and/or of the *Vāda* tradition and/or of the agnostic tradition. Anyhow, if it is accepted that the criticism of Vātsyāyana is directed against *V*, that would give us only a *terminus ante quem* (± 350-450 A.D.: date of Vātsyāyana) for *V*: *V* could be located any time before that *terminus.* Likewise, it cannot be affirmed with certainty that *V* had in mind Vātsyāyana's *Bh*, since many of the *Bhāṣya*'s ideas may be ideas that belong to the previous *Vāda* tradition, or to pre-classical Nyāya.

14. In Section IX, the *V* mentions 'Māṭhara' together with 'Kapila'. Kapila is considered by the Indian tradition as the founder of the Sāṃkhya system, 'but modern scholars are unanimous in considering him also a mythological being'.[29] As regards Māṭhara, Indian tradition regards him as the author of the *Maṭharavṛtti.* Belvalkar, who discovered the *Māṭharavṛtti*, thought that this *vṛtti* was the oldest commentary of the *Sāṃkhyakārikā*, that it was the original of Paramārtha's (sixth century) Chinese commentary, and that as such it was an old text. But this opinion has been rejected and now it is admitted that the *Māṭharavṛtti* is a very late text[30] (*c.* 1000 A.D.). So, owing to his late chronological location, Māṭharā, author of the *Māṭharavṛtti*, has nothing to do with *V*. But, the fact that this *Vṛtti* has to be located in a late period does not mean that Māṭhara is also a late name and that there was not some old author (and even a Sāṃkhya author) called 'Māṭhara'. And in fact in

the *Anuyogadvārasūtra*, a Jain work of the fifth century A.D., there is reference to a text called *Māṭharabhāṣya*.[31] But, anyhow, as there is not more precise information regarding this *bhāṣya* and its author, the name Māṭhara does not throw any light on the problem of the authorship and date of *V*.

15. In *V*, Section LV, we find the quotation of three stanzas containing synonyms of the Sanskrit words '*go*', '*hari*', and '*Nārāyaṇa*'. The two first stanzas present great similarity with two stanzas, III, 3, 25 and III, 3, 175 *c-d*, of the *Amarakośa*, but also differences. According to Indian tradition, Amarasiṃha the author of the *Amarakośa* lived in the sixth century A.D.[32] One of these stanzas is a faithful translation of a stanza quoted in *Abhidharmakośa ad* II, 47 (p. 81 Pradhan ed.), which presents also a great similarity with *Amarakośa*'s corresponding text, but also differences. So, we do not think that the two stanzas quoted by *V* come from the *Amarakośa*. These two stanzas, as well as that one quoted by the *Abhidharmakośa*, have been taken from another work which is still to be located. Until then, the presence of these stanzas in *V* does not help us to decide about its date.

16. In Sections XLVIII, XLIX and LXIV of *V* is expressed the idea of the gradual coming forth of the words and sentences that is also found in Bhartṛhari, *Vākyapadīya* II, 19.[33] Bhartṛhari can be located around 450-510 A.D. (cf. Subrahmania Iyer, *Bhartṛhari*, p. 2).

If we could accept that, *V* has references to Bhartṛhari's doctrine of the graduality, then we would have to accept that *V* was composed after 450-510 A.D.

17. In Section XVIII of *V* we have an argument against the possibility of an external object being the *prameya* of a cognitive act. It is an epistemological argument which reminds us the arguments adduced by Yogācāra authors, as Vasubandhu (fourth century A.D.) (*Viṃśatikā*) and Dignāga (fifth century A.D.) (*Ālambanaparīkṣā*) against the possibility of an external object that could function as a *prameya*.

18. The argument adduced in Section II of the *V* affirming the confusion of *pramāṇa* and *prameya* reminds the *sahopalambha* argument of the Yogācāras in favour of their thesis of the sole existence of consciousness. The *pramāṇa* and the *prameya* are never given separately.

Remarks on points 17-18. If it is accepted that the Idealistic school inspired the arguments of *V*, then we would have to locate it after the appearance of the Yogācāra school more or less in 350 A.D.

19. *V* in Section XXIX expresses that *the water is cold by nature* (and it cannot be compared with fire). This is a Vaiśeṣika doctrine mentioned in *Vaiśeṣikasūtras* 2, 2, 5.

20. *V* in Section IX refers to the doctrine that darkness is only absence of light. This was a thesis of the Nyāya-Vaiśeṣika and some branches of the Mīmāṃsā schools. This thesis appears already in *Vaiśeṣikasūtras* 5, 2, 19-20 and there is a reference to it in *TŚ*. The composition of the *Vaiśeṣikasūtras* is located between 200 B.C. and the beginning of the Christian Era.[34]

Remarks on points 19-20. The *Vaiśeṣikasūtra*, because of its chronological position, does not provide any element to fix the date of *V*.

21. We find, in the commentary, a stylistic device that we find also in Candrakīrti's (600-650 A.D.) *Prasannapadā*. Both texts connect each one of the categories that are successively examined either in the *V* or in the *MMK*, with the preceding one, presenting in this way, these categories in a continuous chain. Does this constitute an imitation of Candrakīrti by the commentary of *V* or did the commentary of *V* inspire Candrakīrti? Both alternatives are possible.

22. Out of the four traditional *pramāṇas* (*pratyakṣa, anumāna, upamāna* and *āgama*) dealt with by Gautama, the treatise mentions only two: *pratyakṣa* (Sections XVII, XVIII), and *anumāna* (Section XVIII), and in dealing with *dṛṣṭānta* refers implicitly to *upamāna*. *Āgama*, as a means of knowledge, is not mentioned by the treatise, not even implicitly referred to.

23. In regard to the *avayavas* or parts of the *nyāya* or syllogism, *V* deals with the five traditional ones (*pratijñā, hetu, udāharaṇa* or *dṛṣṭānta, upanaya* and *nigamana*), but out of these, it duly refutes only the three first of them (*pratijñā, hetu* and *udāharaṇa*) (Sections XL-XLIX, XXV-XXXI); it disposes of the last two in a very succinct way (Section XLIII) and, besides that in Section XLVII, it gives as an example a syllogism comprising only the three first *avayavas*.

Remarks on points 22-23. Could the facts mentioned in the two previous points indicate that the *V* belongs to a somewhat late epoch of the history of Nyāya in India, when there was a tendency towards the reduction of the number of *pramāṇas* and *avayavas*, being the number fixed by the Nyāya unnecessarily prolix?[35]

24. In Section XLIX, we find a reference to the way in which are produced the sounds that constitute the language. This is one of the

themes dealt with by the *Śikṣās*, several of which were composed B.C. So, this reference is of no help for fixing the date of *V*.

25. There is not a single reference to *śūnyatā* in *V*, excepting in the commentary that follows the Sūtra 1, where the word *śūnyatāvādins* (*stoṅ pa ñid du smra ba rnams*) is employed opposing them to the Naiyāyikas. Neither is there any reference to *niḥsvabhāva*. On the contrary, in Section LXVIII, the author of *V*, in the commentary, affirms that in his refutation of the *padārthas* he has not considered the *padārthas* as entities devoid of an own being. This would have produced a *chala*, as the opponent would have been speaking of one thing (the *padārthas* as real logical categories) and he—Nāgārjuna—of another thing (the *padārthas* as void and unreal entities). The commentary has limited itself to deprive the *padārthas* of all validity or to show their logical impossibility to exist, handling them in the same level as the opponent. So, the author of *V* in the commentary declares that his intention has not been to demonstrate the *śūnyatā* or *niḥsvabhāvatā* of the *padārthas*. This is not the way of behaving of Nāgārjuna, who in all the treatises that can be attributed to him, has always as an aim the denial of the own being of the categories he analyzes. Even the *VV*, which criticizes the means of correct knowledge (*pramāṇas*) in a way similar to the *V*, has its main interest centred in the refutation of the objections raised against the theory of *śūnyatā* in order to establish this theory. This lack of metaphysical interest and the predominance of the logical approach may perhaps indicate for *V* an author different from Nāgārjuna, the author of the *Mūlamadhyamakakārikās*.

26. Another characteristic of the *V* commentary that must be taken into account is the numerous connections it presents with so many texts, schools and doctrines, some of which we have enumerated in the preceding points. This does not seem to be a characteristic of the *MMK* and of the *Śū*. These treatises do not show points of contact with other texts, schools and tenets in such a way as the *V* does. They seem isolated, without relation with the other contemporary trends of Indian thought.

27. In order to refute the Nyāya categories, *V* has many times recourse to theories or opinions of the other schools, as for instance, the Vaiśeṣika's theory about water or the Nyāya-Vaiśeṣika theory about darkness, in order to reject the lamp-light *dṛṣṭānta* etc. So in these cases the demonstration depends on something external to the category that is refuted. Thus, *V* does not comply with a strict use of the *prasaṅga*

method. *MMK* refutes the entities it analyzes without having recourse to any external factor, taking that entity in itself, alone and isolated, and showing its logical impossibility by mere reasoning on the elements that constitute that entity.

28. Among modern scholars, Kajiyama ('The Vaidalyaprakaraṇa of Nāgārjuna', p. 130, and 'Vaidalyaprakaraṇa' in *Daijō Butten* 14, p. 186), Lindtner (*Nagarjuniana*, pp. 11 and 87), Ruegg (*The Literature of the Madhyamaka School*, pp. 19 and 21), Yamaguchi (*Chugan Bukkyō Ronkō*, p. 113), Williams, *Review* of Potter's *Indian Metaphysics*, consider the *V* (*Sūtra* and *Prakaraṇa*) as an authentic work of the founder of the Madhyamaka school.

Conclusion. (1) We think that the attribution of *V* to Nāgārjuna is based only in very weak grounds: a tradition, whose first records appear only several centuries after Nāgārjuna (points 1-5) and the similarity of style and tenets between *V* and other works of Nāgārjuna, which does not constitute at all by itself a decisive argument in favour of authenticity. (2) On the other side, the possibility of the *V* referring to Māṭhara, the author of the *Māṭharabhāṣya* who is mentioned in the fifth century (point 15); of the *V* being inspired by Bhartṛhari (point 16), by Idealistic authors (point 17) and by Candrakīrti (point 21) provoke at least a doubt regarding the attribution of *V* to Nāgārjuna, even if all these circumstances may not, by themselves alone, discard in an absolute way the authenticity of the work. (3) But the reductionist tendency in relation to the number of *pramāṇas* and *avayavas* (points 22 and 23); the absence of references to *śūnyatā* or *niḥsvabhāvatā* (point 25); the relational character of the treatise (point 26) and the constant recourse to external theories as supporting elements of the abolishing argumentation (point 27)—all these are facts that, corroborated by the weakness of the grounds that support the attribution of the work to Nāgārjuna and corroborated also by the doubt provoked by the circumstances referred to in point 2 of this conclusion, oblige to consider that neither the Sūtras nor the commentary of the *Vaidalyaprakaraṇa* were composed by Nāgārjuna.

Some Works Related to V

V has not received much attention from scholars. This is the reason why so few works related to *V* can be found. We indicate the authors to whose works we have had access.

S.Ch. Vidyabhusana in his *History of Indian Logic* (first edition 1920), pp. 257-58, refers briefly to *V* under the name of *Pramāṇa-viheṭana* or *Pramāṇa-vidhvaṃsana.*

Mochizuki in his *Dai Jiten* (1933) V, p. 4120*c* refers to the *Vaidalya* in relation to early Nyāya.

H. Ui, in his study on Indian Logic (*Indo Tetsugaku Kenkyu,* V) (1929), pp. 165-66, mentions *V* in relation to the development of Indian Logic.

Susumu Yamaguchi, in *Chūgan Bukkyō Ronkō* (1944), published a Japanese translation of *V* with explanations.

Yuichi Kajiyama wrote in *Indogaku Bukkyōgaku Kenkyū* (1957) an article regarding the relations between *V* and the Nyāya.

Yuichi Kajiyama in *Indogaku Shiron Shū* (1965) 6-7, published a critical text of *V* using the Narthang, Peking and Cone editions.

Yuichi Kajiyama also published a Japanese translation of *V* in *Daijō Butten* 14 (1974), with notes giving parallel texts.

Sempā Dorje published (1974), a Sanskrit translation of the *VSūtra* with explanations in Hindi.

P.M. Williams also dedicated to *V* pages 287-90 in his Review of K.H. Potter's book on *Indian Metaphysics and Epistemology, JIP,* Vol. 6 (1978).

D.S. Ruegg dedicated a short paragraph to *V* in *The Literature of the Madhyamaka School,* (1981), (p. 21).

Ch. Lindtner has a section (pp. 87-93) of *Nagarjuniana* (1982) on *V.* He informs that he is preparing an edition and a translation of *V* 'is forthcoming' in *Indiske Studier.*

J. Bronkhorst, in his article on Nāgārjuna and the Naiyāyikas (1985) refers to the relations among *V* and *VV* and *NS.*

Value of the V

Notwithstanding the weakness of many of the arguments employed and the almost general obscurity of the treatise, we think it is an interesting and valuable text.

It gives a clear idea of the Mādhyamika conception of logic. It deals with many themes of Indian Philosophy. It shows in many places a great subtlety of thought. It reveals a great mastership of language and dialectics which allows it to express its arguments reducing them to an extreme brevity, silencing many steps of reasoning and leaving to the reader's skill the task to complete the author's thought. It manifests on the part of its author, a deep knowledge of the Indian philosophical tradition. And finally, it contributes many elements to the history of Indian Logic.

The Present Work

In the present work we offer the Tibetan text of *V.* We have established it using the Sde-dge, Peking, Cone and Snar thaṅ editions. We have taken as basic text, the Sde-dge edition (Tokyo edition=D and Delhi edition=DD). In the margin of the pages containing the Tibetan texts, we have indicated the beginning of each folio in the four editions, and inside the text we have put the sigla of the four editions in the exact place in which each folio begins. We indicate in the textual notes those readings of P and/or C and/or N editions that differ from D readings, and whenever we have preferred a reading from P and/or C and/or N to the reading of D. DD presents few slight differences from D, which we have also indicated in the textual notes. We have not taken into account the differences among the editions we have employed in relation to the Tibetan letters for *ba* and *pa,* since many times, it is not possible to be sure whether it is the one or the other owing to printing conditions and since this circumstance does not affect the meaning and understanding of the text. We also give a translation of *V.* The translation is accompanied by a running commentary of ours, in which we have tried to make clear the ideas of the treatise (which in some places is rather obscure and written in somewhat hard style) and to express what we consider could have been Nāgārjuna's thought; and also by a good number of notes in which we indicate some parallel texts. The number of these parallel texts could be easily increased (as for instance from the *Shih êrh mên lun=Dvādaśadvāraśāstra*), but we think that the elected ones are sufficient to show the relations of *V* with other texts, schools and teachings and to give some elements that may contribute to solve the problem of its authorship. The division in Sections and titles (in the translation and in our commentary) are ours. In general, our division of the text agrees with Kajiyama's division. Each Section comprises the Sūtra and the parts of the commentary before and after that refer to it.

TEXT

TEXT

Źib mo rnam par ḥthag pa źes bya baḥi rab tu byed pa

D 99b[1]=DD 198[1]
P 114a[8]
C 97a[7]
N 104b[7]

rgya gar skad du / Vaidalyanāmaprakaraṇa /
bod skad du / Źib mo rnam par ḥthag pa źes bya
baḥi rab tu byed pa /

P 114b
C 99b

Ḥjam dpal[PC] *gźon nur gyur pa la phyag*[1] *ḥtshal lo/*

I

rtog ge śes paḥi ṅa rgyal gyis / gaṅ źig rtsod par mṅon ḥdod pa / de yi[N] *ṅa rgyal spaṅ*[1] *baḥi phyir / źib mo rnam ḥthag bśad par bya /* 1

gźan dag ḥdir rgol ba thams cad kyis tshad ma daṅ / gźal bya daṅ / the tshom daṅ / dgos pa daṅ / dpe daṅ / grub paḥi mthaḥ daṅ / yan lag daṅ / rtog ge daṅ / gtan la dbab pa daṅ / rtsod pa daṅ / brjod pa daṅ / sun[2] ci phyin[3] du[4] brgal ba daṅ / gtan tshigs ltar snaṅ ba daṅ / tshig dor ba daṅ / ltag chod daṅ / tshar gcad[5] paḥi gnas rnams gdon mi za bar khas blaṅs nas gtan[6] du byed kyi stoṅ pa ñid du smra ba rnams[7] kyis ni źen pa med paḥi phyir tshad ma la sogs paḥi don khas len par mi byed do[8] źes zer ro /

II

ḥdi la brjod par bya ste /

tshad ma daṅ gźal bya dag gñi ga ḥdres so / 2

ḥdir tshad ma daṅ gźal bya gñi ga ḥdres par mthoṅ ste/

gaṅ gi phyir gźal bya yod na tshad ma ni[1] tshad ma ñid du ḥgyur źiṅ / tshad ma yod na yaṅ gźal bya ni gźal bya ñid du ḥgyur ro / źes gźal bya las tshad ma grub pa daṅ / tshad ma las kyaṅ gźal bya grub par byas nas / tshad ma ni gźal byaḥi gźal byar ḥgyur la / gźal bya yaṅ tshad maḥi tshad mar ḥgyur bas phan tshun ltos[2] nas bdag ñid thob par ḥgyur ba deḥi phyir tshad ma yaṅ gñi gar ḥgyur la / gźal bya yaṅ gñi gar ḥgyur bas na gñis ka ḥdres paḥo /

III

deḥi phyir

raṅ las grub pa ma yin no[1] / 3

gal te tshad ma daṅ gźal bya dag raṅ gi ṅo bos grub par ḥgyur na ni /[2] tshad ma daṅ gźal bya dag tu ḥgyur na /[2] gaṅ gi phyir ltos[3] nas grub pa[4] ni /[2] phan tshun skyed[5] par byed pa źes bya baḥi don yin pa[6] /[2] deḥi phyir raṅ las grub pa ma yin no /

IV

gźan yaṅ

yod pa daṅ med pa daṅ gñi gaḥi dṅos po dag ni ltos[1] *pa can ma yin no* / 4

gal te yaṅ ltos[1] pa can du ḥgrub par ḥgyur na yod
D 100a=DD 199 paḥam / med paḥam[2] gñi ga gaṅ źig yin graṅ[D,DD] na[3] /
de la re źig yod pa ñid kyi[4] phyir yod pa ni ltos[1] pa ma
N 105b yin te / yod paḥi[N] bum[P] pa ni gźan ḥjim pa la sogs pa
P 115a la ltos[1] pa ma yin no / med pa ñid kyi phyir med pa yaṅ
ltos[1] pa ma yin te / ri boṅ gi rwa[5] la[6] sogs pa yaṅ ltos[1] par thal baḥi[7] phyir ro / ñes pa gñi ga yod paḥi phyir gñi ga yaṅ ltos[1] pa ma yin no /

V

smras pa / ji ltar sraṅ la sogs pa med na gźal bya gzuṅ
C 100a ba med pa de bźin du tshad ma med na yaṅ gźal bya gzuṅ[C] ba med do źes smra[1] na[2] brjod par bya ste /

ma yin te[3] *thug pa med par thal bar*[4] *ḥgyur baḥi phyir ro* / 5

gal te tshad ma med pas gźal bya grub pa ma yin par ḥdod na gaṅ gis na tshad ma rnams med par tshad ma rnams grub par ḥdod pa yin te /[5] khyad par gyi gtan tshigs sam mi ḥdra ba ñid[6] brjod dgos so / gal te yaṅ don thams cad tshad mas grub pa yin no[7] źe na / tshad ma rnams de las gźan paḥi tshad[8] mas grub bo źes bya bar thal bar ḥgyur te / tshad ma rnams ni don thams cad kyi naṅ du gtogs paḥi phyir ro / gal te tshad ma rnams ni tshad ma rnams kyis ḥgrub pa ma yin na ni don thams cad tshad mas bsgrub par bya ba yin no[7] źes bya baḥi dam bcaḥ ñams pa yin no /

VI

smras pa /

tshad ma rnams la ni tshad ma med[1] *de / ḥdir mar me bźin tshad ma ni raṅ daṅ gźan sgrub par byed pa yin no* / 6

ji ltar mar me ni raṅ daṅ gźan rab tu[2] gsal bar byed pa mthoṅ ba de bźin du tshad ma rnams kyaṅ raṅ daṅ gźan sgrub par byed pa yin no / de lta bas na thug pa med pa mar me la sogs paḥi skyon srid pa ma yin no/

VII

brjod par bya ste /

mar me ni mun pa daṅ phrad paḥam ma phrad kyaṅ ruṅ ste gsal bar byed pa ma yin no / 7

mar me ni mun pa daṅ phrad nas gsal bar[1] byed dam/
ma phrad par yaṅ[2] gsal bar byed graṅ na[3] / re źig mar
me ni mun pa daṅ phrad nas gsal bar byed par mi
ḥgyur te[4] phrad pa med paḥi phyir ro / gaṅ gi phyir
mar me daṅ mun pa ni phrad pa yod pa[5] ma yin
te /[6] ḥgal baḥi[7] phyir ro / gaṅ na mar me yod pa de na
N 106a mun pa med na[N] ji[D,DD] ltar mar[P] me ḥdi mun pa sel bar
D 100b=DD 200 byed paḥam gsal bar byed par ḥgyur / ma phrad pa yin
P 115b na yaṅ ma phrad paḥi ral gri ni gcod par mi byed pa
bźin no /

VIII

gzaḥi gnod pa bźin du ḥdi yaṅ ḥgyur ro[1] źe na[2] ma yin
te[3] dpe daṅ ḥgal baḥi phyir ro / 8

ḥdi[4] lha sbyin[5] la sogs pa la gzas byas paḥi skyon phrad
nas gnod pa byed paḥam /[6] raṅ gi lus la sogs pa rnams
ḥdsin par byed pa de ltar ni mar mes byas paḥi gnod
pa mun pa la yod pa ma yin pa[7] ji ltar gzas byas paḥi
skyon daṅ mtshuṅs pa yin / gzaḥ la sogs pa lus daṅ ldan
pas skyes bu la sogs pa rnams la byed par ḥgyur ba me
daṅ /[6] thag pa daṅ /[6] chu daṅ /[6] nad daṅ /[6] sbrul[8] daṅ[9]
C 100b rims la sogs pa lus can rnams[C] kho nas gnod par byed
pa de lta bu ni mar me la cuṅ zad kyaṅ yod pa ma yin
te / de nas[10] chos mthun pa ñid ma yin no / gźan yaṅ
thag riṅ po na yod paḥi mar me[11] ni mun paḥi lus daṅ
dbaṅ po la sogs pa la gnod par byed pa ma yin te[3] de
dag med paḥi phyir ro / de lta bas na gzaḥi dpe ni ma
phrad par sgrub par byed pa la rigs[12] pa ma yin no / gal
te yaṅ mar me ni ma phrad par gsal bar byed par ḥgyur
na ni ḥdi na gnas pa kho nas ri thams cad kyi phug gi
naṅ du gtogs paḥi mun pa sel bar byed paḥam gsal bar
byed par ḥgyur ba źig na de ltar ni ḥjig rten na ma
mthoṅ baḥam ḥdod pa yaṅ ma yin no /

IX

bstan bcos las ḥjig rten paḥi spyod pa po de yaṅ seṅ ge

la sogs pa daṅ mtshuṅs par mṅon par ḥdod pa yin no / 9

de la ḥjig rten pa ni byis pa la sogs pa nas ba laṅ rdsiḥi
bar duḥo / spyod[1] pa po ni khyab ḥjug daṅ dbaṅ phyug
daṅ tshaṅs[2] pa daṅ ser skya daṅ ḥug pa daṅ rgyas pa
daṅ gnas ḥjog daṅ bya ghra daṅ ḥbyor ldan daṅ / ga
ga ra[3] daṅ / ma tha ra la sogs pa ste / de dag don gaṅ
N 106b la blo mthun[4] pa de ni dper[5] rab tu grub[N] pa yin no /
P 116a de la khyab ḥjug la sogs pa ni ḥod med pa tsam la mun[P]
par ḥdod de / ji lta[6] źe na / ḥod med pa[7] ni mun paḥo
źes brjod paḥi phyir ro / ḥdi na[8] mun pa yin te / snaṅ
ba med pa źes bya baḥi don to / de ltar gźan dag dpyod
D 101a=DD201 pa po la mun pa źes bya[D,DD] baḥi dṅos po ci ḥdra ba źig
yod pa yin te / su źig la yaṅ yod pa ma yin no / de bas
na mar mes mun pa bsal[9] ba źes bya ba ḥdi ma grub pa
yin no / deḥi phyir gaṅ mar me ni mun pa sel bar byed
paḥo / źes bya baḥi dpe ni[10] ḥdi rigs pa ma yin no / de
mi rigs pas dpe can gyi don tshad ma źes bya ba ma
grub pa yin[11] no / deḥi phyir raṅ daṅ gźan sgrub par
byed paḥi tshad ma źes bya ba yod pa ma yin no /

X

gźan yaṅ

mar me ni bdag ñid gsal bar byed pa ma yin te / mun pa med paḥi phyir / 10

mar me ni raṅ gi bdag ñid kyaṅ gsal bar byed pa ma yin no / mar me la ni mun pa yod pa ma yin na ci źig gsal bar byed de[1] / mar me daṅ gsal ba źes bya ba don gcig pa yin no /[2] de la mun pa yod pa ma yin te ḥgal baḥi phyir ro /[2]

XI

gźan yaṅ

phyin ci log tu thal bar ḥgyur baḥi phyir /[1] *mun pa yaṅ bdag ñid la sgrib par byed par ḥgyur ro* / 11

gal te mar me raṅ daṅ gźan gsal bar byed pa yin na dpe
C 101a ci[C] źig la thob[2] par ḥgyur źe na / phyin ci log paḥi phyir mun pa yaṅ bdag ñid la sgrib par byed par ḥgyur ro / gal te yaṅ mun pa raṅ gi bdag ñid la sgrib par byed pa yin na de la mun pa mi dmigs pa thob par ḥgyur ro / su źig la brjod par bya źe na / mar mes bdag ñid daṅ gźan gsal bar byed par raṅ gis[3] khas blaṅs paḥi[4] deḥi ḥdod pa la ltos[5] nas gal te źes bya baḥi sgra smos so / mun pa yaṅ bdag ñid kho nas bdag ñid sgrib pa na mar me de la[6] gsal bar byed par mi ḥgyur ro /

XII

gźan yaṅ[1]

> *tshad ma daṅ gźal bya dag ni dus gsum du ma grub po* / 12

N 107a tshad ma ni gźal byaḥi don las sṅa rol duḥam phyis[N] sam / tshad ma daṅ gźal bya dag cig car du yin graṅ /
P 116b de la gal te tshad[2] ma gźal byaḥi don las sṅa[P] rol du yin na ni gaṅ gis[3] na de tshad mar brjod par bya ba gźal byaḥi don yod pa ma yin pa[4] gaṅ gis tshad ma yin źiṅ ci źig tshad mas ṅes par byed / ḥon te phyis nas yin na
D 101b = DD202 gźal bya yod pa la ci źig tshad mar ḥgyur /[5 D,DD] ma skyes pa ni skyes paḥi tshad mar ḥthad pa ma yin te / ri boṅ gi rwa[6] la sogs pa yaṅ tshad ma ñid du thal bar ḥgyur paḥi phyir daṅ / ma skyes pa daṅ skyes pa dag lhan cig mi gnas paḥi yaṅ phyir ro / ḥon te cig car ba yin na de yaṅ srid pa ma yin te / dper na ba laṅ gi rwa[7] cig car[8] skyes pa dag rgyu daṅ[9] ḥbras bur mi ḥthad pa bźin no /

XIII

smras pa /

> *dus gsum du tshad ma daṅ gźal bya dag ma grub pas ḥgag*[1] *pa mi ḥthad do* / 13

dus gsum du tshad ma daṅ[2] gźal bya dag ma grub par ḥdod pa deḥi phyir khyod kyis brjod paḥi tshad ma daṅ gźal byaḥi ḥgag[1] pa gaṅ yin pa de yaṅ dgag par bya baḥi don las sṅa rol duḥam phyis nas sam cig car yin graṅ na ḥgag[1] pa de yaṅ dus gsum du mi ḥgrub ste[3] dgag par[4] bya ba med paḥi phyir ji ltar khyod kyi tshig kyaṅ ḥgag[5] par byed par ḥgyur źiṅ ji ltar na deḥi dgag pa grub par ḥgyur / ḥon te dgag pa ḥgrub[6] po źe na / dus gsum gyi brtag[7] paḥi don mtshuṅs pa ñid grub pa na tshad ma daṅ gźal bya grub paḥam[8] mi ḥdra ba ñid brjod dgos so / de ltar dgag par bya ba daṅ / ḥgog par byed pa de dus gsum du ma grub pa[9] na de lta yin[10] daṅ / ḥgag[11] pa yaṅ mi ḥgrub po źe na[12]

XIV

brjod par bya ste /

C 101b *dgag pa*[1] *grub na tshad ma daṅ*[C] *gźal bya yaṅ grub po zer*[2] *ba ni ma yin te / sṅar khas blaṅs paḥi phyir ro* / 14

dus gsum gyi brtag pas dgag pas[3] na tshad ma daṅ gźal byạ dag go źes smras pa de ni ma yin no / gaṅ las śe[4]
N 107b na /[N] sṅar khas blaṅs paḥi phyir te / sṅar ñid khyod kyis tshad ma daṅ gźal bya dag dus gsum du ma grub po / źes khas blaṅs paḥi[5] phyi nas ni ḥdi skyon byuṅ ba mthoṅ nas /[6] de[7] ḥjig[8] pas ḥgag[9] pa yaṅ mi ḥgrub po
P 117a źes yoṅs su brtags te smras pa[P] ma yin no[10] /

XV

gal te tshad ma daṅ gźal bya dag ma grub par khas blaṅs pa yin na ni khas blaṅs pa daṅ dus mñam pa kho nar rtsod pa rdzogs pa yin no / 15

ji lta źe na / yoṅs su tshim pa lha rnams dgaḥ ba khyod kyis gaṅ gi tshe kho nar tshad ma daṅ gźal bya dag dus

gsum du ma grub pa yin na dgag pa daṅ ḥgog par byed paḥi tshig kyaṅ ma grub po źes smras[1] par byed pa deḥi
D 102a = DD203 tshe kho nar raṅ gi[D,DD] skyon spaṅ bar ḥdod pa khyod kyis tshad ma daṅ gźal bya dag med par khas blaṅs pa ma yin nam / tshad ma daṅ gźal bya dag med paḥi phyir ḥgag[2] pa ḥdi gaṅ yin źes smra bar byed / gaṅ gi phyir tshad ma daṅ gźal bya dag med pa de khas blaṅs nas phyi nas ḥgag[2] pa ḥgog par byed paḥi phyir daṅ po khas blaṅs pa na rtsod pa rdzogs pa yin no /

XVI

dgag par byed pa med na ḥgag pa źes bya ba med[1] do źe na /[2] de ni ma yin te /[3]

ma grub paḥi rtog pa spoṅ ba yin no / 16

ḥdi lta ste dper na chu śin tu gtiṅ riṅ ba ma yin pa la / gtiṅ riṅ baḥi blo daṅ mṅon par ldan źiṅ ḥjigs par ḥgyur ba la deḥi ḥjigs[4] paḥi dogs pa spaṅ baḥi don du gźan de śes pas ḥdi la chu gtiṅ riṅ ba yod pa ma yin no[5] / źes smra ba ni de med pa la deḥi blo gsal[6] baḥi don du ḥthad pa yin paḥi phyir dgag bya med pa la yaṅ dgag bya brjod pa las dgag pa byed pa yin no / gźan yaṅ gal te mtshuṅs paḥi skyon khas len na mtshuṅs paḥi skyon khas[7] blaṅs pa ñid kyis rtsod pa rdzogs pa yin no / źes[8] khas blaṅs nas smra bar ḥdod par byaḥo /

XVII

smras pa /

mṅon sum la sogs pa ni yod pa yin[1] *te / gaṅ las śe na / yaṅ dag pa rtogs paḥi phyir ro* / 17

ḥdir[2] mṅon sum gyi don la dmigs nas bya ba daṅ bya
N 108a ba ma[N] yin paḥi yon tan śes pa yaṅ dag par rtogs par ḥgyur ro / lhag ma rnams kyaṅ de bźin no / deḥi phyir tshad ma daṅ gźal bya yod do źe na /

XVIII

brjod par bya ste /

P 117b *mṅon sum la*[P] *sogs pa grub kyaṅ*[C] *gźal bya ni ḥthad*
C 102a *pa ma yin no* / 18

de[1] ni khas blaṅs na[2] brjod par bya ste / mṅon sum la
sogs paḥi tshad ma rnams ni grub na gźan gźal byaḥi
don gaṅ źig yin pa smros śig / gaṅ gi phyir bum pa ñid
mṅon sum yin gyi bum pa ni ma yin te dbaṅ[3] po la rab
tu phyogs paḥi don gaṅ yin pa de ni mṅon sum yin par
byas nas / mig gi dbaṅ po la dbaṅ poḥi[4] brda byas la
de la rab tu phyogs paḥi don gaṅ yin pa de ni mṅon
sum yin źiṅ de yaṅ snaṅ ba la sogs paḥi rkyen la ltos[5]
D102b = DD204 pa ste / de[6] phyir bum pa la sogs pa ñid[D,DD] mṅon sum
du yoṅs su grub pa yin na tshad ma de gaṅ gi yin pa doṅ
gźal byar gyur pa de gaṅ źig yin par ḥgyur / de bźin
du me daṅ du ba la ḥbrel pa las mṅon sum sṅon[7] du
ḥgro ba can rjes su dpag pa yin no / de[8] na rjes su dpag
paḥi śes pa skyes pa na yaṅ gaṅ gi de rjes su dpag par
ḥgyur /[9] rjes su dpag par bya baḥi don gźan gaṅ źig yin
par ḥgyur / lhag ma la yaṅ de bźin no /

XIX

smras pa /

bum pa la/[1] bum paḥi blo ni tshad ma yin la bum pa ni gźal bya yin no[2] źe na[3] brjod par bya ste /

de[A] *rkyen du gyur pa ñid yin paḥi phyir śes pa yaṅ*
ma yin źiṅ śes bya yaṅ ma yin no / 19

gaṅ gi phyir dbaṅ po daṅ don phrad pa las blo skye bar ḥdod pa deḥi phyir[5] bum pa ni rkyen du gyur pa ñid yin pa deḥi phyir blo ni tshad ma ma[6] yin la bum pa yaṅ gźal bya ma yin no /

XX

gźan[1] yaṅ

blo ni tshad ma ma yin te / gźal bya yin par mṅon par brjod paḥi phyir ro / 20

gaṅ gi phyir khyod kyi blo gźal bya yin par rjod[2] par
byed de ji lta[3] źe na / bdag daṅ /[4] lus daṅ /[4] dbaṅ po
daṅ /[4] don daṅ /[4N] blo daṅ /[4] yid daṅ /[4] ḥjug pa
N 108b daṅ /[4] skyon daṅ /[4] srid pa phyi ma daṅ / ḥbras bu
daṅ /[4] sdug bsṅal daṅ byaṅ grol rnams ni gźal bya yin
no źes brjod paḥi phyir ro / deḥi phyir gñi ga yaṅ med
pa yin no /

XXI

P 118a smras pa /[1] tshad ma ñid gaṅ[P] yin pa de ñid gźal bya
yin no[2] źes brjod pa na the tshom za ba yin no / the
tshom yod paḥi phyir tshad ma daṅ gźal bya gñi ga
grub pa yin no / the tshom źes bya baḥi tshig gi don
ni yod pa ñid de ma[3] bden paḥi don la ḥdi yod[4] ma yin
no[2] źe na[5] brjod par bya ste /

dmigs paḥam ma dmigs pa dag la the tshom za ba
C 102b *med pa*[6] *de yod pa daṅ med*[C] *pa ñid kyi phyir*
ro / 21

ḥdir dmigs paḥi don laḥam ma dmigs paḥi don laḥam dmigs[7] bźin paḥi don la the tshom za graṅ / dmigs paḥi don la the tshom za ba mi rigs śiṅ / ma dmigs paḥi don la yaṅ the tshom za bar mi rigs la / dmigs bźin źes bya baḥi don gsum pa yaṅ yod pa ma yin no / de lta bas na the tshom ni yod pa ma yin no /

XXII

smras pa /

the tshom ni yod pa ma[1] *yin te / khyad par la ltos*[2] *pa*
D103a = DD205 *med paḥi phyir*[D,DD] *ro* / 22

ḥdir sdoṅ dum mam skyes bu źes bya ba yul thag riṅ po nas mthoṅ nas phyir ḥdsin pa[3] ḥdi skyes buḥam /[4] ḥon te sdoṅ dum yin źes the tshom za bar ḥgyur ro / gaṅ gi ṭshe byaḥi tshaṅ bcas paḥam ri dags ḥkhrug[5] pa la sogs paḥi khyad par mthoṅ ba deḥi tshe ḥdi ni sdoṅ dum ñid do[6] /[4] źes ṅes par ḥgyur źiṅ de las bzlog pa yin paḥi phyir daṅ / mgo bsgyur ba daṅ /[4] lag pa gyo ba la sogs paḥi bya ba mthoṅ baḥi phyir skyes buḥi blo ḥbyuṅ ba yin no / ḥdi yaṅ yod pa daṅ med pa ñid kyi phyir khyad par la ltos[2] pa yin la de las gźan du na the tshom za ba yin no / deḥi phyir the tshom ni yod pa yin no źe na[7]

XXIII

brjod par bya ste /

> *sṅar bkag zin paḥi phyir the tshom ni khyad par la ltos*[1] *pa ma yin no* / 23

yod pa daṅ med paḥi phyir the tshom med do źes bya
ba ḥdis sṅar ñid bkag pa yin no / ji lta[2] źe na / sdoṅ
N109a dum la byaḥi tshaṅ bcas pa[3N] sogs paḥi rgyu mtshan
dmigs pas ḥdi na[4] sdoṅ dum yin no / źes śes pa skyeḥi
the tshom ni ma yin te / yaṅ dag pa ji lta ba bźin du
P118b yoṅs su śes pa ñid kyi phyir[P] ro / de bźin du skyes bu
yin pa la yaṅ mgo bsgyur ba la sogs paḥi rgyu mtshan
dmigs pas ḥdi ni skyes bu ñid do / źes yaṅ dag pa ji lta
ba bźin du yoṅs su śes pa skye bar ḥgyur ba the tshom
ni ma yin te / yaṅ dag pa[5] ji lta ba bźin du śes pa ñid
khyi phyir ro / gñi ga la yaṅ yaṅ dag paḥi[6] śes paḥi rgyu
mtshan med na ma rtogs pa ñid yin gyi the tshom ma
yin te / ma ṅes pa daṅ / ma rtogs pa daṅ / ma bzuṅ
ba daṅ / mi śes pa daṅ / ma mthoṅ baḥi don rnams
gźan ma yin źiṅ de dag ni mi śes paḥi rnam graṅs yin
te / śes pa las bzlog pa yin paḥi phyir ro / ḥdi skad du
stoṇ par ḥgyur te / khyad par la ltos[1] nas śes par ḥgyur
C 103a la / khyad par ma mthoṅ ba la ni mi śes pa skye[C] bar

ḥgyur ro / mgo bsgyur ba daṅ/[7] lag pa gyo ba la sogs pa mthoṅ na the tshom du ḥgyur ba ma yin la / khyad par med na ni mi śes pa ñid yin no / ḥdi lta bur ḥgyur
D 103b=DD 206 te[8] khyad par yod na śes par ḥgyur źiṅ de med na mi śes pa ñid[D,DD] do / gaṅ la khyad par daṅ khyad par med pa dag cig[9] car ḥgyur ba rtog pa gsum pa ni med paḥi phyir the tshom yod pa ma yin no /

XXIV

smras pa / dgos paḥi don gaṅ la kho bo[1] cag gi śes pa ṅes par[2] ma skyes paḥi dgos pa don[3] de la the tshom yod pa yin no[4] źe na[5] brjod par bya ste /

yod pa daṅ med pa ñid kyi phyir dgos paḥi don ni med pa yin no / 24

don gaṅ gi ched du gñer nas ḥjug pa de ni dgos pa yin no / źes khyod kyis brjod pa yin te / ji ltar bum paḥi don du rdsa mkhan ḥjug pa bźin no / gal te ḥjim pa
N109b la bum pa yod[N] pa deḥi tshe deḥi ḥjug pa don med par ḥgyur ro / ḥon te med na bye ma bźin du med pa ñid kyis[6] de la ḥjug pa ma yin no /

XXV

smras pa /

bye ma la ḥjug pa ni ma yin te / dpe yod paḥi phyir ro / 25

ji ltar snam bu dgos pa na snal ma[1] la sogs pa la ḥjug pa yin gyi ḥjag ma[2] la ma yin pa bźin no[3] źe na[4]

XXVI

brjod par bya ste / de lta bu

P119a *de yaṅ sṅa ma daṅ[P] mtshuṅs pa ñid do* / 26

XXVII

gźan yaṅ[1]

> *thog ma daṅ dbus med paḥi phyir mthaḥ yaṅ mthoṅ ba ma yin no* / 27

gaṅ gis[2] don gyi thog ma daṅ dbus ma mthoṅ ba des ji ltar mthar[3] mthoṅ ba yin te / thog ma daṅ dbus med na mthaḥ yod pa ma yin no / deḥi phyir dpe med pa yin no /

XXVIII

smras pa / ḥjig rten pa daṅ spyod[1] pa po dag don gaṅ la[2] blo mthun pa de ni dpe yin la de yaṅ chos mthun pa ñid daṅ /[3] chos mi mthun pa ñid[4] yin no[5] źe na[6] brjod par bya ste /

> *chos mthun pa ñid kyi phyir me ni meḥi dpe ñid ma yin no* / 28

chos mthun pa ñid kyi phyir dpe źes gaṅ brjod pa de ni ma yin no / gaṅ gi phyir me ni meḥi dpe ma yin te / bsgrub par bya ba daṅ /[3] sgrub par byed pa dag khyad par med paḥi phyir ro / gal te de ñid bsgrub[7] par bya ba yin źiṅ de ñid sgrub par byed pa yin na yaṅ ji ltar na dpe khyad par can du ḥgyur /

XXIX

gźan yaṅ

> *chu ni meḥi dpe ma yin te / chos mi mthun pa ñid kyi phyir*[1] / 29

graṅ bar gtogs paḥi chu ni meḥi dper ḥthad pa ma yin
C103b te /[2] la la dag tu chu ni graṅ ba yin te / dper na me[C]
bźin no[3] źes smras pa de daṅ ḥdraḥo /

XXX

gźan yaṅ

cuṅ zad chos mthun pa las yin no źe na[1] *ma yin te ri rab daṅ skra bźin no* / 30

D104a = DD207 de la[D,DD] cuṅ zad chos mthun pa las dpe yin no[2] źes bya ba de ltar ḥgyur ro[3] źe na[1] de ni ma yin te / ga las śe[4] na /[5] ḥdir ri rab daṅ skra dag kyaṅ yod pa ñid daṅ gcig pa ñid daṅ lus can ñid du cuṅ zad chos mthun pa yin no / gźan yaṅ ri rab daṅ mtshuṅs paḥi skra[6] źes rab tu grags pa ni ma yin no[7] /

XXXI

phal cher chos mthun pa las[1] ḥgyur ro[2] źe na[3] brjod par bya ste /

N110a *sṅar bkag pa ñid kyis phal cher chos*[N] *mthun pas*[4] *ni ma yin no* / 31

ḥdir phal cher chos mi mthun par ḥgyur ba[5] yaṅ[6] ma[7] yin te /[8] de la[9] phal cher chos mthun pa daṅ chos mi mthun pa ñid kyis ma grub pa yin no /

XXXII

P119b smras pa / khyod ni grub pa[1] med pa ñid du brjod[P] pa yin te grub mthaḥ med pa daṅ lhan cig smra bar bya ba ma yin no źe na[2] brjod par bya ste /

thog ma ma grub na tha ma ḥgrub pa yaṅ ma yin no / gal te thog ma ma grub na dbus daṅ mthaḥ gñis ma grub po[3] / 32

XXXIII

smras pa / yan lag daṅ bral ba ni sgrub par byed pa ma yin la khyed cag gi yan lag tu[1] smra ba ni[2] ma yin no /

deś na thams cad ma[3] ḥbrel ba ñid kyis ḥgog pa[4] yin pa deḥi phyir gdon mi za bar yan lag gzuṅ[5] bar byas nas brjod par bya dgos te / rnam pa gźan du na dgag pa mi ḥgrub po źe na[6] brjod par bya ste/

yan lag can med paḥi phyir yan lag yod pa ma yin no / 33

ḥdir dam bcaḥ ba daṅ gtan tshigs daṅ dpe daṅ ñe bar sbyor ba daṅ mjug[7] bsdu baḥi yan lag rnams la yan lag can med paḥi phyir yan lag rnam pa[8] med pa yin no/

XXXIV

smras pa / tshogs pa la yan lag can[1] grub[2] bo źe na[3] brjod par bya ste /

re re la med paḥi phyir tshogs pa la yaṅ mi ḥgrub bo / 34

tshogs pa la yan lag can yod pa źes bya bar brjod pa gaṅ yin pa de ni ma yin te / yan lag re re la yan lag can med paḥi phyir tshogs pa la yaṅ yod pa ma yin no/

XXXV

gźan yaṅ

yan lag can gcig yin paḥi phyir yan lag rnam pa[1] thams cad gcig ñid du thal bar ḥgyur te / 35

skyon ḥdi ni gźan ma[2] yin pa laḥo / ḥon te yan lag lṅa las gźan pa gcig[3] yin na ni drug par thal bar ḥgyur ro/

XXXVI

gźan yaṅ /

D104b = DD208
C104a

dus gsum la ma[D,DD] grub[C] pas yan lag[1] med pa ñid do / 36

dam bcaḥ ba la sogs pa skyes pa daṅ /[2] ma skyes pa
daṅ /[2] da ltar ba rnams la[3] ḥdas pa daṅ /[2] ma ḥoṅs pa
N110b daṅ /[2] da ltar ba rnams yoṅs[N] su brtag bzod pa ma yin
te / rigs pa med paḥi phyir ro / deḥi phyir yan lag can
med pa yin źiṅ yan lag kyaṅ med pa yin no /

XXXVII

ḥon te rtswa bal ba ja bźin du de yaṅ grub bo / 37

ji ltar rtswa bal ba ja gcig gis glaṅ po che ḥchiṅ bar mi
nus kyaṅ rtswa[1] bal ba ja tshogs pas ni nus pa ltar[2] de
bźin du na[3] dam bcaḥ pa la sogs pa[4] tshogs pa la[5] yan
P120a lag can yod pa yin[6] no[7P] źe na[8]

XXXVIII

brjod par bya ste[1]

ma yin te / bsgrub par bya ba daṅ mtshuṅs paḥi phyir ro / 38

ḥdi ni mo gśam daṅ loṅ ba daṅ bye ma lta bu yin te gaṅ
gi tshe mo gśam gcig[2] gis bu bskyed mi nus pa de bźin
du mo gśam stoṅ phrag du ma tshogs pas kyaṅ bskyed[3]
par nus par mi ḥgyur ro / ji ltar loṅ ba gcig la mthoṅ
baḥi nus pa med pa de bźin du loṅ ba stoṅ phrag du
ma la[4] yaṅ mthoṅ baḥi nus pa yod pa ma yin no / ji ltar
bye ma re re la til mar[5] med pa de bźin du/[6] maṅ po
tshogs pas ḥbyin pa med de med pa ñid kyi phyir ro /

XXXIX

ḥon te mo gśam la sogs paḥi dpe ni mtshuṅs pa ñid de
gaṅ gis na de phye[1] ma leb la sogs paḥam / de lta buḥi
ṅo bo ḥgaḥ źig ḥchiṅ bar ḥgyur ba bal ba ja gcig[2] la yaṅ
bal ba jaḥi ṅo bo daṅ rjẹs su mthun paḥi nus pa yod pa

yin[3] la /[4] maṅ po ḥdus pas ni glaṅ po che ḥaṅ ḥchiṅ bar nus par ḥgyur ro sñam du sems na / de yaṅ srid pa ma yin te / gaṅ[5] las śe[6] na[7]

rigs pa med paḥi phyir ro / 39

rab tu grags paḥi yan lag can gyi dper yin na / yan lag can dag la ni ma yin te /[4] lhan cig gnas pa med paḥi phyir ro / dus gcig[2] laḥam[8] kha[9] sgoḥi yul la dam bcaḥ ba la sogs paḥam deḥi yi ge dag lhan cig gnas pa yod pa ma yin te / deḥi phyir bal ba jaḥi dpe ḥdi mi rigs so / de mi rigs paḥi phyir yan lag med do[10] źes bya bar grub pa yin no /

XL

gźan yaṅ /

yan lag dag la yaṅ yan lag yod par thal bar ḥgyur ro / 40

N111a gal te yan lag[1N] ni ma grub paḥi don sgrub par byed[D,DD]
D105a = DD209 pa yin[C] na / de dag kyaṅ grub pa źig sgrub par byed pa
C104b yin nam ma grub pa źig yin graṅ / gal te grub pa źig
sgrub par byed pa yin na sgrub byed gaṅ gis /[2] de dag
sgrub par byed pa de dag la yaṅ sgrub par byed pa gźan
źig yod par ḥgyur la de dag la yaṅ gźan yod pas thug pa
med par thal bar ḥgyur ro / ḥon te de dag la yaṅ gźan
P 120b yod pa ma yin[P] na mi ḥdra ba ñid daṅ dam bcaḥ ba
ñams pa źes bya ba[3] ḥdi dag thams cad yan lag gi sgo
nas yan lag can sgrub par ḥdod pa la brjod par byaḥo/

XLI

gźan yaṅ /

dam bcaḥ ba las gtan tshigs gźan daṅ gźan ma yin paḥi phyir gtan tshigs ma yin no / 41

[1]dam bcaḥ ba daṅ gtan tshigs gźan yin nam gźan ma[2] yin pa yin graṅ / gal te gźan ñid yin na ci źig ḥthob par ḥgyur / dam bcaḥ ba ni snam bu dkar po ñid yin paḥo / gźan yaṅ gtan tshigs gaṅ yin źe na / nag po ñid kyi phyir ro / ḥdod pa ma yin te / gaṅ gi phyir dkar po ñid ni sgrub byed nag pos mi ḥgrub paḥi phyir ro[1]/ ḥon te gtan tshigs daṅ dam bcaḥ ba dag[3] ma yin na ci źig ḥthob par ḥgyur źe na dam bcaḥ ba ni snam bu dkar poḥo[4]/[5] gtan tshigs gaṅ źe na dkar po ñid kyi phyir ro / de ñid ni deḥi sgrub byed ma yin te ḥdi ni bsgrub par bya ba daṅ mtshuṅs pa yin no /

XLII

gźan yaṅ

gtan tshigs la gtan tshigs med paḥi yaṅ phyir ro / 42

gtan tshigs las grub po źes brjod pa gaṅ yin pa de ni ma yin te gtan tshigs la yaṅ gtan tshigs gźan thob par ḥgyur źiṅ de la yaṅ gźan yin no / źes thug pa med par ḥgyur ro / ḥon te gtan tshigs la yaṅ gtan tshigs yod par mi ḥdod na deḥi phyir gtan tshigs med pa yin no / yaṅ na gtan tshigs bźin du thams cad kyaṅ gtan tshigs med par grub par ḥgyur ro /

XLIII

gźan yaṅ /

N 111b *dam*[N] *bcaḥ ba daṅ gtan tshigs*[1] *med paḥi phyir ñe bar sbyor ba daṅ mjug bsdu*[2] *ba dag med pa yin no* / 43

de ltar na dam bcas[3] ba daṅ gtan tshigs daṅ dpe dag med pa ñid kyis ñe bar sbyor ba daṅ mjug bsdu[2] ba dag kyaṅ yod pa ma yin[4] no /

XLIV

gźan yaṅ[1]

lhag ma dag la gtan tshigs med do / 44

P 121a gal te yaṅ dam bcaḥ ba ni gtan tshigs las grub pa yin na dpe la sogs pa sgrub par byed pa la ni gtan tshigs[P] med par thal bar ḥgyur ro /

XLV

gźan yaṅ[1]

D105b = DD210 *gal te grub pa ni gtan tshigs kyis byas pa yin na ci źig*[D,DD] *ḥthob ce na / dpe la sogs pa don med do* / 45

C 105a khyod gtan tshigs kho nas[C] ḥgrub par sems na[2] deḥi phyir dpe la sogs pa dag don med par ḥgyur te gtan tshigs kho nas[3] don ḥgrub paḥi phyir ro /

XLVI

gźan yaṅ

gtan tshigs don med pa ñid dam / 46

ḥon te dpe grub par ḥdod na deḥi tshe gtan tshigs don med par[1] thob par ḥgyur ro / yaṅ na dpe don med pa yin no /

XLVII

smras pa /[1] bdag sgrub pa la gtan tshigs daṅ dpe yin no[2] źe na / brjod par bya ste /

bdag ḥgrub pa ni ma yin no / 47

gtan tshigs kyis ḥgrub par sems te / ji ltar skyes bu rtag pa ni dam bcaḥ baḥo[3] / lus can ma yin paḥi phyir ni gtan tshigs so / dpe ni nam mkhaḥ bźin no[2] źes khyod kyis smras pa yin no / gtan tshigs kyis ḥgrub par[4] rtag pa ma yin te / mi rtag pa ñid kyi phyir ro / gaṅ gi phyir raṅ ñid kyis med pas rtag paḥi ṅo bo ñid med pa yin no / [5]gtan tshigs daṅ dpe la yaṅ de bźin no[5] /

XLVIII

[1]gźan yaṅ/

gcig daṅ gcig brjod baḥi phyir gcig la gcig med do / 48

gaṅ gi tshe dam bcaḥ ba brjod pa[1] deḥi tshe gtan tshigs[2] la sogs pa med la gtan tshigs[2] brjod pa na[3] yaṅ dam bcaḥ la sogs pa med do / deḥi phyir gtan tshigs la sogs pa dag yod pa ma yin no /

XLIX

ḥdir smras pa / khyod kyi[1] yan lag thams cad med do źes dam bcaḥ[2] ba de lta bas na / dam bcaḥ[2] ba khas blaṅs paḥi phyir khyod la lhag ma dag kyaṅ grub pa yin no źe na[3] brjod par bya ste /

N 112a *yi ge*[N] *dag la yaṅ de lta bu yin no* / 49

yan lag ma grub paḥi rnam pa gaṅ yin pa de yi ge thams cad la yaṅ lta bar byed de[4] / ji ltar praḥi yi ge daṅ /[5] tiḥi yi ge daṅ[6] jñaḥi yi ge dag lhan cig gnas pa med paḥi phyir dam bcaḥ ba med pa ñid do / de bźin du praḥi[7]
P 121b yi ge la[8] yaṅ pra la sogs paḥi rim gyis brjod paḥi phyir[P] yi[9] ge med do / rluṅ[10] daṅ /[5] nam mkhaḥ daṅ /[5] lce daṅ /[5] so daṅ /[5] mgrin pa daṅ /[5] rkan daṅ /[5] chu[11] daṅ ḥbad pa la sogs paḥi rkyen las byuṅ baḥi tshe gcig la gcig[12] med pa yin no /

L

smras pa /[1] gaṅ gi phyir brtags[2] na de ma thag tu rab tu rtog pa de[3] phyir rtog ge źes bya baḥi tshig gi don[4] yod pa yin no / de yod paḥi phyir gźan dag kyaṅ grub pa yin no[5] źe na[6] brjod par bya ste /

the tshom bźin du rtog ge yaṅ yin no / 50

D 106a = DD211 ji lta[7] źe na / śes[D,DD] paḥi don la dpyod pa yin nam mi śes paḥi don la dpyod pa yin graṅ / de la gal te śes paḥi don la yin na ci źig dpyod par ḥgyur / ḥon te mi śes paḥi don la[8] yin na yaṅ ci źig dpyod par ḥgyur[1] / rnam
C 105b par rtog pa gsum[C] pa ni med do /

LI

smras pa / rnam par dpyad[1] pas[2] don khoṅ du chud pa ni gtan la phab pa yin la / ṅo śes paḥi rgyu[3] mtshan ni ḥthad paḥo / de kho na ñid śes paḥi don du dpyod par byed pa ni rtog ge yin no[4] źe na[5] brjod par bya ste /[6]

rdsas daṅ yod pa daṅ gcig ñid la sogs pa dag ni gźan daṅ gźan ma yin pa daṅ gñis ka[7] *med paḥi phyir gtan la phab pa med do* / 51

ḥdir bum pa daṅ /[6] yod pa daṅ /[6] gcig[8] daṅ /[6] zlum po daṅ /[6] dmar po la sogs pa[9] dag gcig[8] ñid dam gźan ñid graṅ / de la gal te gcig[8] ñid du ḥdod na gaṅ la yod pa la sogs pa dag gi naṅ nas gaṅ yaṅ ruṅ ba gcig[8] srid pa de la nus pa yod par ḥgyur te / dbaṅ[10] daṅ nus pa[9] ldan daṅ groṅ khyer ḥjig par byed pa bźin no / ḥon te de lta ma yin na de lta bas na gcig[8] ñid med do / ḥon te gźan yin na deḥi phyir bum pa ni yod pa ma yin źiṅ gcig
N 112b kyaṅ[N] ma yin la / zlum po daṅ dmar po yaṅ ma yin no / bum pa ni yod pa yin te / yod pa ñid daṅ ldan paḥi phyir ro[11] źe na[5] de ni ma yin no[12] / gaṅ źig gaṅ daṅ ldan pa de ni de ñid du ḥgyur ba ma yin no / deḥi phyir

gcig ñid daṅ gźan ñid daṅ gñi ga med paḥi phyir gtan la dbab pa med do /

LII

P 122a smras pa /[1] tshad mas sgrub par byed pa klan[P] ka[2] can grub mthaḥ daṅ mi ḥgal ba yan lag lṅa las skyes pa phyogs daṅ mi mthun pa dag yoṅs su ḥdsin pa ni rtsod pa yin la / ḥdir bum pa la sogs pa gsal bar ḥdod pa khyod[3] phyogs daṅ mi mthun pa yoṅs su ḥdsin pa yin no[4] brjod par bya ste /

> *rtsod pa ni /*[1] *yod pa ma yin te / rjod*[5] *par byed pa daṅ brjod bya dag med paḥi phyir* / 52

rtsod pa yaṅ med do / ji ltar rdsas daṅ yod pa daṅ gcig ñid la sogs pa dag ni gźan daṅ gźan ma yin pa gñi ga med pas gtan la phab pa med pa de bźin[6] gal te bum
D 106b = DD212 pa·mṅon par brjod pa daṅ[D,DD] /bum[7] pa gcig[8] ñid yin na bum pa brjod pa bźin du phyi rol yaṅ ḥjim paḥi goṅ bu daṅ /[1] ḥkhor lo daṅ /[1] chu la sogs pa ḥdus pa la ma ltos[9] par grub par ḥgyur te / bum pa la sogs pa mṅon par rtogs[10] nas bum pa la sogs pa ḥgrub par ḥgyur ro / bum pa źes brjod pa na kha gaṅ bar ḥgyur la me źes
C 106a brjod pa na mchu ḥtshig par ḥgyur te de ltar ḥdod[C] pa yaṅ ma yin no / gźan yin na bum pa źes ṅes par brjod pa na bum pa ṅes par mi ḥgyur ro /

LIII

brda byas paḥi brjod paḥi tha sñad yin no[1] źe na[2] ma yin te /

> *don dam pa dpyod paḥi skabs yin paḥi phyir ro* / 53

ḥdi ltar lha rnams dgaḥ baḥi[3] rigs pa phra baḥi phyogs su lhuṅ ba khyod kyi tshig gi don bcu drug yoṅs su śes

pas grol bar ḥgyur ro / źes bya ba ni grub paḥi mthaḥ yin no / gaṅ gi phyir tshad ma la sogs paḥi tshig[4] don bcu drug po ḥdi dag don dam par ḥgyur ba ni ḥdi la
N 113a rigs[5] pa ci źig[N] ces mkhas pa rnams kyis[6] rtogs par byed do / raṅ gis brda byas[7] paḥi miṅ ḥdi dag ni yaṅ dag pa ma yin paḥi don dag la yaṅ mthoṅ ste / ḥdi ltar lha sbyin[8] daṅ dbaṅ pos sbed ces bya ba yin no / gal te ḥjig rten paḥi tha sñad ḥbaḥ źig las grol ba yin na ba laṅ rdsi
P 122b la sogs pa thams cad kyaṅ grol bar ḥgyur ba daṅ /[P] mkhas pa daṅ /[9] rmoṅs pa źes bya baḥi khyad par dag kyaṅ med par ḥgyur ro /

LIV

gźan yaṅ[1]

> *brda byas paḥi miṅ dag ni rnam pa du ma mthoṅ ste* /[2] 54

ḥdi lta ste /[2] ba laṅ la ḍa mi ḍa la sogs pa ni stigs[3] ta daṅ ḥphags pa źes miṅ du byas pa lta bu daṅ / de bźin du yul tshigs[4] ḥjig[5] pa dag gis kyaṅ piṇ ḍa[6] ra sa daṅ skyur[7] rtsi la[8] sogs paḥi rdsas la tshogs can daṅ śa lo ka la sogs pa lta buḥo /

LV

gźan yaṅ

> *ḥjig rten paḥi mkhas pa dag kyaṅ rjod*[1] *par byed pa daṅ brjod par bya ba du mu la sbyor ba mthoṅ baḥi phyir ro* / 55

ḥjig rten paḥi mkhas pa dag ni goḥi sgra du ma la sbyor bar byed de / ha riḥi sgra yaṅ de bźin no / goḥi sgra rnam pa du ma la ḥjug pa ni ḥdi lta ste /

> **ṅag[2] phyogs daṅ ni[3] sa gźi daṅ /[4]**

ḥod zer rdo rje phyugs daṅ mig /
D 107a = DD213 chu[D,DD] daṅ mtho ris don dgu[5] la /
mkhas pas go sgra ṅes gzuṅ bya /

ji ltar

khyab ḥjug seṅ ge glaṅ po sbal /
ñi zla ḥod daṅ spreḥu daṅ /
ser skya ne tsho dbaṅ po klu[6] /
mkhas pas ha rir śes par bya /

sgra gcan gnas ldan khyab ḥjug daṅ /
ha ri ban glaṅ skyoṅ bdag daṅ /
mi yi seṅ ge mi thuṅ sbrul /
sred med bu ḥdi grags pa yin /

de bźin du sgra gźan la yaṅ ñe bar gzuṅ[7] bar
C 106b byaḥo /[C] ḥdi ltar re źig[8] rjod[1] par byed pa gcig la don
du ma yin pa daṅ / brjod par bya ba re re la yaṅ rjod[1]
par byed pa du ma yin no / de bźin du nus ldan
daṅ /[9] dbaṅ po daṅ /[9] groṅ khyer ḥjig[10] daṅ / mchod
sbyin daṅ /[9] kau śi ka daṅ /[9] brgya byin dag gi sgra ni
N 113b brjod par bya ba gcig[11] la ḥjug pa yin no / med[N] pa daṅ
yod pa ma yin pa daṅ mi ḥdogs[12] pa źes bya baḥi[13] miṅ
gi rnam graṅs yin no / de yaṅ don dam par grub pa ma
yin no / deḥi phyir rjod[14] par byed pa daṅ brjod par bya
ba dag rnam pa du ma ḥdres[15] paḥi skyon mthoṅ baḥi
phyir ma ṅes pas[16] ma grub pa yin no /

LVI

gźan yaṅ

gcig ñid yin na rjod[1] par byed pa daṅ brjod par bya ba ma grub pa yin la / gźan ñid yin na ni / 56

P 123a bum pa źes bya[P] baḥi rjod[1] par byed pa sbyor ba na bum
pa la śes pa ṅes par mi ḥgyur ro / de kho na bźin du
gźan la yaṅ gcig ñid yin na / sṅar bśad paḥi skyon ñid
yin no / deḥi phyir rtsod[2] pa ni mi srid do /

LVII

gźan yaṅ

> *brjod pa daṅ sun ci phyin du brgal ba yaṅ de bźin no* / 57

de.bźin źes bya ba ni rnam pa gaṅ gis rtsod pa sun phyuṅ baḥi rnam pa des źes bya baḥi don to[1] / des brjod pa daṅ sun ci phyin du brgal ba dag med pa yin no /

LVIII

smras pa /[1] khyod kyis thams cad gtan tshigs ltar snaṅ bar brjod ciṅ lan daṅ ldan pa ma yin no[2] źe na brjod par bya ste /

> *chos mthun pa ñid daṅ / chos mi mthun pa ñid med paḥi phyir gtan tshigs ltar snaṅ ba ma yin no* / 58

gal te gtan tshigs ltar snaṅ ba yod na de chos mthun pa ñid kyis yin nam chos mi mthun pa ñid kyis yin graṅ / re źig chos mthun pa ñid kyis ni gtan tshigs ltar snaṅ
D 107b = DD214 bar ḥgyur ba ma yin te / ji ltar[D,DD] gser ñid la gser ñid kyi[3] yoṅs su dpyod pa na gser ñid dor bar mi byed pa de ni gser yin gyi gser ltar snaṅ ba ni ma yin no / de bźin du gtan tshigs gaṅ yin pa de ni gtan tshigs kho na yin gyi gtan tshigs ltar snaṅ ba ma yin no / de bźin du chos mi mthun pa ñid kyis kyaṅ gtan tshigs ltar snaṅ bar mi ḥgyur te / ji ltar boṅ ba la sogs pa gser ma yin pa gaṅ yin pa de ni ji ltar na gser ltar snaṅ bar ḥgyur / de bźin du gtan tshigs ma yin pa de ni gtan tshigs ltar snaṅ ba ma yin te[4] / gtan tshigs ñid ma yin paḥi phyir ro / ltar
C 107a snaṅ źes bya ba ni dṅos po de ñid ma[C] yin te / de las
N 114a bzlog[N] pa yin paḥi phyir ro / raṅ gi rgyud yoṅs su ḥgyur baḥi phyir[5] khyad par khams mi mñam pa ñid las mi

ñams paḥam / khams mñam pa las deḥi blo ni śes pa ñid yin pa ltar / yoṅs su[6] brtags na gtan tshigs ltar snaṅ ba źes bya ba cuṅ zad yod pa ma yin no / gaṅ gi phyir
P 123b gtan tshigs ma yin[P] pa daṅ / gtan tshigs las gźan gsum pa ḥdi[7] ḥthad pa ma yin no / de lta bas na gtan tshigs ltar snaṅ ba ni yod pa ma yin no /

LIX

gźan yaṅ /

ma ḥkhrul ba ni ḥkhrul[1] *pa daṅ bral ba las yin no* / 59

ma ḥkhrul ba ñid gaṅ las śe[2] na / raṅ gi bdag ñid la ḥkhrul pa daṅ bcas pa yin par ḥgyur ram ma ḥkhrul bar ḥgyur graṅ / gal te bdag ñid la ḥkhrul par mi ḥgyur ba yin na ḥkhrul pa daṅ bcas par mi ḥgyur te / ji lta[3] źe na / bdag ñid raṅ gi ṅo bo mi ḥdor baḥi phyir ro / bdag ñid des yod pa ñid kyi phyir ḥkhrul pa daṅ bcas par mi ḥgyur ro[4]/ ḥon te raṅ gi ṅo bo ḥdor bar byed pa de lta na yaṅ ḥkhrul pa daṅ bcas pa ma yin te / raṅ gi ṅo bo dor nas de ñid med paḥi phyir ro / rnam pa gźan du na yaṅ rigs pa yod pa ma yin no / ḥdi skad bstan par ḥgyur te /[5] gtan tshigs bsgrub bya sgrub par byed paḥi raṅ bźin can gaṅ yin pa de ni bdag ñid des ḥkhrul pa can ma yin la / bsgrub bya sgrub par byed paḥi raṅ bźin ma yin pa de ni gtan tshigs ma yin pa ñid
D 108a = DD215 kyi phyir ḥkhrul pa daṅ[D,DD] bcas pa ma yin te / rnam par rtog pa gsum pa med paḥi phyir ro /

LX

smras pa /

ḥkhrul pa daṅ bcas paḥi gtan tshigs yod do / 60

ḥdi lta ste /[1] nam mkhaḥ[2] daṅ las źes bya ba dag la

lus can ma yin pa ñid daṅ / rdul phra rab daṅ / bum pa źes bya ba la sogs pa la spyi daṅ khyad par lta buḥo[3]

LXI

N 114b *źe na*[1] *ma yin te / de*[N] *dag ni*[2] *gźan yin paḥi phyir ro* / 61

de ni yod pa ma[3] yin no / gaṅ[4] las śe[5] na de dag gźan ñid yin paḥi phyir ro / nam mkhaḥ[6] la yod paḥi lus can ma yin pa gaṅ yin pa de ni de ñid las daṅ blo la yod par rigs pa ma yin te skyes pa daṅ ma skyes pa ḥgal baḥi
P 124a phyir ro / ḥdir las daṅ blo la sogs pa[PC] dag gi lus can
C 107b ma yin pa ni[7] skye ba daṅ ldan pa yin la / nam mkhaḥi[8] ma yin pa ñid do / nam mkhaḥi[9] lus can ma yin pa ñid gaṅ yin pa de ni las la yod pa ma yin te / gaṅ gi phyir las ni skye ba daṅ ldan paḥi phyir ro / lus can ma yin pa de daṅ lhan cig skye ba na skye ba daṅ / des[10] ḥjig pa na yaṅ ḥjig paḥi phyir ro / deḥi phyir nam mkhaḥ[6] daṅ lus can ma yin pa gźan ñid yin no / nam mkhaḥi[9] lus can ma yin pa ñid gaṅ yin pa de las blo la sogs pa la rigs pa ma yin la las kyi lus can ma yin pa ñid gaṅ yin pa de yaṅ nam mkhaḥ[6] la yod pa ma yin no / sgrub pa daṅ sun ḥbyin pa la rgyu mtshan ḥgaḥ źig yod pa sgrub par byed pa gaṅ yin pa de sgrub par byed pa ñid du mi ḥkhrul la / de bźin du sun ḥbyin pa la yaṅ brjod par byaḥo / deḥi phyir ḥkhrul pa daṅ ldan paḥi gtan tshigs ni yod pa ma yin no / ḥgal ba ñid yin gyi ḥkhrul pa daṅ bcas pa ni ma yin no / deḥi phyir nam mkhaḥi[9] lus can ma yin pa ñid ni rtag pa ñid ni sgrub pa la ḥkhrul pa ma yin no / las[11] la sogs pa la yaṅ de bźin no / daṇḍa

LXII

gźan yaṅ/

skad cig ma ñid kyi phyir yaṅ no / 62

don gaṅ la bsgrub paḥam sun ḥbyin par byed pa de la

ḥjig pa yod pa yin na sgrub paḥam sun ḥbyin par byed
pa rigs pa ma yin no / gñi ga gnas pa yin na gtan tshigs
D 108b = DD216 sgrub paḥam sun ḥbyin par[D,DD] byed pa yin gyi de ḥjig
pa na gtan tshigs de sgrub paḥam sun ḥbyin par byed
par rigs pa ma yin te /[1] gñi ga gnas pa med paḥi phyir
ro / deḥi phyir ḥkhrul pa daṅ bcas paḥi gtan tshigs yod
pa ma yin no /

LXIII

smras pa /

N 115a *khyod kyi[1] gtan tshigs[2] thams[N] cad ḥgal bar brjod
pa yin gyi ḥkhrul pa daṅ bcas pa ni ma yin
no* / 63

ma ṅes pa kho na ḥkhrul pa daṅ bcas pa yin no / sgrub
par byed pa gaṅ yin pa de sgrub par byed pa ñid la ma
P 124b ḥkhrul pa yin la / de bźin du sun ḥbyin[P] par byed pa
la yaṅ brjod par byaḥo / deḥi phyir ḥkhrul pa daṅ ldan
paḥi gtan tshigs med paḥi phyir źes ḥgal ba ñid yin no
źe na[3]

LXIV

brjod par bya ste /

*sṅa ma daṅ phyi mar ḥbyuṅ baḥi phyir ḥgal ba
med do* / 64

ḥgal bar brjod pa gaṅ yin pa de[1] ni med de / re źig sṅa
C 108a ma la ḥgal ba med de phyi[C] ma med paḥi phyir ro /
phyi mar brjod pa la yaṅ ḥgal ba med de / sṅa maḥi
gtan[2] tshigs med paḥi phyir ro / gñi ga dus gcig tu gnas
pa na[3] ḥgal ba yin la / rgol ba daṅ phyir rgol ba dus
gcig[4] kho nar lan daṅ[5] phyir rgol baḥi lan dag smra
baḥi skabs ni med de / lhan cig gnas pa med pa dag ni
ḥgal ba med paḥi phyir ro /

LXV

smras pa / ḥdas paḥi dus źes bya ba gtan tshigs ltar snaṅ ba yod do / de yod pas gtan tshigs ltar snaṅ ba yod do źe na[1] brjod par bya ste /

> *ḥdas pa ni ḥdas paḥo / ḥdas pa źes bya ba ḥdas par gyur paḥo* / 65

ḥdir khyod kyi[2] bum paḥi bdag ñid kyi dus ni da lta ba yin la / ḥjim goṅ gi dus ni ḥdas pa yin źiṅ gyo moḥi bdag ñid ni ma ḥoṅs paḥi dus yin par brjod do / gyo mo ma ḥoṅs pa deḥi phyir[3] yaṅ ḥjim goṅ daṅ bum paḥi dus dag ḥdas par gyur pa yin no / deḥi tshe de dag med paḥi phyir ḥdi ni gaṅ gi ma ḥoṅs par ḥgyur /[4] da ltar daṅ ḥdas pa yod do źe na / de yaṅ ma yin te / da ltar gyi dus la ḥdas pa med paḥi phyir daṅ[5] de bźin du ḥdas paḥi dus la yaṅ da ltar ba med paḥi phyir dus thams cad la ḥthob par ḥgyur ro /

LXVI

> *rjod byed kyi rnam pa thams cad med par thal bar ḥgyur baḥi yaṅ phyir ro* / 66

D109a = DD217 ḥjig[D,DD] rten na ni rjod[1] byed kyi rnam pa du ma yod
N115b de legs par sbyar ba daṅ / legs[N] par sbyar ba ma yin pa daṅ / tha mal paḥo / ḥbyuṅ bar gyur pa ni ḥdas paḥo / yod pa ni da ltar byuṅ baḥo / ḥbyuṅ bar ḥgyur ba źes bya ba ni ma ḥoṅs paḥo / de bźin du[2] legs par sbyar ba ma yin pa daṅ tha mal paḥi rjod[1] par byed pa la yaṅ
P 125a sbyar bar bya ste / gźuṅ ma ṅes[3] paḥi[P] ñes pas ma brjod do /

LXVII

gźan yaṅ /

> *ḥdas paḥi gtan tshigs sam ḥdas paḥi dus ni yod pa ma yin te* /

gaṅ las śe[1] na[2]

mi srid paḥi phyir ro / 67

rna baḥi dbaṅ pos ni gtan tshigs ñid thos pa[3] yin gyi[4] ḥdas pa[5] ma yin te / ḥdas paḥi phyir ro / ḥdas paḥi dus kyaṅ rigs pa ma yin te / gtan tshigs ḥdas pa yin paḥi phyir ro / da ltar gyi dus ni ḥdas paḥi gtan tshigs daṅ ḥbrel pa ma yin te /[6] gaṅ daṅ ḥdi ḥbrel par ḥgyur te de ñid gtan tshigs kyi dus yin no / deḥi phyir de lta bu
C 108b la sogs paḥi rgyu[C] mtshan gyis rnam par dpyad na ḥdas paḥi dus yod pa ma yin źiṅ gtan tshigs kyaṅ yod pa ma yin no /

LXVIII

smras pa /

khyod kyi thams cad tshig don du brjod pa yin gyi don dam par ma yin no źe na[1]

brjod par bya ste /

ma yin te / lan[2] *thams cad la thal bar ḥgyur baḥi phyir ro* / 68

ḥdi ni de lta bu ma yin te / gaṅ cuṅ zad lan du brjod pa de[3] thams cad tshig don ñid[4] du ḥgyur baḥi phyir ro / gaṅ[5] las śe[6] na / smra ba po thams cad ni ḥthad pas gdon mi za bar tshig ñams par byed pa yin no / deḥi phyir lan du ḥthad pa yin[7] no / tshig dor ba med paḥam / yaṅ na tshul ḥdi mi ḥdod na deḥi phyir tshig dor ba med par ḥgyur ro /

LXIX

smras pa /[1] gaṅ la bi gyaḥam stoṅ du lan btab pas ltag chod du thal bar ḥgyur ba ṅes paḥi don la ltag chod ces bya ba tshig gi don yod do źe na[2] brjod par bya ste /

> *skyes pa daṅ ma skyes pa gñi ga med paḥi phyir ltag chod ni med do* / 69

ltag chod ces brjod pa gaṅ yin pa de gaṅ las śe[3] na / skyes paḥam ma skyes paḥam /[1] skye bźin ba skye ba
N116a yin graṅ / re źig skyes pa ma yin te / skyes zin pa[N] ñid kyi phyir ro / ma skyes paḥaṅ ma yin te / ma skyes pa
D109b = DD218 ñid kyi phyir ro /[D,DD] gñi ga med paḥi phyir skye bźin pa yod pa ma yin te skyes pa daṅ ma skyes pa las ma
P 125b gtogs paḥi skye bźin pa bya ba ni yod pa[P] ma yin no /

LXX

smras pa / khyod kyis zlos[1] pa brjod par rtogs par byed de gaṅ gi phyir khyod sna tshogs paḥi don la yod pa daṅ med pa ñid kyis dgag pa byed kyi rnam pa gźan du ni ma yin no / deḥi phyir tshar gcad[2] paḥi gnas yin no / źe na[3] brjod par bya ste[4] /

> *ma yin te sṅa ma phyi ma dag gcig ñid daṅ / gźan ñid du med paḥi phyir* / 70

zlos pa brjod pa ni ma yin no / gal te zlos pa brjod par ḥgyur na gcig gis sam gźan gyis yin graṅ / sṅa ma daṅ phyi maḥi tshig de ni gcig ñid kyi[5] zlos pa brjod pa srid pa ma yin no / ji lta źe na / gaṅ gi phyir brjod pa deḥi phyir zlos pa brjod pa ma yin te / de ñid yin paḥi phyir ro / de ñid yin paḥi phyir lan brgyar brjod kyaṅ ji ltar zlos par ḥgyur / ḥon te sṅa ma las gźan yin no źe na / de yaṅ zlos pa brjod par mi ḥgyur te / gźan ñid yin paḥi phyir daṅ / skad cig ma ñid[6] yin paḥi phyir ro / sgra
C 109a yaṅ brjod pa sṅa ma gźan yin la / phyi ma yaṅ de[C] daṅ ḥdra bar gźan yin no / deḥi phyir zlos[1] pa brjod pa gźan yin no /

LXXI

gźan yaṅ /

> *tshar gcad[1] paḥi gnas kyaṅ de bźin no* / 71

ji ltar skyes pa daṅ ma skyes pa gñi ga med paḥi phyir ltag chod med pa bźin du tshar gcad paḥi gnas kyaṅ med pa yin no / tshar gcad paḥi gnas źes bya ba tshar gcad pa las ḥgyur ram ma gcad[1] pa las ḥgyur graṅ na / rnam pa gñi ga yaṅ srid pa ma yin te / deḥi phyir de ni med do /

LXXII

gźan yaṅ /[1]

tshar gcad[2] paḥi gnas la ni tshar gcad[2] pa med de bciṅs[3] pa bźin no / 72

tshar gcad[2] paḥi gnas la yaṅ tshar gcod par mi ḥgyur te / dper na bciṅs paḥi gnas na gnas pa yaṅ gdon mi
N116b za bar bciṅs par ḥgyur ba ma yin pas na ḥdiḥi[N] ṅes pa ni[4] yod pa ma yin no/

LXXIII

smras pa /[1] tshad ma la sogs pa[2] ḥgag[3] par bya ba bźin du dgag pa yaṅ med pa yin no[4] źe na[5] brjod par bya ste /

P126a *gñi ga khas ma blaṅs[P] paḥi phyir ro / de ma grub na ma grub pa kho nar zad do /*

D110a = DD219 gal[D,DD] te tshad ma la sogs pa dag med pas dgag pa yaṅ med pa yin te / de lta bas na gñi ga yaṅ ma grub bo źes bya bar ḥdod na /

de kho na bźin du brjod pa yin no / mṅon par brjod pa ni med pa ñid do / 73

gcig ñid daṅ gźan ñid daṅ gñi ga med paḥi phyir dṅos po thams cad med par khas blaṅs pa yin no / de lta bas na dṅos po med par mṅon par brjod par bya ba daṅ /

mṅon par brjod pa yaṅ med pa yin no / deḥi phyir mya ṅan las ḥdas pa daṅ byaṅ grol źes bya ba dag don gźan ñid ni ma yin no /

tshad ma la sogs pa tshig gi[1] don bcu drug sel bar byed pa źib mo rnam par ḥthag paḥi rab tu byed pa / slob dpon ḥphags pa klu sgrub kyis mdsad pa rdsogs so //

yoṅs kyi dge baḥi bśes gñen chen po[2] yon tan grags paḥi bkas /

kha cheḥi paṇḍita Jayānanda[3] daṅ / bod kyi lo tsā ba chen po śā-kyaḥi dge sloṅ khu mdo sde ḥbar gyis bsgyur ciṅ źus te gtan la phab paḥo //

TRANSLATION

TRANSLATION

Treatise of the Subtle Pulverization

I

Aim of the Treatise

1. *The* Vaidalya *is to be explained in order to eliminate the arrogance of those*[1] *who are eager of discussions,*[2] *on account of the arrogance (produced in them) by their knowledge of logic.*

Negation of the Sixteen Logical Categories

It is said that all the others who dispute on this matter (of logic), always do it assuming as being beyond doubt (the sixteen following categories:)[3]

1. the means of valid knowledge (*tshad ma; pramāṇa*),
2. the knowable (object) (*gźal bya; prameya*),
3. doubt (*the tshom; saṃśaya*),
4. aim (*dgos pa; prayojana*),
5. example (*dpe; dṛṣṭānta*),
6. the accepted theory (*grub paḥi mthaḥ; siddhānta*),
7. the members (of inference) (*yan lag; avayava*),
8. reasoning (*rtog ge; tarka*),
9. determination (*gtan la dbab pa; nirṇaya*),
10. debate (*rtsod pa; vāda*),
11. discussion (*brjod pa; jalpa*),
12. altercation (*sun ci phyin du brgal ba; vitaṇḍa*),
13. fallacious reason (*gtan tshigs ltar snaṅ ba; hetvābhāsa*),
14. sophism (*tshig dor ba; chala*),
15. irrelevant rejoinder (*ltag chod; jāti*),
16. points-of-defeat (in argumentation) (*tshar gcad paḥi gnas rnams; nigrahasthānāni*)—but the śūnyatāvādins,[4] since they do not adhere (to anything),[5] do not accept the (above-mentioned) categories of means of valid knowledge etc.

PRAMĀṆA AND PRAMEYA

II

Confusion of pramāṇa *and* prameya

On regard to this it must be said:

2. *The means of valid knowledge and the knowable (object) both are confused.*[1]

Here[2] the means of valid knowledge and the knowable (object) both are seen as being confused, because (only) when the knowable (object) exists, the means of valid knowledge becomes means of valid knowledge; and also (only) when the means of valid knowledge exists, the knowable (object) becomes a knowable (object). Thus on account of the knowable (object) the means of valid knowledge is established (as existing); and also on account of the means of valid knowledge, the knowable (object) is established (as existing); consequently the means of valid knowledge becomes the knowable (object) of the knowable (object), and the knowable (object) also becomes the means of valid knowledge of the means of valid knowledge; thereby (only) through (this) mutual relation of dependence they come into existence.[3] Because of this the means of valid knowledge happens to be both, and the knowable (object) happens also to be both; thereby both are confused.[4]

III

Pramāṇa *and* prameya *are not* ex se

Because of this

3. *They are not established (as existing) out of themselves.*

If the means of valid knowledge and the knowable (object) were both established (as existing) with an own being, (then), as they become both of them means of valid knowledge and knowable (object) because they are established in relation of dependence, they would make each other to be born—this is the meaning (of the *sūtra*). For this reason *they are not established (as existing) out of themselves.*

IV

Pramāṇa *and* prameya *as mutually dependent are neither existent nor non-existent nor existent and non-existent.*

Moreover

4. *An existing (thing), a non-existing (thing), and a thing that were both are not dependent (on something other).*

If (something) were established as dependent, (then) it would be either an existing (thing), or a non-existing (thing) or anything that were both (of them). Among these (alternatives) an existing (thing) is not dependent, because it *is*; (so for instance) a pot that *is*, is not dependent on something other, as the clay etc.; a non-existing (thing) is neither dependent (on something else), because it *is not*, by reason of the absurd consequence of even the hare's horn etc. resulting dependent (on something else); (a thing that were) both is neither dependent, because both (previous) defects would exist.[1]

V

The opponent affirms: pramāṇas *must exist in order that* prameyas *may be established. Rejection of this thesis: the* pramāṇas *cannot be established by other* pramāṇas, *because the logical defect of a* regressus ad infinitum *would be produced.*

It is said: In the same way as if the balance etc. does not exist, what is to be weighed (etc.) is not grasped, so if the means of valid knowledge does not exist, the knowable (object) would not be grasped[1]—if it is (thus) said, it must be replied:

5. *It is not (so), because of the absurd consequence of a* regressus ad infinitum.[2]

If it is maintained that without means of valid knowledge, the knowable (object) is not established (as existing), (then we ask:) how is it maintained that without means of valid knowledge, the means of valid knowledge are established (as existing)? and in this case it is necessary to say either the special proof or the difference.[3]

If it is said that all the objects are established (as existing) by the means of valid knowledge, (then) the absurd consequence consisting in the means of valid knowledge being established (as existing) by (other) means of valid knowledge different from them would occur,[4] since the means of valid knowledge belong to the (class of) objects.

If the means of valid knowledge are not established (as existing) by the means of valid knowledge, (then) the thesis that all the objects are to be established (as existing) by the means of valid knowledge is destroyed.[5]

VI

The opponent affirms: the pramāṇas *are* svayaṃsiddha *(auto-established) as the lamplight, so no* regressus ad infinitum *is produced.*

6. *In relation to the means of valid knowledge there are no means of valid knowledge. Regarding this point the means of valid knowledge, like the lamplight,[1] establish themselves and the other (objects).*

In the same way as a lamplight is seen illuminating itself and the other (objects), so the means of valid knowledge also establish themselves and the other (objects). By such a reason there is no possibility of the *regressus ad infinitum* as a defect of the lamplight etc.[2]

VII

The analogy of lamplight and pramāṇas *adduced by the opponent is unfit, because the lamplight cannot illuminate darkness, since no connection is possible between them.*

It must be said:

7. *The lamplight, either connected or not connected with darkness, does not illuminate.*

The lamplight, either illuminates being connected with darkness, or illuminates without being connected (with it).

(We have it that) the lamplight cannot illuminate being connected with darkness, since (that) connection is not (possible), because the lamplight and darkness do not get connected as they are opposed. Where the lamplight is, there darkness is not;[1] consequently, how the lamplight could either remove or illuminate darkness?

Also (the lamplight cannot illuminate) not being connected (with darkness), as the sword that is not in contact (with something) does not cut (it).[2]

VIII

In order to save his thesis of svayaṃsiddhi *the opponent argues that, even without getting into contact with darkness, the lamplight can affect it, adducing in support of his saying the case of the planets that have a hurtful influence on men. That new analogy is also declared to be unfit.*

8. *If it is said that this*[1] *can occur as (in the case of) the hurtful influence of the planets,*[2] *(we answer that) it is not (so), because (the case of the hurtful influence of the planets) is contradictory to the example (of the lamplight and the darkness).*[3]

The evil done by the planets to Devadatta etc. getting into contact (with them) does harm (to them) or takes possession of their body etc., (but) a harm like that done by the lamplight does not exist for darkness. How could (the case of the lamplight and the darkness) be similar to (the case of) the evil done by the planets?

The planets etc. act on men etc. because these have a body; the fire, the rope, the water, the illness, the serpent, the plague etc. do harm exclusively to those possessing a body. So it is not at all in (the case of) the lamplight.

Consequently there is no similitude between the two terms of the comparison: the case of the planets and the case of the lamplight. Moreover a lamplight which is at great distance does no harm to the body and the senses etc. of darkness, because they do no exist.

For this reason the example of the planets, as there is no contact (between the lamplight and darkness), is not suitable for establishing (as valid) (the thesis of the adversary).

If the lamplight, even without contact (with darkness), could illuminate (it), (then a lamplight) just located here would eliminate the darkness that belongs to the interior of the caves of all the mountains or would illuminate (it)—never such a thing has been either seen or admitted in this world.[4]

IX

Darkness does not exist, so it cannot be illuminated or dispelled, and therefore the dṛṣṭānta *adduced by the opponent in Section VI is not valid.*

9. *In (your)* śāstra[1] *the investigators among the inhabitants of the world are considered to be similar to lions etc.*[2]

Here 'inhabitants of the world' (means:) from children etc. up to cow-keepers. 'Investigators' (are:) Viṣṇu, Śiva, Brahmā, Kapila, Ulūka, Vyāsa, Vasiṣṭha, Vyāghra, Samṛddha, Gagara and Māṭhara[3] etc. That matter, in regard to which they[4] are of the same opinion, is established as an example.[5] In (relation to) this (point) Viṣṇu etc. consider the mere inexistence of light as darkness.[6] If it is asked why?, (we answer:) because the inexistence of light is named 'darkness'. (If) there is darkness here, then there is no light—this is the meaning. Similarly for other investigators[7] the thing called 'darkness', of whatever description it may be, is not in any place. For this reason this (assertion) that darkness is dispelled by the lamplight is not established (as valid). Consequently that example which affirms that the lamplight dispels darkness is not logical.[8] Because it is not logical, a so-called 'means of valid knowledge' (as) a category provided with example,[9] is not established (as existing). Thus a so-called 'means of valid knowledge', which establishes itself and the other (objects), does not exist.

X

Impossibility for the lamplight of illuminating itself, because of the inexistence in it of darkness.

Moreover

10. *The lamplight does not illuminate itself, because darkness does not exist (in it).*

The lamplight does not illuminate itself either. As in the lamplight darkness does not exist,[1] what would it illuminate? 'Lamplight' and 'illumination' are the same thing, therein darkness does not exist, because (darkness and light) are contradictory.[2]

XI

Another reason for the impossibility of the lamplight to illuminate itself: the prasaṅga *of the darkness obscuring itself would occur.*

Moreover

11. *Darkness also would obscure itself, because it would occur the absurd consequence of 'the contrary'.*

If it is asked: If the lamplight illuminate itself and other (objects), (then) what would the example obtain?,[1] (we answer that what it obtains is that), because of the (occurrence of) the contrary, darkness also would obscure itself. If darkness also obscures its own self, in that case it would be obtained that darkness would not be perceived. If it is asked in relation to whom (this) is to be said, (we answer that) the word 'if' has been said in relation to the opinion of those who by themselves assume that the lamplight illuminates itself and the other (objects). When darkness also obscures itself by itself, (then) the lamplight would not illuminate it.[2]

XII

Another argument against the existence of pramāṇa *and* prameya: *the impossibility of any chronological relation between them.*

Moreover

12. *The means of valid knowledge and the knowable (object) are not established (as existing) in (any of) the three times.*[1]

The means of valid knowledge may exist before the knowable object or after (it) or the means of valid knowledge and the knowable (object) may exist at the same time.

Among these (alternatives), if the means of valid knowledge existed before the knowable object, (then) thanks to what should it be called 'means of valid knowledge'? There is not a knowable object thanks to which the means of valid knowledge could exist and (thanks to which) something could be ascertained by (that) means of valid knowledge.[2]

Or else, if (the means of valid knowledge) existed after (the knowable object), as the knowable (object) is (already) existing (as knowable object), what could be (in regard to it) a means of valid knowledge? It is not admitted that something not (yet) arisen could be a means of valid knowledge of something (already) arisen, because it would occur the absurd consequence of even the horns of the hare etc.[3] becoming a means of valid knowledge, and because something not arisen and something arisen cannot stay together.[4]

Or else if (the means of valid knowledge and the knowable object) existed at the same time,—that[5] is not possible either.[6] As for instance the (two) horns of the cow arising at the same time are not admitted to be cause and effect (one of the other).[7]

XIII

Opponent's rejection of the negation of the existence of pramāṇa *and* prameya: *the denial implies the existence of the denied object.*

It is said:

13. *Because the means of valid knowledge and the knowable (object) are not established (as existing) in (any of) the three times, (its) denial is not logically possible.*[1]

It is maintained that the means of valid knowledge and the knowable (object) are not established (as existing) in (any of) the three times, therefore, the denial itself of the means of valid knowledge and the knowable (object) expressed by you ought to be before the object that is to be negated or after (it) or at the same time (as it); consequently the denial also is not established (as existing) in (any of) the three times.[2] Since what is to be denied does not exist, how then could your statement itself deny, and how could a denial of them (= the means of valid knowledge and the knowable object) occur?[3]

But if it is said that the denial is established (as existing), (then), since (the means of valid knowledge and the knowable object) have been established as being similar to any examined object of the three times, the means of valid knowledge and the knowable (object) are established (as existing), or else it is necessary to explain their difference.

If it is said that in that case, (only) if what is to be denied and that (statement) which denies were not established (as existing)[4] in (any of) the three times—it would be so (i.e. the *pramāṇa* and the *prameya* would not exist), but (in that case) the denial also would not be established (as existing)[5],

XIV

Nāgārjuna's refusal of the opponent's argument: the existence of something cannot be deduced from its previous negation.

it must be answered:

> 14. *To say that if the negation is established (as existing), the means of valid knowledge and the knowable (object) are also established (as existing)—this is not (possible), because of the previous acceptance.*[1]

To say that, in consequence of the examination of the three times, (we have it that) owing to the negation, the means of valid knowledge and the knowable (object) (exist)—this is not (possible). If one asks: Why?, (the *sūtra* says:) because of the previous acceptance. After having been accepted by you previously that the means of valid knowledge and the knowable (object) are not established (as existing) in (any of) the three times, on seeing the logical defect coming forth (in your reasoning), (we must conclude that) it is not possible to say, after due investigation, that, owing to the elimination (of the means of valid knowledge and the knowable object) through that (previous acceptance of their inexistence in any of the three times), (their) negation also is not established (as existing).

XV

The opponent's previous acceptance of the inexistence of the pramāṇa ***and the*** prameya ***puts an end to the discussion.***

> 15. *If there is acceptance of the non-existence of the means of valid knowledge and the knowable (object), in the very moment of this acceptance, the discussion is over.*

If it is asked: Why?, (we answer:) at the same time it is said by you who are foolish[1] and fully satisfied (with yourself) that, since the means of valid knowledge and the knowable (object) are not established (as existing) in (any of) the three times, the negation and the word which denies are not established (as existing) either, in that very time is not their acceptance by you—desirous of avoiding your own logical defect—of the means of valid knowledge and the knowable (object) as being non-existent? That negation has been said (by me) to exist because of the inexistence of the means of valid knowledge and the knowable (object). After having accepted that (negation, which exists) because of the inexistence of the means of valid knowledge and the knowable (object), (immediately) on having accepted the first (statement: 'the inexistence of the means of valid knowledge and the knowable object'), (although it be just) for the sake of negating the negation, the discussion is over.

XVI

Even if what is to be negated is not existing, the negation is possible, because it has to do with a concept—this is Nāgārjuna's position in regard to negation.

If it is said that when non-existence is to be negated,[1] the so-called negation does not exist,[2] (we answer:) that is not (so),

16. *(Because, in the negation, only) the idea of (something) non-established (as existing) is eliminated.*

As for instance: although the river is not deep, (somebody) being possessed with the idea that it is deep gets afraid and somebody else knowing this (fact), in order to eliminate his fearful apprehension, says to him: 'The river is not deep'. Because that (deep river) does not exist and (that negative proposition of the other man) is appropriate for putting away the (false) idea of that (fearing man), (it results that), even if what is to be denied does not exist, to negate through the naming of what is to be denied is (possible).[3] After having being accepted this: 'If it is accepted the same logical defect (as being in the example of the river as well as in your reasoning), (then) by the (mere) acceptance of the same logical defect (as being in both), the discussion is over', something else is expected to be said.

XVII

The existence of valid acts of knowledge is adduced by the opponent as a new argument in favour of the existence of the pramāṇas.

(And) it is said:

17. *The perception etc. exist. If it is asked: Why? (the answer is:) because (they provide) a correct knowledge.*

If it is said that here the cognition—(that comes) after the grasping of the object of the perception—(of the existence in the object) of the quality of (capability for) performance or non-performance (of its own function) happens to be a correct knowledge;[1] (and) that (about) the remaining (means of valid knowledge) the same (thing is) also (to be said); (and) that because of that the means of valid knowledge and the knowable (object) exist,[2]

XVIII

Refutation of the argument adduced by the opponent in the previous sūtra: even if the pramāṇas *exist, the* prameyas *do not exist. The opponent is asked to say what the* prameya *is.*

it must be said:

18. *Even if the perception etc. exist, the knowable (object) is not admitted.*

If that is accepted, it must be said: If the means of valid knowledge as the perception etc. are established (as existing), you have to say what is the other, the knowable object. Since, although a pot is perceived, the pot itself is not (the *prameya* of that perception)—because (only) that which is the correspondent object of a sense-organ is perceived, (or in other words) taking the sense of the eye as the representative sense-organ, (only) that which is the correspondent object of it (*i.e.* of the eye) is perceived,[1] and besides that (because) it (*i.e.* the perception) depends on (numerous) conditions like the sight etc.[2]—therefore, if the pot etc. are established as perceived, (it is necessary to say) what happens to be that object which has become the knowable (object), (and) of which that means of valid knowledge is (means of valid knowledge)?

In the same way the inference is (produced) from the connection between fire and smoke (and) is preceded by a perception.[3] Being so, when an inferential knowledge arises, what happens to be the other inferable object of which that (inference) happens to be the inference?

In relation to the remaining (means of valid knowledge) the same (thing is) also (to be said).

XIX

Refutation of the new thesis adduced by the opponent in his answer: the pramāṇa *is the idea of pot, the* prameya *is the pot. For Nāgārjuna the pot is only a determining condition of the* pramāṇa.

It is said: In regard to the pot, the idea of pot is the means of valid knowledge and the pot itself is the knowable (object)—if it is (thus) said, it must be replied:

19. *Because it (the pot) is (only) a determining condition,*[1] *(it) is not the cognition and (it) is not the cognizable either.*

Since it is accepted that the idea arises from the connection of the object with the organ of sense, therefore, that pot is (only) a determining condition (of the *pramāṇa*), therefore, the idea is not the means of valid knowledge, and the pot is not the knowable (object) either.

XX

Another argument adduced by Nāgārjuna against the opponent's thesis that the idea is the pramāṇa.

Moreover:

20. *The idea is not a means of valid knowledge, because it has been said*[1] *to be a knowable (object).*

Since, if it is asked how (it is possible) to say that in your opinion the idea is the knowable (object), (it is to be answered: that it is so,) because souls, bodies, senses, objects, *ideas,* minds, activities, faults, reincarnations, consequences (of action), sufferings, emancipations have been said (by you) to be knowable (objects);[2] therefore, both are not existent.

SAMŚAYA

XXI

The doubt is introduced by the opponent as a new argument in favour of the existence of the pramāṇa *and the* prameya. *Nāgārjuna's negation of doubt* (saṃśaya).

It is said: When it is affirmed that what is a means of valid knowledge, that is indeed the knowable (object), a doubt arises.[1] Because of the existence of the doubt, both the means of valid knowledge and the knowable (object) are established (as existing). Concerning the category 'doubt', if it is said that it exists (and) it is not about an unreal object, it must be answered:

21. *The doubt does not exist about something perceived or about something non-perceived, because they are existent (= the perceived one) and non-existent (= the non-perceived one).*[2]

In this respect doubt is either about a perceived object or about a non-perceived object or about an object that seems to be perceived. About a perceived object doubt is not logical, about a non-perceived object doubt is neither logical; the third object, i.e. the one that seems perceived, does not exist either. For this reason doubt does not exist.[3]

XXII

The opponent's argumentation in favour of the existence of doubt, contradicting Nāgārjuna's position expressed in the previous section.

It is said:

22. *The doubt would not exist, if there were not reference to peculiarities.*[1]

Here he who grasps a thing as 'a tree-trunk or a man', because of looking at it from afar, becomes doubtful thinking whether it is a man or a tree-trunk.

At which time the peculiarities like the nest of a bird or a meeting of deers etc. are seen, at that time occurs the certainty: 'This is indeed a tree-trunk'; but (on the contrary) the idea of man arises, because the actions of turning the head, moving the hand, etc. are seen, and because (the idea 'man') is (in the present case) the counterpart to that (= i.e. the idea 'tree-trunk').

Because of the existence and non-existence of these (= the ideas 'tree trunk' and 'man'), there is a reference to peculiarities, and in a manner different from that there is doubt.[2]

If it said that for this reason the doubt exists.

XXIII

The a priori denial of doubt prevents its being in relation with peculiarities according to Nāgārjuna.

it should be answered:

23. *On account of its having been denied at first, doubt has no reference to peculiarities.*

If (peculiarities) exist and (if peculiarities) do not exist, doubt does not exist—with this (the doubt) is denied at first.

If it is asked: Why?, (we answer:) concerning the tree-trunk, on perceiving the characteristics like a bird's nest etc., when the knowledge: 'here there is a tree-trunk' arises, there is no doubt, since there is a cognition of things as they are.[1] In the same way concerning the existence of the man also, on perceiving the characteristics like the turning of the head etc., a cognition of things as they are arises: 'this is indeed a man', there is no doubt, since there is a cognition of things as they are.

When there are not the characteristics proper to a correct knowledge regarding both (= the tree-trunk and the man), while there is the non-exact determination (of any of both), there is no doubt. The meanings of 'non-ascertainment', 'non-exact determination', 'non-perception', 'lack of knowledge', 'non-seeing' are not different, they are synonyms of 'lack of knowledge', because they are the contrary of 'knowledge'.

In this way it should be explained: If there is knowledge through the reference to peculiarities, when peculiarities are not seen, lack of knowledge is produced. When the turning of the head and the moving of the hand etc. are seen, one is not doubtful. And when there are not peculiarities (to be seen), there is only lack of knowledge.

This happens to be: when there are peculiarities there is knowledge, but when this (= knowledge) is not, (there is) lack of knowledge only.

Since the third alternative according to which the peculiarities and the lack of peculiarities occur simultaneously is not (possible), doubt does not exist.

PRAYOJANA

XXIV

Nāgārjuna's denial of the purpose of action (prayojana).

It is said: Doubt exists concerning the object which is the purpose (of action) so long as in regard to it our knowledge does not arise with certainty[1]—if it is (thus) said, it must be answered:

24. *The object which is the purpose (of action) does not exist either if (action) exists or does not exist.*

'That object, aiming at which one acts, that is the purpose'[2]—so it has been said by you—[3] in the same way as the maker of a pot acts having the pot as (his) object. If the pot (already) exists in the clay, then the action of that (maker) would be without object; or if (the pot) does not exist (in the clay), on account of its inexistence, as (in the example of) the sand (and the oil),[4] in regard to it there is no action.[5]

DṚṢṬĀNTA

XXV

The opponent's affirmation of the purpose of action based on the existence of examples (dṛṣṭānta).

It is said that:

25. *In regard to sand action does not exist, but (the purpose of action exists) because there are examples*[1] *(that demonstrate its existence).*

As (for instance) when the woollen cloth is the purpose, there is an action in regard to woollen threads etc., but there is not in regard to blades of grass—if it is said so,

XXVI

Nāgārjuna's refutation of the previous objection.

(then) it must be answered: (An example) of that kind—

26. *It is also similar to the preceding one.*

XXVII

Nāgārjuna's denial of the example (dṛṣṭānta) *as involving a logical impossibility.*

Moreover

27. *Because the beginning and the middle do not exist, the end either is not seen.*

How could the end (*anta*) of an object be seen (*dṛṣṭa*) by whom the beginning and the middle is not seen? If the beginning and the middle do not exist, the end (*anta*) does not exist. For this reason the example (*dṛṣṭa-anta*) is non-existent.

XXVIII

Naiyāyika *definition and classification of* dṛṣṭānta. *Nāgārjuna's refusal of* dṛṣṭānta *through similarity.*

It is said that 'example is that matter in regard to which both the ordinary man and the investigator are of the same mind',[1] and that it is (through) similarity and (through) dissimilarity[2]—if it is thus said, it must be answered:

28. *By reason of similarity, fire is not example of fire.*[3]

What is called 'example by reason of similarity' that does not exist, because fire is not example of fire, since what is to be established and that which establishes would be without difference. If what is to be established is the same as that which establishes, how the example would be something different?

XXIX

Nāgārjuna's refusal of dṛṣṭānta *through dissimilarity.*

Moreover

29. *Water is not example of fire by reason of dissimilarity.*

Water which belongs to cold is not admitted as an example of fire. It is equal to say that somewhere water is cold and is like fire.[1]

XXX

Nāgārjuna's refusal of dṛṣṭānta *through slight similarity.*

30. *Furthermore if it is said that (the* dṛṣṭānta) *exists through a slight similarity,*[1] *(we answer that) it is not (so), as (it is seen through the case of) the (comparison between) the mountain Sumeru and a hair of the head.*[2]

If it is said regarding this matter that it can be so that the example exists through a slight similarity—this is not possible. If it is asked: Why?, (we answer that) in this world even the mountain Sumeru and a hair of the head both are of a slight similarity as regards existence, unity and corporeity.[3] Moreover it is not a general opinion to speak about a hair of the head similar to the Mount Sumeru.

XXXI

Nāgārjuna's refusal of dṛṣṭānta *through partial similarity and through partial dissimilarity.*

If it is said that (the *dṛṣṭānta*) takes place through partial similarity, it must be answered:

31. *Because of the previous refutation (the* dṛṣṭānta*) through partial similarity does not exist.*

In this world it is neither possible that (the *dṛṣṭānta*) be produced with a partial dissimilarity.[1] For this reason (the *dṛṣṭānta*) is not established (as existing) by means of a partial similarity and dissimilarity.

SIDDHĀNTA

XXXII

Nāgārjuna's denial of siddhānta *(the accepted theory).*

It is said: You affirm that (the example)[1] is not established (as existing) (*siddha*), but (this) must not be said (by you) together with (the statement of) the inexistence of the (category) 'accepted theory' (*siddhānta*)[2]—if it is thus said, it must be answered:

32. *If the beginning is not established (as existing), the end is not established (as existing) either; if the beginning is not established (as existing), both the middle and the end are not established (as existing).*

AVAYAVAS

XXXIII

Nāgārjuna's denial of the avayavas, *the parts (of the syllogism) having recourse to the arguments related to the whole and the parts*[1] *discussion.*

It is said: Deprived of parts[2] a demonstration would not exist, and so a speech of yours with parts would not exist. Thereby (your) whole (speech) because of its connectednessless would be discarded. Therefore, at all events it is necessary to speak having assumed the parts. Otherwise a denial (on your part) is not possible—if it is thus said, it must be answered:

33. *Because of the non-existence of the whole the parts do not exist.*[3]

Here because of the non-existence of the whole in the parts[4] which are the proposition (to be proved), the reason, the example, the application and the conclusion, the parts taken separately are non-existent.[5]

XXXIV

The whole does not exist in the parts.

It is said that the whole exists in the aggregate—if it is thus said, it must be answered:

34. *Because it (= the whole) does not exist (separately) in each (of the parts), it does not exist in the aggregate either.*

What is said: 'The whole exists in the aggregate', that is not possible. Because of the non-existence of the whole in each of the parts (separately), it does not exist in the aggregate either.

XXXV

Absurd consequences that occur if the whole is one.

Moreover

35. *If the whole is one,*[1] *it would result the absurd consequence of all the manifold parts being one.*

This error (occurs) not being (the whole) different (from the parts),[2] or else: being (the whole) one, different from the five parts, it would result the absurd consequence of (there) being six (elements).

XXXVI

The whole does not exist in any of the three times.

Furthermore

36. *Because (the whole) is not established (as existing) in any of the three times, the parts do not exist.*

The proposition (to be proved) and the other (parts of the syllogism) are arisen and non-arisen (at the same time as the whole); or (the whole) is past with respect to present (parts); or (the whole) is future and (the parts) present—(these alternatives) do not tolerate an examination, because they are not logical. For this reason being the whole non-existent, the parts also are non-existent.

XXXVII

Opponent's thesis: the whole may exist in the aggregate, although not in the parts.

37. *Or else like (in the example of) the Balbaja*[1] *grass, it (=the whole) is also established (as existing).*

If it is said that in the same way as it is not possible to bind an elephant with one single Balbaja grass, but it is possible with an aggregate of

Balbaja grass,[2] so the whole exists in the aggregate of the proposition (to be proved) and the other (members of the syllogism),

XXXVIII

Refutation of the opponent's objection because it implies a sādhyasama.

it must be answered:

38. *It is not (so), because (the reason adduced to prove) is equal to what is to be proved.*[1]

This is like the barren woman, and the blind and the sand. If by one barren woman a child cannot be procreated, in the same way by a multitude of several thousands of barren women it (= the child) cannot be procreated either. As in a blind person there is not the capacity of seeing, so in several thousands of blind persons there is not the capacity of seeing. As in every grain of sand there is not oil,[2] so by an aggregate of many (grains of sand) (oil) is not produced, because it does not exist.

XXXIX

The opponent's argumentation is not valid for the proposition and its letters.

Or if you think so: 'The examples of the barren woman etc. are indeed equal (to the Balbaja grass example of mine). (But) there is a capacity (of binding) suitable to the nature of the Balbaja (grass) even in one single Balbaja (grass) with which a butterfly etc., and some beings of that kind are bound; and by assembling many (blades of Balbaja grass) even an elephant could be bound'[1]—that is not possible. If it is asked: Why?, (it is)

39. *Because it is not logical.*

(Even) if it[2] is accepted as an example generally admitted of a whole, it is not fit for the two (presumptive) wholes (that follow),[3] because (their parts) do not coexist. The proposition (to be proved) and the other (members of the syllogism), and their (constitutive) letters do not co-exist at the same time and in the (same) place of the mouth.[4] For this reason this example of the Balbaja (grass) is not logical. And because it is not logical, the parts do not exist—so it has been established.[5]

XL

End of the discussion of the whole and the parts argument. Beginning of the refutation one by one of the five avayavas *or members (of the syllogism): Inexistence of the* pratijñā, *the proposition to be proved, the first member of the syllogism, because of the absurd consequences it would produce.*

Moreover

40. *There would occur the absurd consequence of the existence of parts also for the parts.*

If the parts were the establishers of an unestablished thing, they would also be either something established that establishes or something unestablished.

If they were something established that establishes, (then) also for those establishers, through which they (= the parts) have become establishers, other establishers would have to exist; and since for these latter also other (establishers would have to) exist, it would occur the absurd consequence of the *regressus ad infinitum.*

Or else if for these (parts) other (parts that establish them) do not exist, it would be necessary (for you)—after (your) assertion that the whole is established (as existing) through all these parts—to admit either the difference or the destruction of (your just mentioned) proposition.[1]

XLI

Nāgārjuna's refutation of the hetu, *the second member of the syllogism, because it cannot prove either being different from or identical to the* pratijñā.

Moreover

41. *If the reason*[1] *is different from the proposition (to be proved) or if it is not different, the reason does not exist.*

The proposition (to be proved) and the reason are different or are not different.

If they are indeed different, what happens? (Let us take) a proposition (to be proved:) 'The woollen cloth is indeed white'. If it is further asked: Which is the reason?, (we answer:) 'because it is black'. (This) is not admitted, because 'whiteness' is not established through 'black(ness)' (as) establisher.

Or else if the reason and the proposition (to be proved) are not (different), (and) if it is asked: What happens?, (we answer:) (Let us take) a proposition (to be proved:) 'The woollen cloth is white'. If it is asked: Which is the reason?, (we answer:) 'because it is white'. This (latter) indeed is not an establisher of that (former): the (latter) is equal to what is to be established.

XLII

Another proof against the hetu: *it cannot be admitted with or without another reason that supports it.*

Moreover

42. *(The reason does not exist) also, because for the reason there is not a reason.*

What is said to be arisen from a reason, that does not exist, since when for the reason another reason is also at hand, for this (latter) there is also another (reason). So the *regressus ad infinitum*[1] occurs.

Or else if for the reason the existence of (another) reason is not accepted, then the reason does not exist (as such). Otherwise (if it is accepted a reason without a reason, then), like the reason, everything would be established without a reason.

XLIII

Refutation of upanaya *and* nigamana, *the fourth and fifth members of the syllogism: they cannot exist since the* hetu *is inexistent.*

Moreover

43. *Because the proposition (to be proved) and the reason do not exist, the application and the conclusion*[1] *do not exist.*

So on account of the non-existence of the proposition (to be proved), of the reason and the example, the application and the conclusion, both, do not exist either.

XLIV

If the mere hetu *demonstrates, the* ahetuprasaṅga *would occur for the other members of the syllogism.*

Moreover

44. *For the remaining (members of the syllogism) a reason does not exist.*

If the proposition (to be proved) is demonstrated through the reason, (then) for the example and the other demonstrators (members of the syllogism) it would occur the absurd consequence of being without a reason.

XLV

If the mere hetu *demonstrates, the remaining* avayavas *would be useless.*

Moreover

45. *If it is asked what happens if the demonstration is made by means of the reason, (we answer:) the example and the other (members of the syllogism) are useless.*

If you think that it (= the proposition to be proved) is demonstrated through the mere reason, then the example and the other (members of the syllogism) will become useless, because the purpose (of the syllogism) is accomplished by the mere reason.

XLVI

If the example demonstrates, the hetu *would be useless and vice versa.*

Moreover

46. *Or (otherwise) the reason would be useless.*

Or if it is admitted that the example demonstrates, then the reason becomes useless. Otherwise the example is useless.

XLVII

Another argument against the hetu *and the* dṛṣṭānta : *it cannot be accepted that they exist because they demonstrate the soul, since the soul does not exist.*

It is said that for demonstrating the soul the reason and the example exist—if it is (thus) said, it must be answered:

47. *The soul cannot be demonstrated.*

You think that (the soul) can be demonstrated by a reason.[1] For instance it has been said by you: 'The soul is eternal'—the proposition (to be proved); 'because it has no body'—the reason; the example—'like the space'. (The eternity of the soul) being proved by a reason, the soul is not eternal, on account of (its) non-eternal being, since (the soul) is not an eternal nature, because (its eternity) does not exist by itself. So it is with the reason and the example.

XLVIII

Another argument against the existence of the avayavas *in general: they do not coexist.*

Moreover

48. *Because of being expressed one by one,*[1] *when one is there the other is not.*

When the proposition (to be proved) is expressed, then the reason and the other (members of the syllogism) do not exist, and also when the reason is expressed, the proposition (to be proved) and the other (members of the syllogism) do not exist. Therefore, the reason etc. are non-existent.

XLIX

Nāgārjuna rejects the opponent's assertion that he himself, on denying the avayavas *is maintaining a* pratijñā: *the* pratijñā *is impossible because its syllables do not coexist.*

On this respect it is said: It is a proposition (to be proved) of yours: 'All the members (of the syllogism) do not exist', consequently, because of having admitted a proposition (to be proved), for you the remaining (members of the syllogism) are also established (as existing)—if it is (thus) said, it must be answered:

49. *The syllables are also such.*[1]

Concerning all the syllables which are the parts of a non-established member (of the syllogism), that is also seen. In the same way as, because the syllable '*pra*', and the syllable '*ti*' and the syllable '*jñā*' do not exist at the same time, the *pratijñā* (= the proposition to be proved) does not exist; so, concerning the syllable '*pra*' too, because the utterance of '*pra*' etc. is according to a certain order, these syllables do not exist. And when one (syllable)—born out of the conditions which are the air, the space, the tongue, the teeth, the throat, the palate, the saliva and the exertion[2]—is there, the other is not.

TARKA

L

Nāgārjuna's refutation of reasoning (tarka) *in a way similar to the refutation of doubt.*

It is said that, since, when there is hesitation, immediately after one reasons,[1] then the category called 'reasoning'[2] exists; (and) because of its existence, the other (categories) are also established (as existing)—if it is (thus) said, it must be answered:

> 50. *Reasoning also is as the doubt.*

If it is asked: How is it?, (we answer:) the investigation is in relation to an object (already) known or in relation to an object not (yet) known. There, if it is in relation to an object (already) known, what is investigated? Or also if it is in relation to an object not (yet) known, what is investigated? (And) there is not a third alternative.

NIRṆAYA

LI

Nāgārjuna's refutation of determination (nirṇaya) *because of its impossibility either if the object and its attributes are identical or different.*

It is said that the ascertainment of the object after (due) examination is 'determination',[1] and that therefore a cause of the defined ('determination') is admitted; (and) that (the cause,) the examination aiming at the knowledge of reality, is reasoning[2]—if it is (thus) said, it must be answered:

51. *Since the matter and the existence and the unity etc. are not different neither non-different nor both, the determination does not exist.*

On this respect the pot, the existence, the unity, the roundness, the redness etc. are one (and the same) or are different.

In regard to this, if they are admitted to be one (and the same), (then it would result that) where any one from among existence etc. could happen to be, there (the pot) could be able to be, as it is the case with 'Śiva' and 'The Mighty One' and 'The Destroyer of Towns'. Otherwise, were it not so, then they (=existence etc.) would not be one (and the same).[3]

Or else, if they are different, then the pot, not being existent, would not be one neither would it be roundish nor red.

If it is said that the pot exists, because it is possessed of existence, (we answer that) that it is not (so): if something is possessed of something else, the former does not become the latter.

Therefore, since (they) are neither one (and the same) nor different nor both the determination does not exist.

VĀDA

LII

Nāgārjuna's refutation of the debate (vāda) *because of the non-existence of the word and the object designated by the word as they cannot exist either as one and the same or as different.*

It is said: 'The debate is provided with a demonstration and a criticism[1] through the means of valid knowledge; is not in contradiction to the accepted theory; is originated from the five members (of the syllogism); comprehends a thesis and a counter-thesis;'[2] and in this respect your intention to remove the pot etc.[3] comprehends (implicitly) a thesis and a counter-thesis[4]—(if it is said so,) it must be answered:

52. *The debate does not exist, because of the non-existence of both the name and that which is named.*

The debate does not exist either. In the same way as the determination does not exist, because the matter, the existence and the unity etc. are not different neither non-different (nor) both—so if the word 'pot' and the pot were one (and the same), (then) in the same way as the word 'pot' comes into existence outwardly without reference to the coming together of the lump of clay, the wheel, the water etc., (similarly) the pot (itself) etc. would come into existence after (merely) forming in the mind the idea of pot etc. On saying 'pot', the mouth would become full, and on saying 'fire', the lips would be burnt.[5] And it is not possible to accept such (a thing).

If (they = the word 'pot' and the pot itself) were different, on speaking out: 'pot', the pot would not be ascertained.

LIII

Nāgārjuna's denial of the conventional nature of the relation word-object adduced by the opponent because of the absurd consequences it implies when in relation with the opponent's own siddhāntas.

If it is said that there is a common usage of the word which is made by a convention,[1] (we answer:) (this) is not (so),

> 53. *Because there is occasion[2] for an examination of the true reality (attributed to the sixteen categories).*

Such as this: 'Liberation takes place by means of the thorough knowledge of the sixteen categories': this is the accepted theory of yours[3]—(you) foolish,[4] who follow the trifling thesis of logic![5]

Since (in your opinion) these sixteen categories, the means of valid knowledge and the other, exist in truth[6]—in regard to this (opinion of yours) which idea is acknowledged by the wise men?[7] These names, made by a convention of one's own are seen (to be used) just in regard to objects which are unreal—as (it happens with) 'Devadatta' and 'Indragupta'.

If liberation is (effected) through the mere common usages of the world, even all the cowkeepers etc. would be also liberated and the distinctions: 'wise' and 'ignorant' would not exist either.[8]

LIV

Another consequence of the conventional nature ascribed to words: multiplicity of words for the same object.

Moreover

54. *Names made by a convention are seen (to be) of multiple forms.*

As for instance[1] (the cow is called by different names by persons of different groups), and likewise, owing to the differences of languages of the countries, also (the same thing is called in Sanskrit *piṇḍarasa* and by other names or expressions in other languages).[2]

LV

Another consequence of the conventional nature of words: multiplicity of objects for the same word.

Moreover

55. *(And also) because even the wise men of the world are seen connecting many objects with (one) word.*

The wise men of the world connect the word '*go*'[1] to many (objects). The same thing (happens) also with the word '*hari*'. The word '*go*' is combined with many classes (of objects), as for instance:

(with) 'word', 'region', and 'earth-ground',
'ray of light', 'thunderbolt', 'cattle' and 'eye',
'water', and 'heaven'—with (these) nine meanings
the word '*go*' is to be taken by the wise.[2]

(And also) as

'Viṣṇu', 'lion', 'elephant', 'frog',
'sun and moon', 'light' and 'monkey',
'reddish brown', 'parrot',[3] 'Indra', 'snake',
are to be understood as 'hari' by the wise.[4]

'Rāhu', 'The Dweller', and 'Viṣṇu',
'Hari', 'Gopati', and 'The Lord',
'Narasiṃha', 'The Dwarf', 'The Serpent'—
as 'Nārāyaṇa' they are considered.[5]

So (this) is also to be applied to other words. Thus for each single word there are many meanings; and also for each object there are many words. So the words 'The Mighty one' and 'Indra' and 'The Destroyer of Towns' and 'Yajña' and 'Kauśika' and 'Śakra'[6] are combined with a single object. 'Inexistent' and 'non-existing' and 'not known'[7] are synonyms. They also are not established (as existing) in truth. For this reason since the defect of the word and the object being mixed in many ways is seen, (both) because of their uncertainty are not established (as existing).

LVI

Nāgārjuna reiterates his objection against the existence of the word and the object either as one and the same or as different.

Moreover

56. *Being one (and the same) the word and the object could not be established (as existing); and, being different,*

when the word 'pot' is employed, the knowledge referring to the pot would not be certain. Likewise if, being different they were also one (and the same), there would be the already mentioned defects. Because of this the debate does not exist.

JALPA AND VITAṆḌĀ

LVII

Nāgārjuna's refutation of discussion (jalpa) *and altercation* (vitaṇḍā) *by means of the same arguments adduced against the existence of debate* (vāda).

Moreover

57. *So are (to be refuted) also the discussion and the altercation.*

'So': in that same way of refutation in which the debate (has been refuted)—this is the meaning. Therefore, the discussion and the altercation are non-existent.[1]

HETVĀBHĀSA

LVIII

Nāgārjuna's refutation of fallacy or the mere appearance of a reason (hetvābhāsa): *it cannot exist either being similar with or different from a (true) reason.*

It is said: As all (reasons) have been put under discussion by you as being mere appearances of a reason,[1] nothing would have refutation—if it is (thus) said, it must be answered :

58. *The mere appearance of a reason does not exist, because of the non-existence of similarity and dissimilarity.*

If there were a mere appearance of a reason, it would be through similarity or (it) would be through dissimilarity.

Something that could become a mere appearance of a reason through similarity does not exist. In the same way as in a thorough testing of pure gold in (what is) pure gold, one does not discard the gold (and) that, being gold, is not a mere appearance of gold, so what is a reason, being only a reason, is not a mere appearance of reason.

(And) likewise it cannot become a mere appearance of reason through dissimilarity either. The pebbles etc. that are not gold, how would they become a mere appearance of gold?—so in the same way what is not a reason, that could not be a mere appearance of reason, because the very reason does not exist (in it).

The so-called 'mere appearance' (of a thing) is not the thing itself, because (this: the thing itself) is the opposite to (that: the mere appearance of a thing).

As for (the hypothesis of) the transformation of a self-dependent (entity), (this one) cannot be destroyed through peculiarities unequal to its basis, or the representation of that (self-dependent entity), (produced) out of (peculiarities) equal to its basis, is indeed the cognition of it.

Likewise after due examination the so-called 'mere appearance of a reason' does not exist at all.

Since the reason does not exist, and a third (kind of mere appearance of a reason as something) different from the reason is not admitted, therefore the mere appearance of a reason does not exist.

LIX

Nāgārjuna's refutation of a special kind of fallacy, the indecisive or inconclusive (anaikāntika, savyabhicārin) *reason* (hetu), *because the reason's own self of being a probans cannot be lost.*

Moreover

59. *The (reason) non affected by indecision*[1] *(in its own nature) is (produced) out of the lack of indecision.*

If it is asked: Wherefrom the fact of not being affected by indecision (is produced for a reason)?, (we answer that) it (= that reason) in its own self either is accompanied by indecision or it is not affected by indecision.

If it, in its own self, is not affected by indecision, it is not accompanied by indecision. If it is asked: Why?, (we answer that it is so,) because the own nature of one's self cannot be rejected. Because (the reason) exists thanks to its own self (=the fact of being a *probans*), it cannot be accompanied by indecision. Or else rejecting the own nature, even so it could not be accompanied by indecision, because, after rejecting its own nature, an entity cannot exist. Otherwise it would not be logic. So it has been taught. The reason which is provided with the nature of a prover of what is to be proved, thanks to its own self, is not accompanied by indecision. And what is not a nature of prover of what is to be proved, because it is not a reason, cannot be accompanied by indecision; and since there is not a third alternative,

LX

The opponent adduces two examples in order to prove the possibility of existence of an indecisive or inconclusive reason.

it is said:

60. *A reason that is accompanied by indecision is (possible).*

As for instance in regard to both 'space' and 'action' the bodilessness (is a reason accompanied by indecision), and in regard to 'atom' and 'pot' etc. the generality and particularity (are) as well (a reason accompanied by indecision).

LXI

Nāgārjuna refutes the objection of the previous sūtra expressing that the examples given therein are not appropriate, because each of these examples refers to two different reasons and not to one and the same reason.

61. *If it is said (so), (we answer:) this is not (possible), because they (= the reasons) are different (in each case).*

They (=the reasons accompanied by indecision) do not exist. If it is asked: Why?, (we answer:) because they (=the reasons) are different (in each case). What is the bodilessness that exists in the space—it is not logical that it indeed exist in the action and in the mind, because the arising and the non-arising are contradictory. Here while the bodilessness of the action and the mind etc. is provided with arising, (the bodilessness) of the space is indeed not (provided with arising). What is the bodilessness of the space, that does not exist in the action, since the action is provided with arising, because (the bodilessness) arises, when (the action) arises together with that bodilessness, and (the bodilessness) also perishes, when (the action) perishes with it. Therefore, the space and its bodilessness are different (from the action and its bodilessness). What is the bodilessness of the space—that is not logical in the action, in the mind etc., and what is the bodilessness of the action, that also does not exist in the space.

What proves that there is some cause for proving or refuting, that is not affected by indecision in regard to its nature of a prover; the same is to be said also in regard to refutation. Therefore, a reason that is accompanied by indicision does not exist. Even if (a reason) were contradictory, (that does) not (mean that) it is accompanied by indecision. Therefore, the bodilessness of space is not (a reason) affected by indecision in regard to proving (its) eternity. It is the same also in regard to the action etc.

LXII

Another argument against the existence of the inconclusive reason.

Moreover

62. *Also because of the momentariness.*

Proving or refuting are not logically possible concerning that object in regard to which proving or refuting are made, if (when proving or refuting are accomplished), it (= the object) is (already) destroyed. Even if (it could be admitted that) a reason proves or refutes when both (objects of proving or refuting) subsist, (nevertheless) when they (just born, immediately) vanish, it is not logically possible that a reason prove or refute them, because both (objects) are not (anymore) subsisting. Therefore, a reason accompanied by indecision does not exist.

LXIII

An opponent's objection: contradiction exists as a consequence of the confrontation between Nāgārjuna's denial of the inconclusive reason and the Nyāya's *affirmation of it.*

It is said:

63. *In your opinion even if it could be said that all reasons are contradictory, there are not (reasons) accompanied by indecision.*[1]

(In my opinion) only an inconclusive (reason) is accompanied by indecision. (And in your opinion) what proves is not affected by indecision in regard to its nature of a prover; and the same is to be said also in regard to refutation; (and) therefore a reason that is accompanied by indecision does not exist.[2] So there is contradiction—if it is (thus) said (by the opponent),

LXIV

Rejection by Nāgārjuna of the contradictory reason (viruddha hetu) *because of the impossibility of any chronological relation between the* hetu (probans) *and the thesis or proposition to be proved* (pratijña) *to which it is related.*

it must be answered:

64. *(A reason) contradictory (to the thesis) does not exist, because it arises before or after (the thesis).*

What is said to be a contradictory (reason),[1] that does not exist.

(A reason) contradictory to a (thesis that has arisen) before does not exist, because (that reason that arises) after (the thesis) does not exist (at the moment when the thesis has arisen in order to vanish immediately after).

(A reason) contradictory to (a thesis) said afterwards does not exist either, because the reason (that has arisen in order to vanish immediately after) before (the thesis) does not exist (at the moment when the thesis arises).[2]

As for the existence of a contradiction, in case both (= the reason and the thesis) subsisted at one and the same time, (we reject it, because) there is no way for the propounder of a theory and his opponent of saying just at the same time their objections and counter-objections, (and not being possible the coexistence, there is no contradiction,) because two things that do not subsist together are not contradictory.

LXV

Nāgārjuna refutes the existence of the reason 'whose time has passed away' (kālātīta) *or mistimed reason.*

It is said that the mere appearance of a reason called '(a reason) whose time has passed away'[1] exists, (and that) because of its existence the mere appearance of a reason exists—if it is (thus) said, it must be answered:

65. *The past has passed away.*[2] *'(A reason whose time) has passed away' is past.*[2]

On this respect it is said by you (= the opponent) that the time of the pot itself is the present, and that the time of the mass of clay is the past, and that potsherds themselves are the future time.[3] The potsherds are something future, therefore, (in relation to the potsherds) also the times of the mass of clay and of the pot, both, (ought to) become past. (But) since they (=the mass of clay and the pot) do not exist in that moment, those (= the potsherds) of what are they future? If it is said that the present and the past exist, (we answer that) even they do not exist. Because the past does not exist in regard to the present time and because likewise the present also does not exist in regard to the past time, in regard to all (the three) times (the negation) is valid.[4]

LXVI

Another argument presented by Nāgārjuna against the existence of the past time, ground for the existence of the mistimed (kālātīta) *reason: the way of expression in the different languages confirms the inexistence of the past.*

66. (*The past does not exist,*) *because it would result also the absurd consequence of the inexistence of all the kinds of languages.*

In the world there are numerous kinds of languages: the *saṃskṛta* (well-constructed), the *asaṃskṛta* (not well constructed) and the *prākṛta* (the ordinary one). (In *saṃskṛta* it is said:) What has (already) arisen, is the past (*atīta*); what exists is the present (*vartamāna*), and what will arise is the future (*anāgata*). The same is to be applied to the *asaṃskṛta* and the *prākṛta* languages. (Thus) let (the opponent) not speak owing to the defect of (his) *siddhānta* (of the existence of the reason whose time has passed away) not having been ascertained.

LXVII

Denial of the existence of the past as depending on a passed away reason.

Moreover

67. *The passed away reason and the passed away time do not exist.*

If it is asked: Why?, (we answer:)

Because it is not possible.

Although the reason itself is heard by the ear, it does not exist (as) something past, since it has passed away.[1] The passed away time is not logical either, because the reason (on which it should depend) is something that has passed away. The present time does not depend on a passed away reason, (because in that case) this (= the present time) would be the time of the reason on which it (= the present time) depends.[2] Therefore, on being examined according to such and other proofs, the passed away time does not exist, and the mistimed reason does not exist either.

CHALA

LXVIII

Nāgārjuna's refutation of sophism (chala): *he has considered the* padārthas *in the same way as his opponent, so he has not incurred in the sophism-defect the opponent attributes to him.*

It is said:

68. *Although all has been spoken of (by me) as (being real) logical categories* (pada-artha), *in your opinion they do not exist as true entities* (parama-artha).

It must be answered:

No, because it would result the absurd consequence (of a sophism being any refutation.

This is not so, because whatever has been said (by me) as a refutation,[1] all that has been (said) as having the nature of *padārthas.*[2] If it is asked: Why?, (we answer:) all the disputants, by accepting (what you say) would necessarily destroy their own words. Therefore, (whatever is said) is accepted as a refutation, but it is not a sophism. Or else if that principle is not admitted, then a sophism does not occur.

JĀTI
LXIX

Nāgārjuna's refutation of irrelevant rejoinder (jāti), *because 'arising'* (jāti) *is impossible.*

It is said that the category 'irrelevant rejoinder'[1] exists in relation to an ascertained subject, in relation to which takes place, under manifold forms, through refutation, an irrelevant-rejoinder-objection[2]—if it is (thus) said, it must be answered:

69. *Since something arisen, and not arisen, and both (= arisen and not arisen) do not exist, the irrelevant rejoinder* (jāti) *does not exist.*

If it is asked: What is said to be 'an irrelevant rejoinder', how (is it produced)? (It must be answered:) It arises either being something that has already arisen or being something that has not yet arisen or being something that is arising.

Now something that has already arisen is not (something that can arise), because of being already arisen.

Something that has not yet arisen is not (something that can arise), because of not being yet arisen.

(And) since both (= the previous two alternatives of arisen and not arisen) do not exist, something that is arising does not exist; not being separated from being arisen and not being arisen, the action of being arising is non-existent.[3]

NIGRAHASTHĀNĀNI

LXX

Nāgārjuna's refutation of the reiterative statement (punarvacana), *one of the points-of-defeat (in argumentation)* (nigrahasthānāni).

It is said: The demonstration is done by you in a reiterative way. Since you, who denies manifold subjects by means of (the notions of) 'exists' and 'does not exist', do not have another way (of denying than that),[1] then the points-of-defeat (in argumentation)[2] exist—if it is (thus) said, it must be answered:

70. *It is not (so), because what is (said) before and what is (said) after are neither the same nor different.*

Reiteration does not exist. If reiteration existed, it would be through the same or different words. The word (that is said) before and (the word that is said) after cannot be a reiteration of the same. If it is asked: Why?, (we answer:) since it has been (already) said, therefore, it is not (possible for it to be) said again[3] because it indeed (already) exists. Since it indeed (already) exists, even (if it is) said by the hundreds, how could it be repeated? Or if it is said that (what is said after) is different from what is (said) before, (then we answer:) it cannot be a reiteration either, because it is indeed different, and also because they are momentary.[4] Even the word when said before is one thing, and (when said) after, (although) being similar to that (said before), is another thing. Therefore, what is reiterated is different.

LXXI

All the points of defeat in argumentation are to be declared inexistent as the irrelevant rejoinders by similar arguments.

Moreover

71. *The points-of-defeat (in the argumentation) are also likewise.*[1]

In the same way as the irrelevant rejoinder does not exist, because something arisen and not arisen (and) both (=arisen and not arisen) do not exist, so the points-of-defeat (in the argumentation) also do not exist. The so-called 'points-of-defeat (in the argumentation)' could arise either from a point-of-defeat (in the argumentation) or from a not-point-of-defeat (in the argumentation). Both forms (of arising) are not possible either. Therefore, they (= the points of defeat in the argumentation) do not exist.

LXXII

Last argument adduced by Nāgārjuna against the existence of points of defeat in argumentation.

Moreover

72. *For the points of defeat (in argumentation) there is no defeat, as it is the case of enchainment.*

For the very points of defeat there is no defeat. As for instance in the case of the place of enchainment, the place itself undoubtedly is not enchained, and therefore there is no (possibility of) ascertainment of this (place of enchainment).

CONCLUSION

LXXIII

Nāgārjuna's conclusion: the only result reached by the previous discussion is that neither the padārthas *nor their negation exist. And if things do not exist, names also do not exist.*

It is said that in the same way as the means of valid knowledge and the other (categories) are to be denied, the negation itself does not exist—if it is (thus) said, it must be answered:

73. *Because of the non-acceptance of both (i.e. the means of valid knowledge etc. and their negation). As they (the means of valid knowledge and their negation) have not been established (as existing), the only thing that results is that they are not established (as existing).*

If it is admitted that, because of the non-existence of the means of valid knowledge and the other (categories), the negation itself does not exist, and that being so, both are indeed not established (as existing).

One is speaking according to reality. Names do not exist.

Because of the non-existence of identity, difference and both (together) it is accepted that all the things do not exist. Being so, without things there are no objects to be named nor names either. For this reason the so-called '*nirvāṇa*' and 'liberation' are not different things.

(Here) ends the 'Treatise of the subtle pulverization', which removes the sixteen categories, i.e. the means of valid knowledge etc., composed by the *ācārya*, Ārya Nāgārjuna.

By commandment of Yon tan grags pa, the Great Friend of all Virtues, (this treatise) has been translated, revised and fixed by the Kaśmirian *paṇḍita* Jayānanda, and the great lotsāba of Tibet, the Buddhist monk, Mdo sde ḥbar from Khu.

Khu.oom Khu.om Khu.uom Khu.uom Khu.uo

COMMENTARY

COMMENTARY ON THE DOCTRINARY CONTENTS

Section I: **Aim of the treatise. Negation of the sixteen logical categories.**

The author expresses in Sūtra 1 which is the purpose of the treatise: to eliminate the pride of logicians eager of discussions. This purpose will be attained showing that the sixteen logical categories, enumerated in the commentary, whose existence is for them beyond doubt and which are the basis of their debates, do not really exist. This is the position of the *śūnyatāvādins.*

PRAMĀṆA AND PRAMEYA

Section II: **Confusion of *pramāṇa* and *prameya.***

The means of valid knowledge, *pramāṇa,* and the knowable (object), *prameya* are undistinguishably mixed. Only when there is *prameya* it is possible to say that there is a *pramāṇa* and *vice versa.* When there is no *prameya,* it is not possible to say that there is a *pramāṇa* and *vice versa.* The one exists in relation to the other, as a father exists as father in relation to his son and a son exists as a son in relation to his father. So it is thanks to the *prameya* that the *pramāṇa* is established and *vice versa.* No *prameya* can be said to exist without a *pramāṇa,* which brings it into existence. The *pramāṇa* is thus the *bhāvasādhana* of the *prameya.* At its turn no *pramāṇa* is possible without the existence of its corresponding *prameya.* In this sense the *prameya* is also the *bhāvasādhana* of the *pramāṇa.* So *pramāṇa* and *prameya* both have, each one in relation to the other, the two same functions: each one establishes the other, gives rise to the other, is its *sādhana*; and each one is established, is given rise, by the other, is its *sādhya.* Cf. Vātsyāyana *Bh ad NS* 2, 1, 10 (*pūrvapakṣa*): *asati pramāṇe kena pramīyamāṇo 'rthaḥ prameyaḥ syāt? pramāṇena khalu pramīyamāṇo 'rthaḥ prameyam ityetat sidhyati,* and *ad* 2, 1, 11: *asati pramāṇe prameyaṃ na sidhyati, pramāṇena pramīyamāṇo 'rthaḥ prameyam iti vijñāyata iti*, and Uddyotakara *Vārttika*, p. 89, lines 4-5: *sarvaṃ ca pramāṇaṃ svaviṣayaṃ prati bhāvasādhanam.* Now it is admitted by the epistemological Indian tradition that a *pramāṇa* is that which produces (*karaṇa*) the knowledge (*pramā*) of something (*prameya*) (cf. Vātsyāyana *Bh ad NS* 2, 1, 11: *upalabdhihetuś ca pramāṇam*, and *ad* 2, 1, 16: *yadā ca upalabdhiviṣayaḥ kvacid upalabdhisādhanaṃ bhavati, tadā pramāṇaṃ prameyam iti caiko 'rtho'bhidhīyate*), consequently it can also be considered that a *prameya* is the *pramāṇa* of the *pramāṇa*, since it is that which makes possible, produces the knowledge of the *pramāṇa*, is its unavoidable cause; and the *pramāṇa*, as that whose knowledge is produced by the *prameya* (in its *pramāṇa* function), becomes a *prameya*. So we have, as the commentary says, that the (original) *pramāṇa* has become the *prameya* of its own (original) *prameya* and the (original) *prameya* has become the *pramāṇa* of its own (original) *pramāṇa*. As a consequence of all that has been said, the *pramāṇa* and the *prameya* come into existence only through their mutual relation of dependence.

Section III: ***Pramāṇa* and *prameya* are not *ex se*.**

This Sūtra expresses a consequence that results from the fact of *pramāṇa* and *prameya* being mutually dependent: they cannot be established, they cannot exist, out of themselves, they are not *ex se*. This proposition is corroborated by an argument *ex absurdo*, a *prasaṅga*, developed in the commentary. If it is supposed that the *pramāṇa* and the *prameya* are really existent, have an own being, then the *pramāṇa* would exist out of itself. But, as the *pramāṇa* (according to the previous *sūtra*) is also the *prameya*, it would happen that the *pramāṇa* is produced out of the *prameya*. And inversely, as the *prameya* (according to the previous *sūtra*) is also the *pramāṇa*, it would likewise happen that the *prameya* is produced out of the *pramāṇa*. All this implies, on one side, a mutual causality: the *pramāṇa* produces the *prameya* and at the same time the *prameya* produces the *pramāṇa*; and, on the other side, a contradiction: the *prameya*, although having an own being, is produced out of something else (the *pramāṇa*); and the *pramāṇa*, although having an own being, is produced out of something else (the *prameya*). Because of these absurd consequences (mutual causality and contradiction) it cannot be admitted that the *pramāṇa* and the *prameya* have an existence *in se et per se*.

Section IV: ***Pramāṇa* and *prameya*, as mutually dependent, are neither existent nor non-existent nor existent and non-existent.**

The Sūtra 4 states a general principle: what exists, what does not exist and what exists and does not exist at the same time cannot be in relation of dependence on something else. The commentary gives the logical foundation of this principle: (1) An existing thing cannot be dependent on anything. If a pot exists, then it does not depend for its existence on anything else, as for instance its constituent parts, like the clay etc. For the Buddhist nothing has an existence independent and apart from its constituent parts; but for the Naiyāyika (whom the author of this treatise is refuting) everything has an existence independent and apart from its constituent parts (for instance: the clay). From the Naiyāyika's point of view it can be affirmed that the pot, as having an existence independent and apart from its constituent parts, does not depend on anything. (2) Something inexistent, as for instance the hare's horn, cannot obviously be in relation of dependence with anything else. (3) The hypothesis of an existing and non-existing thing depending on something else cannot be admitted because both elements of this alternative have been already discarded.

This general principle is to be applied to *pramāṇa* and *prameya*: if they are mutually dependent, they cannot exist, not exist or exist and not exist at the same time.

Of these three alternatives it is the first one (impossibility of existence for *pramāṇa* and *prameya*) that will be dealt with in the following Sūtras.

Section V: **The opponent affirms: *pramāṇas* must exist in order that *prameyas* may be established. Rejection of this thesis: the *pramāṇas* cannot be established by other *pramāṇas*, because the logical defect of a *regressus ad infinitum* would be produced.**

In the commentary that precedes the Sūtra an objection is raised against the thesis of the non-existence of *pramāṇa*: if the *pramaṇas* did not exist, the things that constitute the objects of knowledge would not be perceived—what is contrary to the daily common experience. The Sūtra answers this objection in a very concise way. The implied reasoning is as follows: the *pramāṇa* cannot attest the existence of the *prameya* (*ma yin te*), because its own existence or validity must be proved by another *pramāṇa*, and this other *pramāṇa* at its own turn needs another *pramāṇa* in order to be proved, and so on. In this way the logical defect (*thal ba, prasaṅga*) of a *regressus ad infinitum* (*thag pa med pa, anavasthā*) would be produced.

The commentary after the Sūtra begins referring to the opponent's objection expressed in the commentary that introduces the Sūtra: how can the *prameyas* be established without *pramāṇas*? The idea underlying this objection is that the *prameyas* are proved by the *pramāṇas*. This gives rise to a question on the part of our author: how at their own turn are the *pramāṇas* established (as existing)? Two alternatives are possible: (1) the *pramāṇas* are established (as existing) by means of other *pramāṇas*, and (2) the *pramāṇas* are not established (as existing) by means of other *pramāṇas*.

The basis of the first alternative (expressed in the commentary) is that the *pramāṇas* belong to the category of objects (*don*) and as such are to be established through *pramāṇas*. This alternative results in a *regressus ad infinitum* and therefore cannot be admitted.

The second alternative cannot be adopted, because it does not respect the logicians' principle that all object is to be established (as existing) by a *pramāṇa*; this principle would be destroyed. With this second alternative there would be a kind of objects, the *pramāṇas*, that would not comply to this principle. This principle is precisely the foundation of the objector's argumentation expressed in the beginning of this Section: all *prameyas*, as objects, must be established by *pramāṇas*.

Then if we have no recourse to a *pramāṇa* in order to establish the existence or the validity of a given *pramāṇa*, which is the special *probans* (*khyad par gyi gtan tshigs, viśeṣahetu*) that establishes it? Which is the difference (*mi ḥdra ba, visadṛśatva*) between the *pramāṇa* and the other objects (*don*) which require a *pramāṇa* in order to be established?

Section VI: **The opponent affirms: the *pramāṇas* are *svayaṃsiddha* (auto-established) as the lamplight, so no *regressus ad infinitum* is produced.**

The objector answers that the *pramāṇas* do not need other *pramāṇas* in order to be established; they establish themselves, they are *svayaṃsiddha* (auto-established) besides establishing the *prameyas*, as the lamplight which illuminates itself and things around it.

In order to avoid falling in the *regressus ad infinitum*, a special *probans* of the validity of the *pramāṇas* is presented by the objector: their *svayaṃsiddhatva*. This special *probans* implies a difference between the *pramāṇas* and the other objects (*don*): the *pramāṇas* are *svayaṃsiddha*, the other objects are not so.

The defence of the opponent is constituted by an *upamāna* reasoning. The lamplight makes things 'appear' before our eyes out from darkness and the *pramāṇas* similarly makes things 'appear' before our mind out of non-cognition. Based on this likeness the opponent ascribes to *pramāṇas* an attribute of the lamplight: the power of self-illumination, which, in the case of the *pramāṇas*, is the power of self-establishing.

And, as is said in the last sentence of the commentary of this Sūtra, as there is not *regressus ad infinitum* for the lamplight since, owing to its attribute of self-illumination, it does not need another lamplight in order to be illuminated, so there is not *regressus ad infinitum* for the *pramāṇas* since, owing to their attribute of self-establishment, they do not need other *pramāṇas* in order to be established.

Section VII: **The analogy of lamplight and *pramāṇas* adduced by the opponent is unfit, because the lamplight cannot illuminate darkness, since no connection is possible between them.**

The author of the treatise refutes in Sūtras 7-11 the argument of *svayaṃsiddhi* put forward by the opponent denying the lamplight the capacity to illuminate itself and others. In this way the lamplight analogy is rejected as useless for proving that the *pramāṇas* can establish themselves and the *prameyas*. If nevertheless the analogy of the lamplight and the *pramāṇas* were maintained, it would turn itself against the thesis it was intended to support: as the lamplight cannot illuminate either itself or others, so the *pramāṇas* cannot establish either themselves or even the *prameyas*.

The argumentation against the capacity of the lamplight to illuminate others is carried on in Sūtras 7-9, and the argumentation against the capacity to illuminate itself in Sūtras 10-11.

The author of the treatise introduces in these Sūtras the concept of darkness, because darkness has to be illuminated or removed in order to allow other things, concealed by it, to be perceived. In the Sūtra 7 it is affirmed that the lamplight cannot illuminate darkness. Theoretically there are two possibilities: (1) the lamplight gets in contact with darkness and (2) the lamplight does not get in contact with darkness. The first possibility cannot be accepted, because a connection between the lamplight and darkness is impossible, since they are contradictory and thus the existence or presence of the one excludes that of the other. So there remains only the second possibility of non-connection between the lamplight and darkness. Without connection the lamplight cannot affect darkness, as a sword cannot cut a body that it does not touch.

Section VIII: **In order to save his thesis of *svayaṃsiddhi* the opponent argues that, even without getting into contact with darkness, the lamplight can affect it, adducing in support of his saying the case of the planets that have a hurtful influence on men. That new analogy is also declared to be unfit.**

In the first half of the Sūtra the opponent argues without entering into details that it is possible that the lamplight affect or illuminate darkness (even without getting into contact with it), in the same way as the planets affect or do harm to men. In the last part of the Sūtra Nāgārjuna answers that that objection in not well grounded, because there is not equivalence between the lamplight in regard to darkness and the planets in regard to men affected by their influence, as the commentary will explain more in detail.

The commentary begins with Nāgārjuna's affirmation that the evil done by the planets affects Devadatta or takes possession of his body because it gets into contact with Devadatta. This is the first difference between, on one side, the case of the planets and Devadatta etc. and, on the other side, the case of the lamplight and darkness: the planets do really get into contact with Devadatta etc.; the lamplight (in the alternative which is being analyzed) does not get into contact with darkness.

Moreover the planets, like the fire etc., do harm exclusively to what possesses a body. This is not so in the case of the lamplight and darkness, because the latter does not have a body. This is the second difference between both cases.

A last difference between both cases is that the planets can do harm to Devadatta's body and senses from a far distance, because Devadatta has a body, but the lamplight does not have the power to affect something from a far distance and, even if it had that power, it could not affect the body and the senses of darkness, by the mere reason that these do not exist.

Nāgārjuna rejects in this way the example of the planets adduced by the opponent as an argument in favour of his thesis that the lamplight can illuminate darkness: in the case of the planets there is contact (and there is contact, because what is affected by the planets has a body), in the case of the lamplight there is not (and there is not, because darkness does not possess a body). So both examples cannot be matched.

In the last part of the commentary Nāgārjuna examines the second hypothesis, that of the lamplight illuminating darkness even without being in contact with it. This hypothesis would lead to an absurd consequence, contradictory to facts: the lamplight would illuminate even the darkness existing in far removed places.

Section IX: **Darkness does not exist, so it cannot be illuminated or dispelled, and therefore the *dṛṣṭānta* adduced by the opponent in Section VI is not valid.**

This Sūtra and its commentary adduce another argument against the possibility of the lamplight illuminating darkness.

The Sūtra simply states that those who are philosophers among common people are said to be comparable to lions, i.e. are most important persons, whose opinions must be accepted.

The commentary explains who are 'common people' (*ḥjig rten pa, laukika*) and who are philosophers or investigators (*spyod pa po, parīkṣaka*) and mentions some of them. Then the commentary expresses that 'that matter in regard to which they are of the same opinion, is established as an example'. This sentence corresponds exactly to *NS* 1.1.25: *laukikaparīkṣakāṇāṃ yasminn arthe buddhisamyaṃ sa dṛṣṭāntaḥ*. Now these philosophers maintain that 'darkness' (*mun pa, tamas*) is only a name for the inexistence of light. The commentary refers also to other investigators who affirm that, whatever be its nature, darkness is not found anywhere. Consequently, because of the inexistence of darkness as a real entity, because its being only an *abhāva*, the statement that the lamplight, illuminating or dispelling darkness, establishes itself and the other objects as existing is not true; the lamplight cannot illuminate or dispel a non-existing thing like the hare's horn or darkness. And this false statement cannot serve as an analogy (*upamāna*) to establish that also the *pramāṇas* establish themselves and the other objects as existing. An erroneous analogy cannot prove anything. Thus the conclusion is that there is not a category *pramāṇa* which has been provided with an example (*dṛṣṭānta*) that founds, supports or demonstrates its existence. The commentary ends by affirming that the category *pramāṇa* established by an example and establishing other objects does not exist, whereby the opponent's thesis is rejected.

Section X: **Impossibility for the lamplight of illuminating itself, because of the inexistence in it of darkness.**

After having refuted the second alternative presented in the opponent's statement of Sūtra 6, (the lamplight illuminates the other objects), Nāgārjuna proceeds to refute the first one (the lamplight illuminates itself). In the Sūtra it is said why the lamplight does not illuminate itself: because darkness does not exist.

What the Sūtra denies here is not the existence of darkness in itself but the existence of darkness in the lamplight, as is made explicit by the commentary. Darkness would have to be in the lamplight, in order that the lamplight could illuminate itself. And this is impossible because the opposite natures of both.

Section XI: **Another reason for the impossibility of the lamplight to illuminate itself: the *prasaṅga* of darkness obscuring itself would occur.**

This Sūtra adds another argument against the possibility of the illumination of the lamplight by itself. If the lamplight illuminates itself, it would result the necessary absurd consequence (*thal bar ḥgyur ba, prasaṅga*) of darkness obscuring, i.e. concealing itself. The *prasaṅga*, that would occur in this case, consists (taking into account the commentary) in it that, if we grant the opponent's contention that the lamplight illuminates itself and other objects, it can be deduced the conclusion that the contrary also would occur, i.e. that darkness, the contrary to lamplight, would also accomplish the action contrary to illuminating: it would obscure or conceal itself. And, as a consequence thereof, darkness would not be perceived (*mi dmigs pa thob par ḥgyur*)—a conclusion which is palpably absurd as it is directly contradicted by experience. The absurdity of the consequence proves the groundlessness of the opponent's contention.

Moreover, the lamplight cannot reach the darkness that is concealed by itself and consequently is not seen, in the same way as it cannot reach anything else in the same condition.

In this way has been discarded the example of the lamplight as something able to illuminate itself and other objects, which the opponent had adduced in Sūtra 6 in order to establish the *svayaṃsiddhi*, autovalidity, of the *pramāṇas*—a means of avoiding the *anavasthā* or *regressus ad infinitum* that would occur (Sūtra 5) if the *pramāṇas* were to be established by other *pramāṇas*.

Section XII: **Another argument against the existence of *pramāṇa* and *prameya*: the impossibility of any chronological relation between them.**

The Sūtra sets forth a new argument against the existence of the *pramāṇa* and *prameya* logical categories reinforcing that of Sūtras 5-11: they cannot exist 'either in the present or in the past or in the future'. This expression is to be understood in the sense that the anteriority, posteriority and simultaneity of the *pramāṇa* in relation to the *prameya* is not logically possible.

The idea underlying the demonstration that follows is that *pramāṇa* and *prameya* are relational concepts: a *pramāṇa* cannot exist without a *prameya* and *vice versa*; both are meaningless if considered isolated, apart one from the other. Cf. our commentary of Section II.

If the *pramāṇa* existed before the corresponding *prameya*, we would have a *pramāṇa* existing before the *prameya* that it requires in order to come into existence. And, if the *prameya* does not exist when the *pramāṇa* arises, what would be ascertained by the *pramāṇa*, whose essence and reason of being is to ascertain *something* else?

If the *pramaṇa* comes into existence after the *prameya*, we would have a *prameya* existing alone, without a *pramāṇa*. How would it be possible for something to be 'knowable' without a corresponding 'knowledge'? If there could be an inexistent *pramāṇa* of an existent *prameya*, an absurd consequence would result: any non-existing thing as e.g. the horns of the hare, could become a *pramāṇa*. Furthermore it is not possible that in a relation between two entities, as *pramaṇa* and *prameya*, one be inexistent and the other existent.

If the *pramāṇa* and the *prameya* arise together, come together into existence (as for instance the two horns of the cow), the relation of cause and effect, that they have in the mutual dependence that links them one another, would be impossible, as the two horns of the cow that are born together have no cause-effect relation between them.

Section XIII: **Opponent's rejection of the negation of the existence of *pramāṇa* and *prameya*: the denial implies the existence of the denied object.**

The opponent in the Sūtra argues that, if the existence of the *pramāṇa* and *prameya* is not admitted either in the past, or the future or the present (in the meaning we have explained in the commentary of the previous Sūtra), then the denial of the *pramāṇa* and *prameya* would become impossible. The idea upon which this argument is founded is that no negation (*pratiṣedha*) is possible if there is no object to be negated (*pratiṣedhya*).

The commentary develops the opponent's argument. If Nāgārjuna's statement of Sūtra 12 (*pramāṇa* and *prameya* do not exist in any of the three times) is accepted, the reasoning that supports it should also be accepted and there would result that the negation of the *pramāṇa* and *prameya* at its turn should not be admitted, since the same reasoning that Nāgārjuna applied in Sūtra 12 to the *pramāṇa* in regard to the *prameya* in order to deny both of them, could be applied to the negation in regard to what it denies: it is not possible for the negation either to precede or to follow or to be simultaneous with the deniable object.

The conclusion implicit in the opponent's reasoning is that the elimination, because of its impossibility, of the negation of the *pramāṇa* and the *prameya*, put forward by Nāgārjuna, leaves as a result the existence of the *pramāṇa* and the *prameya*. Furthermore with the inexistence of the *pramāṇa* and the *prameya* (Sūtra 12) (if accepted), the negation would remain without an object. In this situation two questions arise: (1) How could a non-existing negation deny something? and (2) How could something non-existing (*abhāva*), as the *pramāṇa* and the *prameya* (in Nāgārjuna's opinion), be denied? So the negation of the *pramāṇa* and the *prameya* is impossible.

But if, notwithstanding the foregoing argumentation, it is maintained that the negation exists, then the *pramāṇa* and the *prameya* must also be admitted as existing, because the *pramāṇa* and the *prameya* belong to the category of objects. (This belongingness was adduced by

Nāgārjuna in his commentary of Sūtra 5). And, as in the case of any other object, their negation implies their existence. We must have in mind here the universal and fundamental principle of ancient Nyāya: as *jñāna* presupposes *jñeya*, so *pratiṣedha* presupposes *pratiṣedhya*. (See note 1 of the translation of this Section). If the similarity of *pramāṇa* and *prameya* to all the other objects present, past and future, were not admitted, one would be obliged to say that there are two different classes of objects: objects that need to exist in order to be negated and objects that could be negated without existing. This difference is against the principle just mentioned.

The commentary ends with a paradoxical presentation by the Naiyāyika opponent of the problem in discussion: the only way to invalidate the negation, which by the mere fact of its existence, gives existence to the negated object, would be if two absurd conditions take place: (1) that the thing itself (object of the presumed negation) do not exist, and (2) that at the same time no utterance of the negation take place. But, if these two conditions are fulfilled, no negation of the *pramāṇa* and the *prameya* would occur, and consequently, according to *NS* 5, 1, 20 (*pratiṣedhānupapatteśca pratiṣeddhavyāpratiṣedhaḥ*) the *pramāṇa* and the *prameya* would stand unrefuted. The implicit conclusion of this opponent's argument is the impossibility for Nāgārjuna to deny the *pramāṇa* and the *prameya*.

As is seen, two alternatives have been considered by the opponent: (1) the negation does not exist, because of the application to it of the same reasoning that Nāgārjuna applies to the *pramāṇa* and the *prameya* concerning the three times and (2) the negation exists and therefore what it denies exists, because of the similarity of the *pramāṇa* and *prameya* to all objects and the principle that a negation implies the existence of the negated object. The next Sūtra takes into account the second alternative.

Section XIV: **Nāgārjuna's refusal of the opponent's argument: the existence of something cannot be deduced from its previous negation.**

Nāgārjuna in this Sūtra refutes what the opponent has adduced in the previous Sūtra—that, since there is a negation of the *pramaṇa* and the *prameya*, the *pramāṇa* and the *prameya* have to exist. Nāgārjuna's reasoning, by which the opponent's argument is refuted, is that 'there has been a previous acceptance'.

The commentary develops Nāgārjuna's elliptical reasoning. The opponent has accepted the non-existence of the *pramāṇa* and the *prameya* in any of the three times (as affirmed by Nāgārjuna), and then draws the conclusion that the *pramāṇa* and the *prameya* must exist, because when there is a *pratiṣedha*, there must be a *pratiṣedhya*. Nāgārjuna rejects the opponent's argumentation, which results in the existence of the *pramāṇa* and the *prameya*, because he finds in it a logical defect consisting in it that, if one accepts the negation of the *pramāṇa* and the *prameya* in any of the three times, one has thereby eliminated from existence the *pramāṇa* and the *prameya*, but from this elimination one cannot deduce the disappearance of the negation itself. It is indeed absurd that, from the previous acceptance of the non-existence of anything, be inferred the existence of that same thing.

Section XV: **The opponent's previous acceptance of the inexistence of the *pramāṇa* and the *prameya* puts an end to the discussion.**

In this Sūtra and its commentary Nāgārjuna reiterates his position against the conclusion of the opponent that *pramāṇa* and the *prameya* have to exist because they have been negated, expressing which is 'the previous acceptance', referred to in Sūtra 14 and its commentary, and which is the logical defect that renders the opponent's reasoning fallacious.

In Sūtra 13 the opponent has accepted that the *pramāṇa* and the *prameya* do not exist in any of the three times just in order to deny afterwards the existence of their negation. This acceptance is what Nāgārjuna calls in Sūtra 14 'the previous acceptance'. Be what it may be the purpose of the opponent, what is evident is that he has accepted, as the first stage of his reasoning, that the *pramāṇa* and the *prameya* do not exist. As soon as he admits the non-existence of the *pramāṇa* and the *prameya* (the first proposition), he is in agreement with Nāgārjuna and so there is no place for a further discussion.

Section XVI: **Even if what is to be negated is not existing, the negation is possible, because it has to do with a concept—this is Nāgārjuna's position in regard to negation.**

The opponent has adduced the argument that the negation is impossible when what is to be negated does not exist. So, if Nāgārjuna's negation of *pramāṇa* and *prameya* is accepted, we must accept also the existence of the negated *pramāṇa* and *prameya*. In a similar way the Naiyāyika opponent maintains in *VV kārikā* 11: *sata eva pratiṣedho*. . . and the commentary adds: *sato'rthasya pratiṣedhaḥ kriyate nāsataḥ*.

Nāgārjuna refutes this argument saying that what the negation does is only to reject the *idea* or *concept* of the non-existent thing. When one, while being in front of a river that is not deep, says that there is not a deep river, he is referring just to the *concept* of 'deep river': he has in mind 'deep river' as a *designatum* and not 'deep river' as a *denotatum*.

If it is admitted that in the example of the river it would be a logical defect to deduce the impossibility of the negation of the deep river from the non-existence of the deep river, one has also to admit that in the reasoning of the opponent there is a similar logical defect, that defect consisting in deducing the impossibility of the negation of the *pramāṇa* and *prameya* from the non-existence of the *pramāṇa* and the *prameya*. It is possible to deny the deep river and the *pramāṇa* and *prameya* in the conceptual level, even if they do not exist in the ontological level. The implicit conclusion of this section is that it was possible for Nāgārjuna to deny the *pramāṇa* and the *prameya* even if they are inexistent and that they do not become existent on account of their refutation.

Section XVII: **The existence of valid acts of knowledge is adduced by the opponent as a new argument in favour of the existence of the *pramāṇas*.**

In this Sūtra the opponent introduces a new argument in favour of the existence of the *pramāṇas*: the *pramāṇas* exist because there are in fact valid acts of knowledge.

In the commentary the *pramāṇa* perception is analyzed from the point of view of Nyāya principles. In the first moment there is the mere grasping of the object of perception by the subject of knowledge. This perceptual knowledge is just the manifestation of the object. There is nothing in it that determines its truth or falsity. In a further moment there is the knowledge of the qualities or attributes possessed by the object grasped in the previous perceptual grasping and consisting in what it can or cannot do. And how the knowledge of these qualities or attributes is produced? By the direct experience of their effects. I see water; I do not know whether this water is real water or a mirage, whether this perceptual grasping is true or false. Afterwards, that water quenches my thirst. I have ascertained through a direct experience that that water has quality or attribute, that I expected it had, proper to water, of quenching my thirst. So I have known a quality or attribute of that object, a quality or attribute *really* existing as it has *real* effects. This knowledge is correct because it reaches reality.

In this way the validity of the knowledge of the qualities or attributes of the object (water), verified by a pragmatic test (the drinking of the water and the quenching of the thirst), gives at its turn validity to the initial perceptual grasping which originated all this complex process.

The conclusion is that there are acts of valid knowledge and consequently there are also means of valid knowledge which make them possible. In other words the correct knowledge provided by the perception and the other *pramāṇas* is a proof of the existence of the *pramāṇas*. And from the existence of the *pramāṇas* the existence of the *prameyas* must be deduced.

Next Sūtra contains the refutation of this argument in favour of the existence of *pramāṇa* and *prameya*.

Section XVIII: **Refutation of the argument adduced by the opponent in the previous Sūtra: even if the *pramāṇas* exist, the *prameyas* do not exist. The opponent is asked to say what the *prameya* is.**

In Nāgārjuna's opinion the existence of the *pramāṇas* (perception etc.), which give rise to valid acts of knowledge, do not imply the existence of the corresponding *prameyas*.

If one accepts the existence of the *pramāṇas* (perception etc.), one is obliged to say what is the object that is to be known and that constitutes the other pole of the *pramāṇa-prameya* relation, because the pot, which is considered by the opponent as the *prameya*, cannot be the *prameya*.

The pot cannot be the *prameya* of the perception because of the following reasoning. Taking the eye as the representative sense-organ one can admit that a perception of a pot can be formed in the mind, but from this one cannot deduce that a real and external pot is the *prameya* of that perception. The perception is a mental process, its counterpart can only be something mental. The perception and its object remain both within the limits of the mental realm.

The author has recourse to an analogy with the inference in order to make clear his argument. The inferential knowledge (there is fire on the hill, because there is smoke on it) is possible thanks to the necessary conjunction (we could say the invariable concomitance) between two entities (fire and smoke) and follows the perception (of one of these two entities: the smoke). When one knows by inference that 'there is fire on the hill', the object of this inference, the *anumeya*, is a mere product of the mind, since one does not perceive directly the fire that is on the hill; in other words: the *anumeya* is not something external to the mind.

Similarly, in the case of the perception, something external to the mind is not the *prameya* of the perception. The pot etc., external objects, which the opponent considered as the *prameya* of the perception, are not such. So the opponent has to say what really is the *prameya* of the perception. Therefore, even if the *pramāṇa*-perception existed, from that fact the existence of the *prameya*-pot cannot be deduced.

Section XIX: **Refutation of the new thesis adduced by the opponent in his answer: the *pramāṇa* is the idea of pot, the *prameya* is the pot. For Nāgārjuna the pot is only a determining condition of the *pramāṇa*.**

In the commentary preceding the Sūtra the opponent adduces in his answer a new thesis: the *pramāṇa* is the idea or representation of the pot, the *prameya* is the pot. Nāgārjuna's answer is contained in the Sūtra and explained in its commentary. The pot cannot be either the cognition or the cognizable object, because it is a mere *pratyaya* or determining condition.

In fact the pot in union with some other factors, as the sense-organ etc., gives rise to an idea: the idea of pot. So the pot is a mere *pratyaya* of the idea that comes forth in the mind. Nāgārjuna concludes from all this (1) that the idea of pot is not a *pramāṇa* and (2) that the pot is not a *prameya*.

The first conclusion seems to be founded in the following reasoning. The idea of a pot (*bum paḥi blo*) that arises in the mind cannot be a *pramāṇa*, because, if it were so, it would be the *pramāṇa* of the *prameya* pot, i.e. the means that would provide a correct knowledge of the pot, but the pot itself is not the *prameya*, it is only one of the factors (*pratyaya*) that, together with the sense-organ, the light etc., provoke in the mind the idea of a pot. Anyone of the other factors that produce the *pramāṇa* has the same right as the pot to be considered the *prameya*. There is no reason to give to the pot a preferential status.

As to the second conclusion, the pot itself, being (as already said) *only* one of the conditions that give rise in the mind to the idea of a pot, is not the *prameya* of that idea, even if (as the opponent thinks) that idea would be considered as a *pramāṇa*.

Section XX: **Another argument adduced by Nāgārjuna against the opponent's thesis that the idea is the *pramāṇa*.**

Nāgārjuna adds a new argument against the opponent's opinion that the idea is a means of valid knowledge: the idea is considered a *prameya* by the opponent himself, since the Naiyāyikas have explicitly affirmed that the idea (*blo, buddhi*) is a *prameya*, as the souls, the bodies, the senses etc. In fact in the *NS* 1, 1, 9 the *idea* is enumerated among the *prameyas*. Therefore, the idea cannot be considered *prameya* and *pramāṇa* at the same time.

The last sentence of the commentary expresses Nāgārjuna's conclusion that comes forth from the arguments adduced in Sūtras 17-20: neither *pramāṇas* nor *prameyas* are possible, since whatever the opponent has presented as such (the pot as *prameya* and the idea of pot as *pramāṇa*) has been rejected.

But this conclusion concerns also the whole argumentation against the existence of the two first Nyāya categories.

SAMŚAYA

Section XXI: **The doubt is introduced by the opponent as a new argument in favour of the existence of the *pramāṇa* and the *prameya*. Nāgārjuna's negation of doubt.**

In the commentary, which precedes the Sūtra 21, the opponent gives a new argument in favour of the existence of *pramāṇa* and *prameya*, introducing in the debate a new *padārtha*, the doubt (*the tshom; saṃśaya*): if somebody maintains that what is a *pramāṇa* that is a *prameya*, a doubt arises. The existence of the doubt would allow to infer the existence of the *pramāṇa* and the *prameya* to which it refers, since the doubt is an existing *padārtha* and cannot concern an unreal object.

Nāgārjuna answers this objection in the Sūtra 21 expressing in a very concise way that the doubt does not exist in relation to something that is perceived or to something that is not perceived, since the first exists and the second does not exist.

In the commentary Nāgārjuna adds that the doubt may be in relation to something that is perceived, or to something that is not perceived, or to something that seems to be perceived, and that doubt is not logical in any of these three alternatives. His conclusion is that doubt, therefore, does not exist.

The idea underlying Nāgārjuna's reasoning seems to be the following one: If I see a thing, all that is there is merely the mental representation of that thing. If I see a thing and I perceive it as a man or as a tree-trunk, the only thing that has been produced in my mind is the representation of that thing perceived as a man or as a tree-trunk. As Nāgārjuna will say in Section XXIII, if that thing is a man and I perceive it as a man, there is a correct cognition; if on the contrary that thing is a tree-trunk and I perceive it as a man or *vice versa,* there is a lack of cognition of the real object. The perceptive act gives us a *datum* but this *datum* has not itself any element upon which a doubt may be constructed. If I see a man, this mere representation of a man has nothing in itself that could induce me to think that perhaps what I am seeing as a man is not a man, i.e. has nothing in itself that can provoke in me a doubt.

In the same way, in the mere absence of a perception there is only absence of perception; there is no element to provoke our doubt.

And the same thing happens in relation to something that seems to be perceived. In the perception of a rope as if it were a serpent, there is only the (false) representation of a serpent, the lack of representation of a rope, but there is—as in the case of the mere absence of a perception—no element that can give rise to a doubt.

In the next Sūtra the opponent will indicate that there are elements which on being added to the mere act of perception give rise to the doubt.

Section XXII: **The opponent's argumentation in favour of the existence of doubt, contradicting Nāgārjuna's position expressed in the previous section.**

The opponent affirms in the Sūtra 22 that only if there were not reference (*ltos pa, apekṣā*) to specific attributes or peculiarities (*khyad par, viśeṣa*), doubt would not exist.

We can distinguish three parts in the exposition of the opponent's view in the commentary. In the first part he gives a description of a case of doubt: on seeing from afar an object, there arises an uncertain cognition, a wavering judgment (*vimarśa*) which cannot ascertain whether that object is a man or a tree-trunk.

This description of a process of doubt can be completed with *NS* 1, 1, 23 and Vātsyāyana's *Nbh ad locum.* The only qualities of the object that are perceived are those which are common to the man and to the tree-trunk: the length and the breadth.

We could say that to this first part corresponds the first explicit definition of doubt given by Vātsyāyana *ibidem: tad anavadhāraṇaṃ jñānaṃ saṃśayaḥ.*

In the second part it is explained how doubt comes to an end: when the distinctive features of either a man or a tree-trunk *are perceived,* doubt ceases to be, because there arises in mind a certainty: 'it is a man' or 'it is a tree-trunk'.

In the third part a new element is added to the description of doubt previously given: because the perceived object can be or cannot be a man or a tree-trunk (as only the qualities common to the two things are seen), this oscillation in the mind produces a looking for (*ltos pa, apekṣā*) those qualities that would distinguish one thing from the other (*khyad par, viśeṣa*).

As when the distinctive features *are perceived* doubt comes to an end, so, 'in a manner different from that' (*de las gźan du na*), when these features are *looked for,* it is because doubt has arisen. This looking for, this search of, this reference to (*ltos pa, apekṣā*), 'this desire to know' (*bubhutsā* as Vātsyāyana understands *apekṣā*) the peculiarities of the things, constitutes the new element that enriches the definition of doubt, making it more precise and subtler.

We could say that for Nāgārjuna the process referred to in these Sections XXI-XXIII contains two moments: (1) a perception with a correct cognition or with an erroneous cognition and (2) the perception of special characteristics which confirms the right cognition or rectifies the wrong one. For the opponent there is a third moment between the first and the second ones: the mind wavers, cannot ascertain what is the thing perceived, and it is this circumstance that induces it to look for the special characteristics.

We could also say that to this third part of the explanation of the commentary (that contains the larger notion of doubt) corresponds the second explicit definition of doubt given by Vātsyāyana in his *Bhāṣya: viśeṣāpekṣo vimarśaḥ saṃśayaḥ.*

Section XXIII: **The a priori denial of doubt prevents its being in relation with peculiarities according to Nāgārjuna.**

This Section contains the refutation by Nāgārjuna of the argument adduced by the opponent in favour of the existence of doubt. According to the opponent the looking for the peculiarities that distinguish one thing from the other, produced by the wavering judgment, is the essential feature of doubt, it is the element that makes it possible. In Nāgārjuna's opinion, expressed in the Sūtra, the *first fact*, that is established by reasoning, is that doubt does not exist, is a mere fiction; and that consequently there is no place for any relation between doubt and peculiarities.

In the commentary he begins by reiterating what is expressed in the Sūtra: doubt is to be denied *in first place, before anything*, either if peculiarities are given or not, by force of the arguments he develops immediately after this assertion. In the case of the tree-trunk as well as in the case of the man, when the characteristics that distinguish them, are perceived, in this very moment there is no doubt; there is only a certain cognition, a correct knowledge which presents things as they are (*yaṅ dag pa ji lta ba bźin du, yathābhūta*) a tree-trunk as a tree-trunk, a man as a man. And on the contrary if in regard to both there are not the characteristics proper to a correct knowledge of them (as for instance the grasping of peculiarities), then there is no doubt, there is only 'a lack of knowledge' (*mi śes pa, ajñāna*) that can be designated by different names.

In the last part of the commentary, Nāgārjuna indicates what results from the reference to peculiarities: if peculiarities exist and are perceived, there is knowledge; if peculiarities do not exist or are not perceived, there is lack of knowledge. But from reference to peculiarities doubt does not come forth in any of both cases. A third alternative, which admits at the same time the existence and non-existence of peculiarities, is excluded by Nāgārjuna.

The general conclusion is that doubt does not exist.

PRAYOJANA

Section XXIV: **Nāgārjuna's denial of the purpose of action (*prayojana*).**

This Section begins with the last argument adduced by the opponent in favour of the existence of doubt: the purpose of action can be considered as an object of doubt.

Nāgārjuna answers this argument by denying in the Sūtra the existence of the purpose of action, either in the case of the existence or in the case of the non-existence of action.

The commentary after the Sūtra starts quoting *NS* 1, 1, 24: *yam artham adhikṛtya pravartate tat prayojanam*: 'that object, aiming at which one acts, is *prayojana*, the purpose'. And then gives an illustration of that definition of *prayojana* according to Nyāya: the action of the pot-maker has the pot as its aim; the pot is the purpose of the activity of the agent.

Against this Nyāya conception of *prayojana* Nāgārjuna argues: if the pot existed already in the clay, it cannot be anymore the goal of a pot-producing activity of the pot-maker, because it is already there. A goal cannot pre-exist the action that intends to give rise to it. In this case the action, whose aim is to produce a pot, remains without object; there is no aim for that action; the *prayojana* does not exist. If on the contrary the pot does not exist in the clay, there cannot be an action of the pot-maker that produce a pot out of the clay in which it does not exist, as according to the *sikatātailanyāya* (referred to several times by Candrakīrti in his *Prasannapadā*: p. 81, 1.13; p. 195, 1.7; p. 382, 1.14; p. 392, 1.2; p. 393, 1.5) nothing can be produced out of something, in the whole or in the parts of which it does not exist; and therefore there is no action that could produce it. Oil cannot be produced out of the sand as a whole neither out of its grains; an action that extracts oil out of the sand is impossible to exist. And, if the action is impossible to exist there cannot be a purpose of that non-existing action. In this case also there is no *prayojana*.

The Nyāya's definition of *prayojana* relates *action* to an object which is the purpose of action. The conclusion of Nāgārjuna is that nothing can be the purpose of an action or what is the same that the *prayojana* does not exist: if the object which would be the purpose of the action exists prior to the action, it cannot be the aim of that action that intends to produce it; and if the object which would be the purpose of the action does not exist prior to the action, it cannot be—being impossible the action which would have it as its aim—the aim of that non-existent action.

This reasoning can be extended to any action, and so there is not any possibility for anything of becoming a purpose of an action. Objects, as the pot, the oil etc., can exist or cannot exist as objects, but can never become *purposes* of the action.

DṚṢṬĀNTA

Section XXV: **The opponent's affirmation of the purpose of action (*prayojana*) based on the existence of examples (*dṛṣṭānta*).**

This Sūtra is the opponent's answer to the argument of Nāgārjuna adduced in the last part of the previous commentary:

Nāgārjuna has said that, if the pot (that would be the purpose of the action) does not already exist in the clay, there cannot be any action in regard to it, and he adduces the example of the sand and the oil: if oil does not already exist in the sand, oil can never be produced from the sand, there can never be an action that produce oil out of the sand.

The opponent admits that there cannot be an action applied to the sand in order to extract from it an oil that does not exist in it. But he affirms that the purpose of action still exists, since there are other examples that prove its existence and he adduces one of these examples: a woollen cloth can be the purpose of an action applied to woollen threads with the aim of producing it. But it is obvious that there is not an action applied to blades of grass in order to produce a woollen cloth. The example of the pot and the clay is parallel to the example of the woollen cloth and the woollen threads; and the example of the sand and the oil is parallel to that of the blades of grass and the woollen cloth.

Section XXVI: **Nāgārjuna's refutation of the previous objection.**

In Nāgārjuna's opinion the example of the woollen threads and the woollen cloth is similar 'to the preceding one', i.e. similar to the example of the clay and the pot adduced by himself in the commentary of Sūtra 24, because to both the same reasoning can be applied: the woollen cloth can exist in the woollen threads or cannot exist; in the first case, it could not be anymore the goal of a cloth-producing activity of the weaver, because it is already there; in the second case there could not be an action of the weaver that produces a cloth out of the threads in which it does not exist, according again to the *sikatātailanyāya*; in both cases the *prayojana* is not logically possible, and there is no *dṛṣṭānta* that can serve to demonstrate it.

Section XXVII: **Nāgārjuna's denial of the example, *dṛṣṭānta*, as involving a logical impossibility.**

In this Section Nāgārjuna maintains that the example, *dṛṣṭānta*, does not exist. The argument developed by Nāgārjuna in support of his denial of the *dṛṣṭānta* is based on the etymology of the Sanskrit word *dṛṣṭānta* = *dṛṣṭa-anta,* whose meaning is 'something whose end is seen'. Of course the Tibetan translation of *dṛṣṭānta, dpe,* cannot reflect this etymological reference. In the word *dṛṣṭānta* there is the affirmation that the end of a thing is seen, but there is no mention of a beginning and a middle being seen. And it is not possible to see the end if the beginning and the middle are not seen. Moreover if a beginning and a middle do not exist, an *end* does not exist. The word *dṛṣṭānta* is, therefore, denoting an impossibility: something of which *only* the end is seen or exists.

Section XXVIII: **Naiyāyika definition and classification of *dṛṣṭānta*. Nāgārjuna's refusal of *dṛṣṭānta* through similarity.**

In the commentary before the Sūtra the definition of *dṛṣṭānta* is given. This definition corresponds to Gautama's definition of *NS* 1, 1, 25: *laukikaparīkṣakāṇāṃ yasminn arthe buddhisamyaṃ sa dṛṣṭāntaḥ.* In the commentary to Sūtra 9 this definition has already been quoted. The classification of *dṛṣṭānta* into *dṛṣṭānta* through similarity (*sādharmya*) and *dṛṣṭānta* through dissimilarity (*vaidharmya*) is also given. The first kind of *dṛṣṭānta* is also called 'affirmative' or 'homogeneous' and the second one 'negative' or 'heterogeneous'. On the classification of *dṛṣṭānta* into these two classes see *NSBh ad* 1, 1, 34-35 and also *Nyāyapraveśakasūtra* p. 1, lines 15-16.

Definition and classification are presented as the opponent's opinion, against which Nāgārjuna argues in this Sūtra and in the commentary after the Sūtra and in the next Sūtra 29 and its commentary.

The *dṛṣṭānta* through similarity which Nāgārjuna has in mind in his criticism is the absolute similarity referred to in *NS* 2, 1, 44 (*atyantasādharmya*) and in *Bh ad* 2, 1, 45 (*kṛtsnasādharmya*). This kind of *sādharmya* is not admitted even by the Nyāya, and it is considered as a *doṣa* by Gautama in *NS* 2, 1, 45.

Dṛṣṭānta through similarity would imply two terms that are related; one of them is the *dṛṣṭānta* itself and the other is the thing which is to be illustrated, made intelligible, made known, set in a clear light. If there is absolute resemblance between the example and the thing to be exemplified, the example does not serve any purpose, is useless, because it does not add anything to the knowledge of the thing in itself.

As the *pūrvapakṣa* in *NSBh ad* 2, 1, 44 affirms, in relation to analogy (*upamāna*) on the basis of complete resemblance, (*atyantasādharmya*): *na caivaṃ bhavati yathā gaur evaṃ gaur iti* or as Nāgārjuna says in this section, concerning *sādharmyadṛṣṭānta, me ni meḥi dpe ma yin*: fire cannot be example of fire.

If that which illustrates, the *dṛṣṭānta,* and that which is to be illustrated are the same, the *dṛṣṭānta* does not exist as a separate category.

Section XXIX: **Nāgārjuna's refusal of *dṛṣṭānta* through dissimilarity.**

After having refuted the example through similarity (*sādharmya dṛṣṭānta*), Nāgārjuna in this Section rejects the other case of example, the example through dissimilarity (*vaidharmyadṛṣṭānta*).

As in the case of *sādharmyadṛṣṭānta* the *vaidharmyadṛṣṭānta* would imply two terms. If these two terms belong to absolutely different classes of things, as water (which is cold by nature according to *Vaiśeṣikasūtra* 2, 2, 5, and *Nyāya* as for instance *Tarkasaṃgraha* 11) and fire, one (water) cannot be example of the other (fire), because, being contradictory, the use of one of them as example of the other would only produce an erroneous knowledge about the exemplified one, as providing it with an attribute contrary to its nature.

Moreover, if fire is said to be 'like water', it is also possible to say, making a conversion of the equation, that water, which is cold by nature, is 'like fire'. In this way the irrationality of the example 'the fire is like water' becomes more manifest.

The implicit conclusion of this Section is that the *dṛṣṭānta* through dissimilarity is not logically possible.

Section XXX: **Nāgārjuna's refusal of *dṛṣṭānta* through slight similarity.**

In Section XXVIII Nāgārjuna has dealt with the example through similarity (*sādharmyadṛṣṭānta*), corresponding to the analogy (*upamāna*) on the basis of absolute resemblance (*atyantasādharmya*) (*NS* 2, 1, 44 or total resemblance, *kṛtsnasādharmya*, as it is called in *Bh ad* 2, 1, 45). In the present Section Nāgārjuna refers to another kind of *sādharmya*: the slight resemblance, which finds also its correspondence in *NS* 2, 1, 44: *ekadeśasādharmya* (or *alpasādharmya*, as it is called in *Bh ad* 2, 1, 45).

Nāgārjuna's rejection is founded in the following reasoning: if one accepts the existence of a *dṛṣṭānta* only through a slight similarity between two things, it would even be possible to compare Mount Sumeru and a hair of the head, because all things possess at least the slight similarities constituted by the general, universal, extensive attributes as existence, unity, corporeity or materiality mentioned in the commentary. This would result in the absurd consequence that 'all things could be conceived of as resembling one another': *ekadeśasādharmyāt upamānaṃ na sidhyati, na hi sarveṇa sarvam upamīyata iti* (*NSBh ad* 2, 1, 44).

At the end of the commentary Nāgārjuna presents another argument against the existence of a *dṛṣṭānta* through slight similarity: when the resemblance is so insignificant, as in the case of a hair of the head and Mount Sumeru, there is no more a universal agreement about it, and therefore the Nyāya definition of *dṛṣṭānta* is not valid anymore.

Section XXXI: **Nāgārjuna's refusal of *dṛṣṭānta* through partial similarity and through partial dissimilarity.**

The opponent affirms that there still remains the possibility of a *dṛṣṭānta* through partial similarity (*prāyasādharmya*). This kind of *dṛṣṭānta* corresponds to the second kind of analogy (*upamāna*) rejected in *NS* 2, 1, 44 and 45 and *Bh* together with the *atyantasādharmya* (or *kṛtsnasādharmya*) and the *ekadeśasādharmya* (or *alpasādharmya*).

Nāgārjuna in the Sūtra denies the possibility of the existence of an example through partial similarities on the basis of what has been denied by him in previous Sūtras. We must understand that Nāgārjuna is referring to the negation of *dṛṣṭānta* through slight similarity (Sūtra 30). The *dṛṣṭānta* through partial similarity must be discarded by the same arguments used for discarding the *dṛṣṭānta* through slight similarity.

In the first sentence of the commentary after the Sūtra a new concept is introduced, that of *prāyavaidharmyadṛṣṭānta*, '*dṛṣṭānta* through partial dissimilarity'. This *dṛṣṭānta* is also negated by Nāgārjuna. We think that this *dṛṣṭānta* through partial dissimilarity is negated by Nāgārjuna because it is a kind of *vaidharmyadṛṣṭānta* which has already been negated (Sūtra 29).

We could also say that, concerning the *dṛṣṭānta* through partial similarity, it always implies a partial dissimilarity, in the same way as a *dṛṣṭānta* through partial dissimilarity always implies a partial similarity.

The *dṛṣṭānta* through partial similarity cannot be accepted since it involves dissimilarity and this latter has been negated as a basis for a *dṛṣṭānta* (Sūtra 29).

So the *dṛṣṭānta* is logically impossible.

SIDDHĀNTA

Section XXXII : Nāgārjuna's denial of *siddhānta* (the accepted theory).

In the commentary before the Sūtra the opponent argues that Nāgārjuna has concluded (at the end of the previous Sūtra) that 'the *dṛṣṭānta* is not established (as existing)'. For the opponent this constitutes a *siddhānta*, an accepted theory, something already established, on the part of Nāgārjuna. Consequently it is not logically possible for Nāgārjuna to state at the same time that 'the category *siddhānta* does not exist'; he is obliged to accept therefore the existence of that category, from the very moment he has accepted a theory regarding the example.

Nāgārjuna replies in the Sūtra, which has no commentary, giving his argument in favour of the inexistence of *siddhānta* category. His reasoning is similar to that developed in Section XXVII. It is based on the etymology of the Sanskrit word *siddhānta* = *siddha-anta*, i.e. 'something whose end is established (as existing)'. In the word *siddhānta* there is the affirmation that the end is established as existing, but there is no mention in it of a beginning and a middle being established as existing. And it is not possible to establish anything as existing if the beginning and the middle are not established. The word *siddhānta* denotes an impossibility : something of which *only* the end is established or exists.

AVAYAVAS

Section XXXIII: Nāgārjuna's denial of the *avayavas*, the parts (of the syllogism) having recourse to the arguments related to the whole and the parts discussion. The whole does not exist in the parts separately taken.

In the commentary before the Sūtra the opponent affirms that the parts of demonstration (i.e. of a *nyāya* or syllogistic reasoning) must exist in order that a demonstration be accomplished. If Nāgārjuna maintains that the parts of the syllogism do not exist, his own speech would be deprived of these parts. Consequently Nāgārjuna's speech would be deprived of the structure constituted by these parts, and obviously deprived also of the logical connections among them. Such a speech cannot demonstrate anything, cannot reach any definite conclusion. If Nāgārjuna wants that his speech be efficient in his purpose of denying or refuting the opponent's statements, he has to acknowledge the existence of these parts.

An implicit consequence of the previous reasoning is that the *siddhānta* (that Nāgārjuna has denied in the previous Sūtra) has to exist, since a *siddhānta* is a thesis that has been established through a reasoning.

Nāgārjuna answers in the Sūtra expressing that, as the whole (*avayavin*) does not exist, the parts do not exist either. We must understand that with the word 'whole' the *nyāya* or syllogistic reasoning is designated. The parts referred to by Nāgārjuna are the parts of that *nyāya: pratijñā* (the proposition to be proved), *hetu* (the reason or *probans*), *udāharaṇa* (the example), *upanaya* (the application) and *nigamana* (the conclusion), as the same Nāgārjuna says in the commentary.

In the commentary of this Sūtra Nāgārjuna begins the demonstration of the inexistence of the whole; he simply states that the whole does not exist in the parts, without giving any argument to support his affirmation. Cf. in note 4 of the translation of this Section some texts which present Buddhist arguments for the non-existence of the whole in the parts. And from this Nāgārjuna concludes that the parts separately taken are inexistent, also without any further explanation. In favour of the conclusion that the parts do not exist because of the inexistence of the whole perhaps it can be said (within the limits and inspiration of Nāgārjuna's thought) that if the whole is inexistent, its parts also must be inexistent because it is not logically possible that a non-existing thing (as the flower in the sky) have parts (as bud, petals etc.). It could also be said that if the whole as such is not established as existing, its parts, that can be at its turn considered as wholes in relation to their parts, do not exist as such either. Cf. note 3 of the translation of this Section.

Section XXXIV: **The whole does not exist in the parts as an aggregate.**

In the previous Section Nāgārjuna has dealt with the alternative of the whole existing in the parts separately taken. In this Section he refers to the alternative of the whole existing in the aggregate or combination of parts. He also discards this possibility, adducing the argument that if the whole is not in the parts separately taken, it cannot be in the aggregate constituted by these parts. As in the previous Section in this commentary there is no further explanation on this matter.

Section XXXV: **Absurd consequences that occur if the whole is one.**

In this Section Nāgārjuna posits the problem of the whole being one, as the Nyāya and the Vaiśeṣika systems affirm. If the whole is one, two alternatives are possible; and each of them results in an absurd consequence: if the whole is not different from the parts, the numerous parts of the whole would also be one—this contradiction is indicated in the Sūtra; if the whole is different from the parts, it would happen that the whole would constitute an additional element. Thus in the case of the syllogistic reasoning, this one would become a sixth element besides the five parts enumerated at the end of the commentary of Sūtra XXXIII.

Section XXXVI: **The whole does not exist in any of the three times.**

Nāgārjuna offers in this Section another argument against the existence of the whole: it does not exist either in the present or in the past or in the future; consequently its parts do not exist. The whole is of course the syllogistic reasoning; the parts of the syllogism enumerated in *NS* 1, 1, 32 are the parts of the whole.

The reasoning developed in this Section is the same as that of Section XII, applied to *pramāṇa* and *prameya,* and that of the texts quoted in note 7 of the same Section, applied to *pratiṣedha* and *pratiṣedhya, sādhana* and *sādhya* etc. The whole cannot exist in any of the three times because the chronological relation of the whole with its parts is impossible, in the same way as the *pramāṇa-prameya, pratiṣedha-pratiṣedhya, sādhana-sādhya,* cause-effect, knowledge-vision chronological relation is impossible. And if the whole does not exist in any of the three times, it does not exist in an absolute way. And, as a consequence of that inexistence, the parts do not exist either. As in Section XXXIII no argument is given to support the statement that because of the inexistence of the whole, the parts do not exist.

Section XXXVII: **Opponent's thesis: the whole may exist in the aggregate although not in the parts.**

This Sūtra contains the opinion of the opponent, presenting a new proof in favour of the existence of the whole. This proof is the *dṛṣṭānta* of the Balbaja grass: a single Balbaja grass cannot bind an elephant, but a rope made of Balbaja grass, which can be considered as an aggregate of Balbaja grass, can do it. The capacity of binding the elephant is not in each single Balbaja grass, but certainly is in the aggregate of Balbaja grass. The aggregate of Balbaja grass, the rope, is thus different from its constituent parts, since it has an attribute, which does not exist in the parts. This fact makes the aggregate of Balbaja grass an entity apart from its components. In the same way the syllogistic reasoning (*nyāya*), i.e. the whole in the present case, exists in the aggregate constituted by the *pratijñā* etc., although it does not exist in each of these elements of the syllogistic reasoning. In the same way as a rope, as something different from its own parts, can serve to bind an elephant, what cannot be done by each Balbaja grass that compose it, so a syllogistic reasoning as something different from its own constituent elements, can serve to demonstrate a thesis, what cannot be done by the *pratijñā* etc. separately taken.

Section XXXVIII: **Refutation of the opponent's objection because it implies a *sādhyasama*.**

Nāgārjuna answers in the Sūtra, rejecting the *dṛṣṭānta* given by the opponent as a proof for his thesis of the existence of the whole, because it implies a *sādhyasama* defect. This defect is defined in *NS* 1, 2, 8 as *sādhyāviśiṣṭaḥ sādhyatvāt sādhyasamaḥ.* The reason adduced by the opponent is similar in nature to the thesis he wants to establish, as both are to be proven. In fact Nāgārjuna provides in the commentary three new examples that show that what is not in the parts cannot be in the aggregate or whole constituted by these parts. A barren woman, a blind man and a grain of sand cannot give birth to a child, see or produce oil respectively; likewise thousands of barren women, blind men or grains of sand joined together are not able either to give rise to those effects. In the same way the capacity to bind or to demonstrate cannot exist in the rope of Balbaja grass or in the syllogistic reasoning since it does not exist in their constituent parts.

So the *dṛṣṭānta* adduced by the opponent cannot be accepted as a proof because it is under discussion, and requires at its own turn to be ascertained.

Section XXXIX: **The opponent's argumentation is not valid for the proposition and its letters.**

In the commentary before the Sūtra Nāgārjuna presents an objection that could be made by the opponent to Nāgārjuna's own argument of the previous Sūtra in the following terms: The examples adduced by Nāgārjuna in Sūtra XXXVIII against the existence of the whole could be considered as equal to the example of the Balbaja grass in it that in each of these examples we have a single part (a Balbaja grass, a barren woman, a blind man, a grain of sand) and an aggregate of parts (a rope made of Balbaja grass, thousands of barren women etc.). But there is a great difference: in each Balbaja grass there is a small capacity of binding that has to do with its own nature, so a single Balbaja grass can bind a small being, as a butterfly; when many Balbajas are put together as in a rope, their individual small capacities of binding are summed, and they can bind an elephant. We can add that in the case of the barren woman, the blind man and the grain of sand, there is an incapacity of giving birth etc. according to their own nature; when barren women come together by thousands their individual incapacities are equally summed.

Nāgārjuna rejects this objection as being not logical. He accepts that the Balbaja grass is commonly considered as a *dṛṣṭānta* in relation to the whole, but it has not application to the cases of the syllogistic reasoning in relation to its parts (*pratijñā* etc.) and of the word on relation to its parts (the letters). In the rope made of Balbaja grass all the Balbaja threads are together in the same place at the same moment. In the cases of the syllogistic reasoning and of the word their constituent elements (*pratijñā* etc. and the letters) never coexist, but come forth successively. Nāgārjuna ends the commentary expressing that the example of the Balbaja grass, not being fit for the syllogistic reasoning because of their intrinsic differences, is not logical for proving the existence of the whole at least in this case. Thus, if the whole has not been proven, its parts do not exist.

Section XL: **End of the discussion of the whole and the parts argument. Beginning of the refutation one by one of the five *avayavas* or members**

(of the syllogism): Inexistence of the *pratijñā*, the proposition to be proved, the first member of the syllogism, because the absurd consequences it would produce.

In this Section Nāgārjuna puts an end to the discussion about the whole and the parts and moreover he refutes the existence of the first member of the syllogism, *pratijñā* or the proposition to be proved, the thesis.

In the Sūtra Nāgārjuna expresses that, if it is maintained that the parts of the syllogistic reasoning (*pratijñā* etc.) exist as establishers of the whole, in this case the *nyāya*, there would occur the *anavasthāprasaṅga*, i.e. the *regressus ad infinitum* of the parts.

In the commentary Nāgārjuna indicates that there are two alternatives. The first alternative is: the parts, as establishers of a whole/*nyāya* not yet established, require other parts that establish them. Adopting this alternative hypothesis, the absurd consequence of a *regressus ad infinitum* would occur because each part used to establish the others would need at its turn other parts to establish it and so on. The defect of the *regressus ad infinitum* deprives the demonstration, the parts that constitute that demonstration and the *pratijñā* (which is one of those parts) of all validity. This alternative is the one referred to in the Sūtra.

The second alternative is: the parts do not require other parts to establish them, i.e. they are self-established. And the *pratijñā*, one of the parts of the syllogism, on being self-established as the other parts, would lose its own nature of being something to be demonstrated, a *probandum*, a *sādhya*; it would become a *siddha*, something already proved, what is in contradiction with the Nyāya definition of *pratijñā*. Cf. *NS* 1, 1, 33: *sādhyanirdeśaḥ pratijñā; Bh ad locum: prajñāpanīyena dharmeṇa dharmiṇo viśiṣṭasya parigrahavacanaṃ pratijñā*, and *Vārttika: siddhatvād dharmiṇo na sādhyateti kecit-dharmī kila dharmalakṣaṇaḥ siddha eva, siddhaś ca sādhyo na bhavati / naiṣa doṣaḥ prajñāpanīya-dharmaviśiṣṭasyeti vacanāt / na brūmo dharmimātraṃ sādhyam api tu prajñāpanīyadharmaviśiṣṭo dharmīti.* With this last alternative the opponent has to face two undesired consequences, between which he has to choose.

1. If the opponent, in order to avoid the *pratijñā* becoming from a *sādhya* a *siddha* and losing thereby its own nature, says that the *pratijñā* is different (non-established) from the other parts of syllogism (assumed to be established), he would have had to explain that difference

(what has not been done). And as something non-established, the *pratijñā* would not have the capacity to establish the *avayavin*, the *nyāya*, what destroys the statement of the opponent: 'the whole is established through all the parts'.

2. If the opponent prefers to affirm that the *pratijñā* is not different from the parts assumed to be self-established, and thereby is itself self-established, not taking into account if the *pratijñā* loses thereby its own nature of being a *sādhya* and is transformed into a *siddha*, it would occur that, as the *pratijñā* has ceased to be a *pratijña*, there would remain only four members of the *nyāya* or syllogism in order to establish it. In this case also the thesis of the opponent that 'the whole is established through *all* the parts' is destroyed. Cf. *NS* 1, 1, 32 quoted in note 2 of the translation of Section XXXIII. Consequently the whole (the *nyāya* or syllogism) as such is not logically possible.

Section XLI: **Nāgārjuna's refutation of the *hetu*, the second member of the syllogism, because it cannot prove either being different from or identical to the *pratijñā*.**

In this Section Nāgārjuna adduces an argument against the existence of the second member of the syllogism, the *hetu* or reason. Two alternatives are possible: (1) the proposition to be proved (*pratijñā*) is different from the *hetu*, and (2) the proposition to be proved is not different. The first case is not logically possible because nothing can be proved by its contrary, as for instance: 'the cloth is white, *because* it is black'. The second case, as for instance: 'the cloth is white, *because* it is white', is not logically possible either, because the reason is only a reiteration of the proposition to be proved.

In fact the two instances of *hetu* adduced by Nāgārjuna are not real *hetus*. In the first case, the *hetu* ('*because* it is *black*') attributes to the subject of the proposition to be proved a quality (black) which hinders the existence in the subject of the quality (white) whose existence the *hetu* intends to prove, and it hinders it, because one (black) is opposite to the other (white) and where the one is the other cannot be. In the second case, the *hetu* ('*because* it is *white*') states the existence in the subject of the proposition to be proved of a quality (white) which is the same quality whose existence in the subject has to be proved, being it so that the *hetu* must state the existence in the subject of the proposition to be proved of a quality different from the quality whose existence is to be proved. This different quality is precisely what (with the intervention of the *udāharaṇa*) will have the capacity to prove the *probandum.*

The Naiyāyika opponent could object to Nāgārjuna that the Nyāya concept of *hetu* is in terms of similarity and dissimilarity (cf. *NS* 1, 1, 34-35 and *Bh*) and that the same happens with the concept of *udāharaṇa* tightly related to that of *hetu*; and also that Nyāya in relation to the theory of *upamāna* (cf. *NS* 2, 1, 44-45, quoted in note 2 of Section XXVIII) expressly rejects the *atyantasādharmya* or 'similarity in all points' (as for instance : *yathā gaur evaṃ gauḥ*: the cow is just like the cow); and that he, Nāgārjuna, is objecting the existence of *hetu* adducing examples that imply absolute dissimilarity or absolute similarity.

Section XLII: **Another proof against the *hetu*: it cannot be admitted with or without another reason that supports it.**

In this Section another argument is given against the existence of the *hetu*. The Section takes into account two alternatives: (1) The *hetu* needs another *hetu* to establish it. The *regressus ad infinitum* would occur. (2) If, for avoiding the *regressus ad infinitum* it is maintained that there is no need of another *hetu* (this is the alternative mentioned in the Sūtra), then the reason would not exist. The commentary does not give any ground for this conclusion. But we could complete Nāgārjuna's thought with arguments given by himself in relation to similar instances. It could be said that, if the *hetu* does not need other *hetu* to be proved, it would be *svayaṃsiddha,* and as *svayaṃsiddha* it cannot exist because the *svayaṃsiddhatva* has been previously rejected by Nāgārjuna as logically impossible in relation to *pramāṇa* and *prameya.* And, if the *hetu* is accepted without a *hetu* that establishes it, then nothing would need a *hetu,* unless a difference be admitted between things which need to be established and the *hetu* which does not need it. And such a difference has not been explained nor demonstrated, and even more, when it is adduced in such a way, it introduces an element of arbitrariness in reasoning (explicitly referred to by Nāgārjuna at the end of his commentary to this same Sūtra): everything could be established without a reason.

Section XLIII: **Refutation of the *upanaya* and *nigamana*, the fourth and fifth members of the syllogism: they cannot exist since the *hetu* is inexistent.**

Nāgārjuna founds his negation of the application (*upanaya*) and the conclusion (*nigamana*) on the inexistence of the proposition to be proved (Section XL), the reason (Sections XLI and XLII), and the example (Sections XXV-XXXI). This negation is logical, because the application and the conclusion essentially depend on the example, the reason and the proposition to be proved, as it is clear from *NS* 1, 1, 38, where *upanaya* and *nigamana* are defined: *udāharaṇāpekṣas tathetyupasaṃhāro na tatheti vā sādhyasyopanayaḥ*, and 1, 1, 39: *hetvapadeśāt pratijñāyāḥ punarvacanaṃ nigamanam.*

Section XLIV: **If the mere *hetu* demonstrates, the *ahetuprasaṅga* would occur for the other members of the syllogism.**

If the function of the *hetu* is to demonstrate the *pratijñā*, then the other members of the syllogism would remain without *hetu*, i.e. would remain without anything that supports or establishes them, and consequently would be unable to contribute to the demonstration of the *pratijñā*, because they are themselves non-established.

Section XLV: **If the mere *hetu* demonstrates, the remaining *avayavas* would be useless.**

In Sūtra XLV Nāgārjuna rejects the possibility of the demonstration of the *pratijñā* being carried on by the mere *hetu*, because in this case the other members of the syllogism would become useless, since the aim of the syllogism would be fulfilled by one of its members. This is against the Nyāya conception of syllogism as defined in *NS* 1, 1, 32 (quoted in note 2 of Section XXXIII).

Section XLVI: **If the example demonstrates, the *hetu* would be useless and vice versa.**

In this Section Nāgārjuna continues the reasoning of the previous Section. So we can understand that this Sūtra refers to the case that the demonstration is not made by means of the reason, and that the burden of the proof is in the example: the reason would be useless.

Section XLVII: **Another argument against the *hetu* and the *dṛṣṭānta*: it cannot be accepted that they exist because they demonstrate the soul, since the soul does not exist.**

The opponent argues that the *hetu* and the *dṛṣṭānta* exist because the soul is demonstrated through them. Nāgārjuna denies in the Sūtra the possibility for the soul of being proved. And he presents in the commentary a syllogism, according to the Nyāya principles: the soul is eternal (*pratijñā*), because it is bodiless (*hetu*), like the space (*dṛṣṭānta*). Nāgārjuna declares that this reasoning is not valid: the soul for being eternal depends on a *hetu* (the bodilessness); depending on a *hetu*, it is not eternal *ex se*, it is not an eternal entity. And, if the so-called 'soul' is not an eternal entity, it cannot be the *soul* as defined by the Nyāya, to whose essence belongs the eternity. Cf. *NS* 3, 1. As the soul does not exist, so also neither the *hetu* nor the *dṛṣṭānta* (whose existence depended on their capacity to prove the existence of the soul) exist.

Section XLVIII: **Another argument against the existence of the *avayavas* in general: they do not coexist.**

In this Section also another argument is adduced by Nāgārjuna against the existence of the *avayavas* or members of the syllogism. When anyone of the *avayavas* is formulated the other do not exist, because they have been already formulated or they have not yet been formulated. There is not the possibility for the *avayavas* of existing together at the same time. Therefore, the *nyāya* or syllogistic reasoning, which according to Nyāya (cf. *NS* 1, 1, 32) is constituted by five members, can never come to existence. If there is not *nyāya* as a whole, there cannot be parts independently existing of that inexistent whole.

The reasoning of Nāgārjuna in this section and in the following one is based on the idea that sentences, words and syllables are submitted to temporality and as such are gradually produced.

Owing to the fact that they are gradually produced it is impossible for the sentences, words and syllables to give rise to a whole, which presupposes the co-existence of its parts.

Section XLIX: **Nāgārjuna rejects the opponent's assertion that he himself, on denying the *avayavas* is maintaining a *pratijñā*: the *pratijñā* is impossible because its syllables do not coexist.**

The opponent objects that, when Nāgārjuna says that the *avayavas* or members of the syllogism do not exist, this statement constitutes a *pratijñā* in itself and consequently he has to admit the existence of the *pratijñā* and the other members of the syllogistic reasoning. Nāgārjuna answers that the syllables of words are similar to the members of the syllogism in that they also are parts of a whole (the *pratijñā* etc.), are pronounced gradually one after the other, and do not coexist. This is exemplified with the word '*pratijñā*' (used in the text in its Sanskrit form) and its analysis into syllables. From this it can be concluded that the syllables, the word and sentences they form do not exist. Consequently a *pratijñā* cannot be attributed to him.

Besides that, the syllables are *pratyayasamutpanna,* i.e. born out of the conditions enumerated in the commentary. These factors cooperating can produce one syllable but not several at one time.

TARKA

Section I.: Nāgārjuna's refutation of reasoning (*tarka*) in a way similar to the refutation of doubt.

This Section refers to the Nyāya category of *tarka. Tarka* is dealt with in *NS* 1, 1, 40: *avijñātatattve 'rthe kāraṇopapattitas tattvajñānārtham ūhas tarkaḥ* and *Bh: avijñāyamānatattve 'rthe jijñāsā tāvaj jāyate jānīyemam artham iti / athajijñāsitasya vastuno vyāhatau dharmau vibhāgena vimṛśati— kiṃ svid ittham ahosvin netham iti/ vimṛśyamānayor dharmayor ekaṃ kāraṇopapattyā 'nujānāti, sambhavatyasmin kāraṇaṃ pramāṇaṃ hetur iti kāraṇopapattyā syād evam etan netarad iti.* These texts allow us to understand why Nāgārjuna says in the Sūtra that *tarka,* reasoning, is like *saṃśaya,* doubt, dealt with in Sections XXI-XXIII. There is an intrinsic similarity between both categories derived from the fact that in both of them there is a vacillation of the mind between two ideas followed by the effort to establish which of these two ideas correspond to reality. As a consequence of this similarity, the refutation of *tarka* in this Section is similar to the refutation of *saṃśaya* in Section XXI.

The opponent argues that the category 'reasoning' (*tarka*) exists because when one is in a state of doubt, one reasons in order to reach the truth. Nāgārjuna's argument in order to discard the existence of *tarka* is the following one: reasoning is always related to an object which is either already known or not yet known. In the first case reasoning becomes useless, because the object it has to establish is already established, and in the second case nobody can reason about an object that has not come into the range of his knowledge.

NIRṆAYA

Section LI : Nāgārjuna's refutation of *nirṇaya*, determination, because of its impossibility either if the object and its attributes are identical or different.

In the commentary previous to the Sūtra a possible objection on the opponent's part is presented against Nāgārjuna's denial of the existence of reasoning (*tarka*): reasoning must exist because, being an examination or inquiry aiming at the knowledge of reality, it is the cause of determination (*nirṇaya*). Nāgārjuna negates in the Sūtra and in its commentary the existence of determination (the effect) negating thereby the possibility of reasoning (the cause) also. The argument of Nāgārjuna is that anything, a pot for instance, must be either identical with or different from the matter which constitutes it and its attributes as existence, unity, roundness, redness etc. which belong to it. Nāgārjuna analyses both alternatives.

If the pot, matter, existence, etc. are identical, if they are all one and the same thing, wherever any one of them (as for instance, wherever any matter) would happen to be, there the pot (identical with matter) would also be. Nāgārjuna illustrates his thought with an example. Being 'Śiva', 'the Mighty One' and 'the Destroyer of Towns' one and the same god, wherever we say that Śiva is, we must assume that The Mighty One, and The Destroyer of Towns are also understood to be. But the most important consequence of the identity of pot, matter, existence etc. would be that any determination (as for instance, *kriyāvad dravyam*, which is an example given by *NSBh ad* 1, 1, 41) would be impossible, because of the essential identity of all things with matter, existence and other attributes, and therefore of all things among themselves, which hinders all predication aiming at determining the real nature of something.

If, on the contrary, pot, matter, existence etc. are different among them, then it would follow that the pot, as being different from existence, roundness, redness, etc. would be inexistent, would not be round neither red etc. As in the previous case any determination of the pot would be impossible, because of its inexistence.

It could be argued by the opponent (as a third alternative derived from the second one) that, although the pot *is not* existence, roundness, redness, etc., it *possesses* existence, roundness, redness etc., and thereby it exists, and consequently its determination is possible through what it possesses. Nāgārjuna refutes this objection observing that the possessor of a thing does not become the thing itself. An example for Nāgārjuna's way of thinking would be: a man can *possess* a sword and is not the sword. And Nāgārjuna concludes that the pot can *possess* existence, roundness, redness etc. and notwithstanding it is not existent, round or reddish, and in this case, if attributes are denied, there is no place for determination of the object.

Perhaps we are facing two irreducible points of view. The idea of the opponent would be that even if an individual (a pot) is not an universal (existence, roundness etc.), anyhow it can participate of the universal, i.e. can have the quality indicated by the universal, if it 'possesses' the universal, or the universal is in it, or it has any kind of relation with the universal. And this idea makes determination of an object possible through the attributes represented by the universals which it 'possesses', i.e. which it participates of. Nāgārjuna's refutation takes into account the relation between two individuals, but not the relation between an individual and a universal—which seems to be the relation the opponent has in mind. Nāgārjuna handles the relation between an individual and a universal as if it were the relation between two individuals. These two relations are different: a man can possess a sword and he is not the sword, but if a man possesses (= is in relation with) existence or redness, he is not the existence or the redness themselves, but he is existent or reddish.

Having disposed of the two alternatives (identity or difference between the object, pot, and its attributes, existence etc.), the alternative of the object being both, identical with and different from its attributes, is logically impossible as each one of them has been already discarded, and being so, the category *nirṇaya* is out of question.

VĀDA

Section LII: **Nāgārjuna's refutation of the debate (*vāda*) because of the non-existence of the word and the object designated by the word as they cannot exist either as one and the same or as different.**

In the commentary before the Sūtra Nāgārjuna expresses that the opponent, in order to save the existence of the *nirṇaya*, could argue that Nāgārjuna himself, on trying to reject the possibility of determining the specific nature of an object (the pot etc.), has been involved in a debate which comprehends the defense of a thesis and the criticism of the antithesis, and consequently implies the existence of *nirṇaya.* The concept of *vāda* referred to by Nāgārjuna closely corresponds to that of *NS* 1, 2, 1: *pramāṇatarka sādhanopālambhaḥ siddhāntāviruddhaḥ pañcāvayavopapannaḥ pakṣapratipakṣaparigraho vādaḥ.*

Nāgārjuna answers this objection of the opponent denying in the Sūtra the existence of the debate on the ground of the inexistence of names and named objects. In the commentary, employing an argumentation similar to that of the previous Sūtra, he affirms that the relation between the name and the object designated by the name could be of identity or of difference.

In the case the word and its object were one and the same, in the same way as the *word* pot is produced (without the intervention of matter, instrument and pot-maker etc.), in that same way the *object* pot would be produced (without the intervention of matter, instrument and pot-maker etc.). And at the same moment the *word* pot is uttered, at that same moment the *object* pot would come into existence. And furthermore, as the *word* pot and the *object* pot are one and the same, on pronouncing the *word* pot, the *object* pot would fill the mouth. These absurd consequences are produced if one admits the identity of word and object.

In the second case, i.e. of the word and the object being different, when the *word* pot is uttered, the *object* pot would not be ascertained because a thing (a pot) cannot be ascertained or made known in its real nature through a thing different from it (a cow).

As a consequence of the previous argumentation there is not the possibility of words related to objects and of objects related to words, and therefore without words and objects the debate is not possible either.

Section LIII: **Nāgārjuna's denial of the conventional nature of the relation word-object adduced by the opponent because of the absurd consequences it implies when in relation with the opponent's own *siddhāntas*.**

In the beginning of this Section Nāgārjuna presents an objection that the opponent could adduce in order to save the existence of words and thereby of *vāda,* the debate. Even if it is not admitted any kind of relation based on identity or difference between the word and the object, there is still a third possibility of explaining that relation:

convention. The relation between the word and the object is a product of conventional agreement (*sāmayika*).

Nāgārjuna in the Sūtra rejects this possibility, expressing that the adduced objection gives him the occasion for examining the true reality that the opponent attributes to the *padārthas.* From this examination will come forth the absurd consequences indicated at the end of the commentary.

According to the opponent's opinion (*siddhānta*) the knowledge of the sixteen categories produces the attainment of the supreme good, liberation. This idea is expressed in *NS* 1, 1, 1 already quoted in note 1 of Section I. The opponent also believes in the true reality of the sixteen *padārthas.* They are reals, absolutely objective facts. Nāgārjuna opposes to this thesis of the true reality of the *padārthas* the opinion of the sages, according to whom names are due to convention and besides that refer to inexistent objects, giving as *dṛṣṭāntas* the names 'Devadatta' ('given by the gods') and 'Indragupta' ('protected by Indra'). These names can be given to any child, just by a decision of the parents any do not really denote a person given or protected by a god. So the same thing happens with the sixteen *padārthas*: if their names are due to convention, as the same opponent affirms, then as it happens with all the names, they designate unreal things. In this Nāgārjuna has put the opponent in contradiction with his own *siddhānta*: 'all the *padārthas* exist in truth'. In the last paragraph of the commentary Nāgārjuna indicates another absurd consequence of the first thesis of the opponent: 'liberation is attained through the *padārthas*'. Liberation would be reached by means of merely wordly conventional creations as are the *padārthas*; common persons would be liberated without any special knowledge or effort as they participate in the wordly conventions to which the *padārthas* belong, and finally there would be no difference between 'wise' and 'ignorant' because they all handle only conventional products to which nothing real corresponds.

Section LIV: **Another consequence of the conventional nature ascribed to words: multiplicity of words for the same object.**

Although it is not possible to give a literal translation of the commentary of Sūtra 54, its general meaning is clear. As the Sūtra says, owing to the fact that words are made by convention, there are manifold words to designate one and the same thing. The commentary gives examples of this.

In the commentary of the next Sūtra will be explained that the conventional nature of the words leads to their inexistence; and from this we can conclude that if words do not exist, the debate is not possible.

Section LV: **Another consequence of the conventional nature of words: multiplicity of objects for the same word.**

In the Sūtra Nāgārjuna expresses that everybody employs one and the same word for denoting many objects, and in the commentary gives two examples, the Sanskrit words '*go*' and '*hari*', to illustrate his assertion, enumerating in the first and second quoted stanzas the many things denoted by these words.

The third quoted stanza presents another example which has not been announced together with *go* and *hari*. We understand this third example in the same way as the two previous examples: the different beings enumerated in the stanza are denoted by a single name *Nārāyaṇa*'.

In the commentary Nāgārjuna reiterates the idea expressed in Sūtra LIII that a single object can be designated by many words and gives two examples of this: the different names under which Indra is known, and the synonimic value of three words that denote the absence of existence.

Nāgārjuna concludes the commentary asserting that the words do not exist with a true reality, since due to the conventional nature of their relation with objects they are the product of human arbitrariness (which makes possible that a single word designates many things and *vice versa*) and this arbitrariness creates uncertainty as words can be applied to anything. And it is obvious that through words of arbitrary and uncertain nature the debate is not possible, the truth cannot be reached, and liberation is not to be attained.

Section LVI: **Nāgārjuna reiterates his objection against the existence of the word and the object either as one and the same or as different.**

Nāgārjuna adduces a new argument against the existence of the word and the object. In the Sūtra he says that if they are one and the same, they could not exist, since the identification of both would mean the elimination of both as individual entities. And if they are different (alternative expressed in the Sūtra and developed in the commentary), no word could ascertain any object as has been explained in our commentary to Section LII. The third alternative of the identity and difference of the word and the object is not possible either, because it carries on the defects proper to the first and the second alternatives.

Because of all the arguments exposed in Sections LII-LVI the Nyāya category of 'debate' (*vāda*) does not exist.

JALPA AND VITAṆḌĀ

Section LVII : **Nāgārjuna's refutation of discussion (*jalpa*) and altercation (*vitaṇḍā*) by means of the same arguments adduced against the existence of debate (*vāda*).**

In relation to the *padārthas* '*jalpa*' and '*vitaṇḍā*' Nāgārjuna only says that a refutation similar to that of the *vāda*, debate, is to be applied to them. This procedure is easily understandable, since among these three categories there is not an essential difference, as it is clear from what is expressed in *NS.* In the beginning of *NSBh* 1, 2, 1 it is said that *vāda, jalpa* and *vitaṇḍā* are three kinds discourse (*kathā*): *tisraḥ kathā bhavanti-vādo, jalpo vitaṇḍā ceti*; and the definitions of these three *padārthas* have several points in common: *NS* 1, 2, 1: *pramāṇatarka-sādhanopālambhaḥ siddhāntāviruddhaḥ pañcāvayavopapannaḥ pakṣa-pratipakṣaparigraho vādaḥ*; 1, 2, 2: *yathoktopapannaś chalajātinigraha-sthānasādhanopālambho jalpaḥ* and *Bh: yathoktopapanna iti-pramāṇa-tarkasādhanopālambhaḥ siddhāntāviruddhaḥ pañcāvayavopapannaḥ pakṣapratipakṣaparigrahaḥ / chalajātinigrahasthānasādhanopālambha iti-chalajātinigrahasthānaiḥ sādhanam upālambhaś. cāsmin kriyata iti evaṃviśeṣaṇo jalpaḥ /* and *NS* 1, 2, 3: *sa pratipakṣasthāpanāhīno vitaṇḍā* and *Bh: sa jalpo vitaṇḍā bhavati / kiṃviśeṣaṇaḥ? pratipakṣasthāpanayā hīnaḥ / yau tau samānādhikaranau virudhau dharmau pakṣaprati-pakṣāv-ity uktaṃ tayor ekataraṃ vaitaṇḍiko na sthāpayatīti parapakṣapratiṣedhenaiva pravartata iti.*

HETVĀBHĀSA

Section LVIII : **Nāgārjuna's refutation of fallacy or the mere appearance of a reason (*hetvābhāsa*): it cannot exist either being similar with or different from a (true) reason.**

In the commentary before the Sūtra Nāgārjuna expresses an objection that could be adduced by the opponent: Nāgārjuna has presented all the reasons adduced till now by the opponent as false reasons (*hetvābhāsa*). And it must also be taken into account that Nāgārjuna has affirmed in Sections XLI and XLII that the *hetu* does not exist; consequently anything presented as a *hetu* is not a *hetu*, is a false *hetu*, something that is only an appearance of a *hetu*. As a consequence of this affirmation nothing can be refuted, since all refutation needs *hetus* in order to be fulfilled, and therefore the refutations done by Nāgārjuna of the opponent's thesis are groundless and as such have no validity. Another implicit consequence is that, since Nāgārjuna maintains that all *hetu* is nothing else than *hetvābhāsa*, at least he is admitting the existence of the logical category '*hetvābhāsa*'.

Nāgārjuna answers in the Sūtra that a mere appearance of a *hetu*, a false *hetu*, does not exist, because there is not the possibility of a similarity or a dissimilarity between the so-called false *hetu* and a (true) *hetu*. In other words a false *hetu* cannot exist either if we assume that it is similar to a true *hetu* or that it is different from it. These are the two possible alternatives for the relation between both. Nāgārjuna analyses these two alternatives in the commentary.

1. An assertion, that is similar to a (true) reason, that has all the characteristics of a (true) reason, that consequently is a (true) reason, cannot be the mere appearance of a (true) reason, because being not different from a (true) reason, being similar to a (true) reason, it is nothing else than (true) reason. An example founds this thesis. If a rigorous testing is made in order to ascertain the pure gold that is in a given piece of gold, nothing can be discarded as not being gold, and the gold, being gold and nothing else than gold, cannot be said to be a mere appearance of gold since it is not different from gold. In the same way a (true) reason, being only a (true) reason and nothing else than a (true) reason, cannot be said to be a mere appearance of a (true) reason: it *is* a true reason and nothing else; there is no place in this case for a mere appearance of a (true) reason.

2. Likewise an assertion, that is different from a (true) reason, that has not a single characteristic of a (true) reason, that consequently is not a (true) reason, cannot become the mere appearance of a (true) reason with which it has nothing in common. Another example serves as a ground for this thesis. A heap of pebbles is not gold, is different from gold, has nothing that identifies it with gold. Consequently it cannot be said to be a mere appearance of gold, since it is different from gold, nothing of gold dwells in it, and it has nothing in common with

gold. In the same way any assertion that in itself has nothing of a (true) reason, that has nothing in common with a (true) reason, cannot be said to be something that can appear as a (true) reason.

In the last paragraph of this Section a third alternative is introduced which has in common with the two previous alternatives the notions of dissimilarity ('unequal') and similarity ('equal'), which Nāgārjuna has employed in the refutation of this fallacy. This alternative takes into account the hypothesis of a transformation in the (true) reason, thanks to which transformation the (true) reason could become a mere appearance of reason, i.e. a false reason. Two cases are taken into consideration in general terms, in relation to a self-dependent entity, i.e. something that has an own nature, an individuality well defined by essential characteristics, as is the (true) reason whose essential characteristic is to be a *probans.* (Another example could be fire as distinguished by its heat and its capacity to burn.)

1. It is not possible that, in order that the self-dependent entity get transformed into something else, such a self-dependent entity (true reason or fire) be connected with peculiarities opposite to its essential nature—essential nature which would serve as a 'basis' (*dhātu=khams*) to which these peculiarities will inhere. (For instance incapacity to prove, and cold and capacity to wet cannot be connected to (true) reason or to fire respectively.) Such a connection would mean the disappearance of that entity and consequently it would be impossible to say that it has been transformed into something else.

2. To such a self-dependent entity would be added peculiarities similar to those it already possess, i.e. not opposite to the nature of that entity. In this case these peculiarities will change nothing in the self-dependent entity; and the representation, that one gets of this entity after the addition of these peculiarities and that is gained through these same peculiarities, will be the same as we had before, will be a true cognition of that entity. (For instance if peculiarities of capacity to prove, and of heat and capacity of burning are added to true reason and fire respectively, the representation of the (true) reason and of fire before and after the addition will be the same, it will give us the true nature of both.) So no transformation is possible.

Nāgārjuna concludes this Section expressing that, as a consequence of the previous analysis, the mere appearance of a reason does not exist, and besides that he adds two observations more against the existence of *hetvābhāsa*: (1) the (true) reason has been proved to be inexistent (in

Sections XLI and XLII) so it is not possible to affirm that there is something that is a mere appearance of an inexistent reason, and (2) as the relations of similarity and dissimilarity between the *hetvābhāsa* and the *hetu* have been discarded, all the possibilities of a relation between them (i.e. between the *hetu* and a *hetvābhāsa* different from it) have been exhausted, not being place for a third one.

Section LIX: **Nāgārjuna's refutation of a special kind of fallacy, the indecisive or inconclusive (*anaikāntika, savyabhicārin*) reason (*hetu*), because the reason's own self of being a *probans* cannot be lost.**

In the Sūtra Nāgārjuna says that a reason non-affected by indecision—i.e. which is not an *anaikāntika, savyabhicārin,* inconclusive, indecisive, indeterminate reason—is produced out of the inexistence of indecision in its own self. The commentary makes clear Nāgārjuna's thought. The commentary begins asking why a reason cannot be affected by indecision. And immediately affirms that a reason in its own essence can be (1) accompanied by indecision, and (2) non-affected by indecision.

The alternative (1) will be dealt with in next Sūtra. With regard to it must be indicated that if a reason is accompanied by indecision it is because its own nature is affected by indecision, as a reason non-affected by indecision cannot be accompanied by indecision as the commentary will assert.

The commentary of this Ṣūtra deals with the alternative (2), and expresses that a reason non-affected in its own nature by indecision cannot be accompanied by indecision, i.e. cannot have indecision as its attribute. The ground for this assertion is very simple: a reason (*hetu*) is a *probans*; its nature is to prove; it exists thanks to its own nature; this own nature cannot be rejected; it cannot receive as attribute something that is in contradiction with that nature, something that hinders that nature to fulfil itself, accomplishing its effects. But it could be thought that the reason non-affected by indecision could reject its own nature and be affected by it. In this case even so, reason could not be accompanied by indecision, because for anything the rejection of one's own nature means the destruction of that thing.

Nāgārjuna concludes the commentary expressing that a reason that is a *probans* cannot be accompanied by indecision which is the contrary to its nature. And what is not a reason cannot be accompanied by indecision, i.e. cannot be *anaikāntika* or *savyabhicārin* since these are attributes only of reason.

Besides these two alternatives: (1) being a reason, and (2) not being a reason, there is not a third alternative, and in both cases there is not possibility of being accompanied by indecision. Consequently the opponent has only one possibility to defend his thesis of the existence of the indecisive reason, and this is only to accept the alternative (1) mentioned at the beginning of this Section: a reason, which has his own nature affected by indecision, can be accompanied by indecision. This is dealt with in the next Section.

Section LX: **The opponent adduces two examples in order to prove the possibility of existence of an indecisive or inconclusive reason.**

The opponent affirms that there can be a reason accompanied by indecision, i.e. there can be an indecisive or *anaikāntika hetu* even if it is necessary to accept that reason has its own nature of *probans* affected by indecision. And he gives two examples of indecisive reason. The first example is bodilessness as a *hetu* for eternality in regard to space and action. In this case bodilessness is an indecisive or *anaikāntika* reason, because it accompanies something (the space) that is eternal and also something (action) which is not eternal. The second example of an indecisive reason is generality, *genus* (*sāmānya*) and particularity, species (*viśeṣa*) as a *hetu* for eternality in regard to the atom and the pot. (Atoms and pot are *dravya* and as such they possess generality and particularity according to the *Vaiśeṣikasūtra* 1, 1, 8: *sad anityaṃ dravyavat kāryaṃ kāraṇaṃ sāmānyaviśeṣavad iti dravyaguṇakarmaṇām aviśeṣaḥ.*) In this second case of atoms and pot generality and particularity are also an indecisive reason, since *genus* and *species* accompany atoms which are eternal, but also pots which are not.

Section LXI: **Nāgārjuna refutes the objection of the previous Sūtra expressing that the examples given therein are not appropriate, because each of these examples refers to two different reasons and not to one and the same reason.**

In the Sūtra Nāgārjuna denies the objection of the opponent, because he says that the reasons are different. The commentary develops this assertion. The bodilessness of the space is different from the bodilessness of action (and mind or idea), because arising and non-arising are contradictory notions, and the bodilessness of space arises, while the bodilessness of action does not. Bodilessness of action, as an attribute of action, comes forth when action arises and ends when action ends. Bodilessness of space cannot be the same since, as an attribute of an eternal entity, it must also be eternal. Thus there is an essential difference between both, and therefore bodilessness of space cannot be in action and bodilessness of action cannot be in space.

This difference between bodilessness of space and bodilessness of action obliges to reject the opponent's examples adduced for proving the existence of an inconclusive reason. In order that a reason be inconclusive, it is necessary that it proves in some cases and that it does not prove in other cases. There is ambivalence in it. If there were only *one* bodilessness, it would prove eternality in the case of the space, and it would not prove it in the case of action. It would be an inconclusive reason. But there are *two* kinds of bodilessness, one kind, that of the space, which proves eternality, and another one, that of action, which does not prove eternality. And in this case there is not that ambivalence that is characteristic of the inconclusive reason.

In the last paragraph of this Section Nāgārjuna expresses that all that has been said in regard to the inconclusive reason adduced in order to prove something, must be applied to the inconclusive reason adduced in order to refute something, since both are, in their essence, reasons. As an example of inconclusive reason adduced in order to refute, the opponent could present 'tangibility' in regard to atoms and jar: tangibility in order to deny the eternality of the jar is an inconclusive reason, since tangibility is also an attribute of the atoms that are eternal. Nāgārjuna could answer that there are two kinds of tangibility as there are two kinds of bodilessness, and because of similar reasons.

Nāgārjuna adds that, if there were a contradictory reason, that could not mean that it is a reason accompanied by indecision since both classes of reason (contradictory and indecisive) are two different species of the *genus* 'mere appearance of a reason' (or fallacies), *hetvābhāsa*, with different attributes and consequently different definitions.

Section LXII: **Another argument against the existence of the inconclusive reason.**

A new argument against the existence of the inconclusive reason is constituted by the momentariness of all things. This is, according to

Buddhism, an attribute of all things, not admitted by many of the non-Buddhist philosophical schools of India. Proving and refutation cannot be made in regard to a thing which disappears while it is being proved or refuted, even if we accept that proving and refutation are possible in regard to a thing that subsists. Nothing can be attributed or negated in relation to a non-existing thing.

After dealing with the inconclusive or indecisive (*anaikāntika*) reason, Nāgārjuna will refute in the next Sections the existence of the contradictory reason, another kind of fallacy, following in this way the same order that is found in *NS* 1, 2, 5: *anaikāntika hetu* and 1, 2, 6: *viruddha hetu*.

Section LXIII: **An opponent's objection: contradiction exists as a consequence of the confrontation between Nāgārjuna's denial of the inconclusive reason and the Nyāya's affirmation of it.**

This Sūtra and its commentary contains an objection made by the opponent to Nāgārjuna. On one side, according to the Naiyāyika opponent, a reason (*hetu*) can be accompanied by indecision, and that reason must belong to the class of 'inconclusive reasons' (*anaikāntika*). This is the Nyāya conception of inconclusive reason, as shown by its definition in *NS* 1, 2, 5 quoted in note of Section LIX. On the other side, according to Nāgārjuna's statements, as a reason is by nature a prover (*sādhyasādhanaṃ hetuḥ, NS* 1, 1, 34) and as such it cannot be affected by indecision (because indecision is contradictory to its own nature of a prover), therefore, a reason accompanied by indecision does not exist. In this way the two thesis, that of Naiyāyika opponent and that of Nāgārjuna, are confronted one another and are found contradictory by the opponent. As a consequence of this he affirms that contradiction is possible, exists. Nāgārjuna in next Section will examine the notion of 'contradiction' in relation to *pratijñā-hetu* (*probandum-probans*), and in itself as a basic logical principle.

Section LXIV: **Rejection by Nāgārjuna of the contradictory reason (*viruddha hetu*), because of the impossibility of any chronological relation between the *hetu* (*probans*) and the thesis or proposition to be proved (*pratijñā*) to which it is related.**

In the Sūtra Nāgārjuna rejects the existence of the contradictory reason, because it arises before or after the proposition it has to prove or to refute.

Before dealing with the commentary it is necessary to make two remarks.

1. In the commentary Nāgārjuna refers to the contradictory reason, but all his arguments against the existence of a contradictory reason can be applied also to the contradiction in itself, a most important logical principle.

2. *NS* 1, 2, 6 defines a contradictory (*viruddha*) reason in the following terms: *siddhāntam abhyupetya tadvirodhī viruddhaḥ* and the *Bh* comments: *taṃ viruṇaddhīti tadvirodhī abhyupetaṃ siddhāntaṃ vyāhantīti*, and *Vārttika: ko 'sya sūtrasyārthaḥ/ abhyupagatārthavirodhī viruddhaḥ.* Therefore, according to these texts it is essential for the contradictory reason as considered by the Nyāya that it contradicts the already accepted thesis that it intends to prove or defend. But the commentary of the present Sūtra gives the notion of contradictory reason a much broader meaning: this reason can contradict either the thesis it should prove (or defend) or the thesis of an opponent. This is seen by the last part of the commentary which refers to the propounder of a theory and his opponent.

The argumentation of Nāgārjuna against the existence of a *hetu* that contradicts a thesis is based on the impossibility of a chronological relation between the *hetu* and the thesis it must support or destroy. It is an argumentation similar to that developed in Section XII. A reason, which comes into existence after the thesis (of the *vādin* or of the *prativādin*) that it has to support or destroy, does not exist as a reason, since a reason in order to be a reason, must have a thesis related to it. A reason, which arises before the thesis (of the *vādin* or of the *prativādin*) that it has to support or destroy, does not exist either as a reason because of the same motive. It can be supposed that, according to the momentariness theory already adduced by Nāgārjuna in Section LXII, both the reason and the thesis related to it arise in order to vanish immediately.

Nāgārjuna rejects the third alternative of the simultaneous existence of the objections and counter-objections of the propounder of a theory (*vādin*) and of his opponent (*prativādin*), because these objections and counter-objections cannot be formulated at the same time. The same can be said about any reason and the thesis it intends to defend or discard.

In this way Nāgārjuna has disposed of the second kind of *hetvābhāsa*: the *viruddha* one. In the next Sūtra Nāgārjuna will analyze a third kind of *hetvābhāsa*: the *kālātīta* one, 'the reason whose time has passed away', the mistimed reason.

Section LXV: **Nāgārjuna refutes the existence of the reason 'whose time has passed away' (*kālātīta*) or mistimed reason.**

In the commentary that precedes the Sūtra Nāgārjuna presents an objection that could be made against his assertion that the mere appearance of a reason (*hetvābhāsa*) does not exist: the reason called '*kālātīta*' ('whose time has passed away') exists and consequently, if the *species* exists, the *genus*, the *hetvābhāsa*, exists also. The existence of the *kālātīta* reason derives from the reasoning developed by Nāgārjuna against the contradictory reason. If a reason comes forth before the thesis it has to defend or refute, and, just on coming forth, disappears, it can be said that its time has passed away, that it is mistimed. So the same Nāgārjuna has accepted the existence of the *kālātīta* reason in particular and consequently of the *hetvābhāsa* in general.

Nāgārjuna observes that, according to the opponent, in relation to the pot three times exist: (1) the present is the time of the existence of the pot as such; (2) the past is the time of the mass of clay wherefrom the pot will originate, and (3) the future is the time of the potsherds, the pieces into which the pot is broken. The potsherds are something future in relation to the pot and the clay; these on their turn should become past in regard to the potsherds. Present, past, future, are correlative notions; each of them needs the others in order to exist; no one of them can exist without the others. But, when the potsherds exist, the clay and the pot are not anymore there; consequently it is not possible to say that the potsherds are the future of the clay and the pot, that are already inexistent; nothing can have any relation to an inexistent thing. So the future does not exist, since the present and the past (to which it should be related in order to exist) are not anymore there.

If it is argued that the past and the present exist, it should be answered that this is not possible, because in order to exist the past should exist in regard to the present and *vice versa*, but that is not logically possible, since when the past exists the present (to which it should be related) has not come forth yet, and when the present is there, the past (its necessary correlative element) has passed away. Consequently, if the past is logically impossible, there cannot be a reason related to an inexistent past.

Section LXVI: **Another argument presented by Nāgārjuna against the existence of the past time, ground for the existence of the mistimed (*kālātīta*) reason: the way of expression in the different languages confirms the inexistence of the past.**

In this Section Nāgārjuna puts forward a new argument against the existence of the past based on a linguistic consideration. All languages as the Sanskrit etc. confirm the thesis that the past time does not exist. In fact languages affirm that what exists is the present, what actually is before us; what has already arisen and, not being the present, does not exist anymore is the past; and what has not yet arisen and, not being the present, does not exist yet is the future. Thus if the past, according to the testimony of languages, is inexistent, the opponent cannot affirm anymore his *siddhānta* that the *kālātīta* or mistimed reason exists, since for its existence the past time would be required, and the existence of this latter has been discarded.

Section LXVII: **Denial of the existence of the past as depending on a passed away reason.**

In the Sūtra Nāgārjuna repeats his assertion that the passed away reason and also the passed away time do not exist because of the impossibility of their existence. It is not denied that a reason is heard by the ear, but immediately after being heard, it passes away, becomes a passed away entity, and as such is an inexistent entity.

It is necessary to take into account that time is always referred to things (in this case: a reason): a thing that has arisen and has ceased to be receives the name of 'past'; if it arises, in the very short instant it arises, it is said to be 'present'; if it has not yet arisen into existence, it is called 'future'. Time, so to say, adheres to things, exists depending on them, does not exist as something apart and independent.

Now it is impossible for any time, past or present, to depend on a passed away reason. As regards the past time, it cannot depend on a passed away and therefore inexistent reason; and besides that, being at its own turn also a passed away and therefore inexistent time, it cannot be said to depend on anything. As regards the present time it cannot depend on a passed away reason, because in this case present time and past reason would have to coexist in order that a relation could be established between them. As a conclusion of all his reasoning carried on in Sections LXV - LXVII the past time and the reason whose time has passed away, the mistimed, *kālātīta* reason, do not exist.

CHALA

Section LXVIII: **Nāgārjuna's refutation of sophism (*chala*): he has considered the *padārthas* in the same way as his opponent, so he has not incurred in the sophism-defect the opponent attributes to him.**

The category *chala* (sophism, quibble, casuistry, purposive distortion) is the subject of *NS* 1, 2, 10-17. A general definition is given in *NS* 1, 2, 10: *vacanavighāto 'rthavikalpopapattyā chalam*, and in 1, 2, 11 three kinds of *chala* are enumerated: *tat trividhaṃ vākchalaṃ sāmānyacchalam upacāracchalam ceti.* Their definitions are given in the three following sūtras and their *Bhāsya*: 1, 2, 12: *aviśeṣābhihite 'rthe vaktur abhiprāyād arthāntarakalpanā vākchalam,* and *Bh*: *navakambalo 'yaṃ māṇavaka iti prayogaḥ/ atra navaḥ kambalo 'syeti vaktur abhiprāyaḥ/ ...tatrāyaṃ chalavādī vaktur abhiprāyād avivakṣitam anyam arthaṃ nava kambalā asyeti tāvad abhihitaṃ bhavateti kalpayati, kalpayitvā cāsambhavena pratiṣedhati eko'sya kambalaḥ kuto nava kambalā iti/*; 1, 2, 13: *sambhavato'rthasyātisāmānyayogād asambhūtārthakalpanā sāmānyacchalam,* and *Bh: aho khalvasau brāhmaṇo vidyācaraṇasampanna ityukte kaścid āha sambhavati brāhmaṇe vidyācaraṇasampad iti/ asya vacanasya vighāto 'arthavikalpopapattyā 'sambhūtārthakalpanayā kriyate-yadi brāhmaṇe vidyācaraṇasampat sambhavati vrātye 'pi sambhavet, vrātyo 'pi brāhmaṇaḥ, so 'pyastu vidyācaraṇasampanna iti/ yad vivakṣitam artham āpnoti cātyeti ca tad atisāmānyam/*; and 1, 2, 14: *dharmavikalpanirdeśe'rthasadbhāvapratiṣedha upacāracchalam,* and *Bh: abhidhānasya dharmo yathārthaprayogaḥ, dharmavikalpo 'nyatra dṛṣṭasyānyatra prayogaḥ, tasya nirdeśe dharmavikalpanirdeśe / yathā mancaḥ krośantīti arthasadbhāvena pratiṣedhaḥ, mañcasthāḥ puruṣāḥ krośanti na tu mañcāḥ krośanti.*

It could be said that the common characteristic of these three kinds of *chala* is that there is not agreement between a disputant and his opponent in regard to the meaning of a word employed by the former. The disputant attributes the word a certain meaning; his opponent, in order to achieve his refutation, maliciously attributes to that same word another meaning (not taken into account by the disputant). We could say that both the disputant and his opponent are speaking of two different things or about the same thing from two different perspectives or in two different levels. When such a procedure takes place in debate it is said that there is a case of *chala*, quibble, purposive distortion or sophism.

We think that, in a way similar to what happens in other Sections, it is necessary to find in the present Section a reproach made by the opponent to Nāgārjuna: that in his refutation of the reality of the *padārthas* he has incurred in the defect called '*chala*'.

We understand that in the first part of the Sūtra the opponent criticizes Nāgārjuna saying that he (the opponent) in his previous argumentations has referred to the *padārthas* or logical categories as real entities, as *data* of our common, ordinary experience, while Nāgārjuna has referred to them as not being existent in reality. Both have had in mind two different things, viewed from diverse perspectives, located in opposite levels. So Nāgārjuna has incurred in the logical defect of *chala*.

Nāgārjuna denies this opponent's assertion, saying in the Sūtra that, if that assertion were true, the same *prasaṅga*, the same defect of sophism would occur in any discussion between Naiyāyikas and Śūnyatāvādins, constituted by assertions and refutations. Whatever the Naiyāyika would affirm would be in reference to the empirical status of the *padārthas* considered as real, while whatever the Śūnyatāvādin would reply would be from the point of view of true reality (*paramārthataḥ*), according to which the *padārthas* are unreal.

The commentary throws some light on the cryptic discussion contained in both parts of the Sūtra. It says that what the opponent affirms in the first part of the Sūtra is not true, because all that he (Nāgārjuna) has said as refutations of the *padārthas*, has been said by him considering them (= the *padārthas*) as *padārthas* in the same sense as the Naiyāyika considers them. And it is from this point of view that he has denied to the *padārthas* any validity. He has not taken into account his own conception of reality, he has only handled logical principles and categories in his discussion. So he has not incurred in a sophism, because he has maintained himself in the same level as the Naiyāyika opponent.

If the opponent asks how is it possible that Nāgārjuna has behaved in that way, he would answer assuming two alternatives: (1) If it is accepted that the Naiyāyika assertion and the Śūnyatāvādin refutation are *a priori* in different levels, owing to their opposite philosophical positions, then all discussion between them would be impossible, because both disputants would incur in sophism as each of them would be giving to words a meaning different from that given by his adversary. In this way, each disputant would nullify his own statements, his own words. As a consequence of all this what has been said by him (i.e. Nāgārjuna) has to be considered as a refutation and not as a sophism. As regard the second alternative, if the affirmation made by the opponent in the first part of the Sūtra is not accepted, then he has been unable to demonstrate the existence of *chala*, and we must conclude that *chala* does not exist.

JĀTI

Section LXIX : **Nāgārjuna's refutation of the irrelevant rejoinder (*jāti*), because 'arising' (*jāti*) is impossible.**

NS 1, 2, 18 gives the definition of *jāti*, 'futile rejoinder', in the following terms: *sādharmyavaidharmyābhyāṃ pratyavasthānaṃ jātiḥ* and *Bh* comments thereon: *prayukte hi hetau yaḥ prasaṅgo jāyate sa jātiḥ / sa ca prasaṅgaḥ sādharmyavaidharmyābhyāṃ pratyavasthānam upālambhaḥ pratiṣedha iti...jāyamāno 'rtho jātir iti.* *NS* 1, 2, 20, indicates that *jātis* (as well as *nigrahasthānas*) are numerous owing to the diverse forms that refutation can assume: *tadvikalpāj jātinigrahasthānabahutvam* and *Bh: tasya sādharmyavaidharmyābhyāṃ pratyavasthānasya vikalpāj jātibahutvam. . . / nānā kalpo vikalpaḥ, vividho vā kalpo vikalpaḥ*, and *Vārttika ad locum: tadvikalpāj jātinigrahasthānabahutvam iti / sādharmyavaidharmyābhyāṃ pratyavasthānasya vikalpāt. . .bahvyo jātayo. . .bhavanti.* It is necessary to lay stress in four concepts of these texts: (1) *jāti* is something that is born (*jāyate, jāyamāno*), (2) *jāti* is a *prasaṅga, pratyavasthāna, upālambha, pratiṣedha*, (3) the *pratyavasthāna* that constitutes the *jāti* may assume numerous forms (*vikalpa* of the *pratyavasthāna*), and (4) owing to the fact indicated in point (3) the *jātis* (as well as the *nigrahasthānas*) are numerous.

We must understand the commentary before the Sūtra having in mind the texts we have already quoted. In this part of the commentary Nāgārjuna presents an argument that could be opposed to his negation of the Nyāya categories: the *jati* or futile rejoinder exists, since it arises whenever, against a well ascertained thesis, a *jāti*-objection belonging to any of its numerous kinds is made under the form of a refutation.

Nāgārjuna in the Sūtra denies the existence of *jāti*, because nothing can arise, either being already arisen or not yet arisen or both. In the commentary after the Sūtra Nāgārjuna refutes the possibility of arising in any of these three alternatives: (1) something already arisen (past) cannot arise again, for a second time; (2) something not yet arisen (future) is inexistent and as such cannot be the agent of any action or process, and (3) something that is arising (present) does not exist since it partakes of 'being already arisen' and of 'not being yet arisen'. So there is not possibility of 'arising'.

NIGRAHASTHĀNĀNI

Section LXX: **Nāgārjuna's refutation of the reiterative statement (*punarvacana*), one of the points-of-defeat (in argumentation) (*nigrahasthānāni*).**

In *NS* 1, 2, 19 *nigrahasthāna*, 'point of defeat', is defined: *vipratipattir apratipattiś ca nigrahasthānam*, and in *NS* 5, 2, 1-2 twenty-two kinds of *nigrahasthāna* are treated in detail. One of these *nigrahasthānas* is the *punarukta* or *punarvacana*, repetitive or reiterative statement, repetition or reiteration, dealt with in *NS* 5, 2, 14-16. Its definition is *śabdārthayoḥ punarvacanaṃ punaruktam anyatrānuvādāt* (14).

After refuting the existence of *jāti* in Section LXIX, Nāgārjuna has to refute the existence of the last Nyāya category, that of the *nigrahasthānas*. He does it rejecting in the first place the *punarukta nigrahasthāna* in Sūtra LXX and then the *nigrahasthānas* in general in Sūtras LXXI and LXXII.

In the commentary that precedes the Sūtra LXX an objection referring to the repetition or reiteration that the opponent could set forward is presented in the following terms: Nāgārjuna has denied the existence of the diverse categories having recourse always to the notions of 'existence' and 'non-existence'; this constitutes a reiterative way of speaking; consequently he has incurred in the *punarukta* defect in argumentation; so it is not possible to deny at least the existence of the *nigrahasthāna* category.

Nāgārjuna denies the possibility of a reiterative statement expressing that two alternatives are possible: either what is said before and what is said after are the same thing or they are different things. Regarding the first alternative he says that no statement can be the repetition of another one, previously uttered, because if something already exists, it cannot come again into existence. It is not possible to produce two times the same things. As regards the second alternative, if the second statement is *different* from the first one, then it is not possible to speak of repetition, which means that *one and the same* thing is stated several times; the only thing we can affirm is that several *different* statements have taken place one after the other. Another reason that Nāgārjuna adduces in order to demonstrate the impossibility of repetition is the momentariness of the statements (as of the all things): it is not possible to say that one statement, that as soon as it is produced vanishes, is similar to another one, that likewise as soon as it is produced vanishes. The commentary ends indicating that, even if a statement is *similar* to another one previously expressed (for instance in their contents), we cannot say that they are one and the same thing.

So anything that is said is different from any other thing that has been already said, and there is no possibility of a reiterative discourse.

Section LXXI: **All the points of defeat in argumentation are to be declared inexistent as the irrelevant rejoinders by similar arguments.**

This Section maintains that the points of defeat are like the irrelevant rejoinder (*jāti*), i.e. inexistent. It has been explained in Section LXIX that a *jāti* cannot exist, because of its impossibility to be produced in any alternative that could be imagined: (1) it was already arisen before being produced, (2) it was not yet arisen, and (3) it was arisen and not arisen. The same thing happens with the *nigrahasthāna* category. Three similar alternatives are contemplated in relation to the *nigrahasthānas*: (1) A point of defeat arises from another point of defeat; in this case *either* the produced one is the same as the producer—then the produced one was already existing when it was produced by the producer (i.e. by itself); this is absurd since nothing can come twice into existence and nothing can originate out of itself; *or* the produced one is different from the producer—then the produced one did not exist when it was produced by the producer; this is also absurd since it is not possible that the action of coming forth be connected to something that does not exist. (2) The point of defeat arises from something that is not a point of defeat. This alternative is absurd since it would imply that anything can originate from anything. (3) The third alternative—the point of defeat arises from something that at the same time is a point of defeat and is not—is equally to be rejected, since nothing can be something and its opposite at the same time, and to each of the elements of this alternative could be applied the objections already indicated in regard to the previous ones.

Section LXXII: **Last argument adduced by Nāgārjuna against the existence of points of defeat in argumentation.**

In this Section a last argument is offered by Nāgārjuna against the existence of the *nigrahasthānas* in general. According to Nyāya the *nigrahasthānas* are deficiencies in the argumentation, that one has to avoid in one's own argumentation and to discover in the opponent's argumentation (*NSBh* 1, 1, 1 at the end). When a disputant discovers that any of his opponent's arguments is nothing else than what is called a *nigrahasthāna*, he points it out and on doing so immediately defeats the *nigrahasthāna*-argument of his opponent.

But in Nāgārjuna's opinion for a *nigrahasthāna*, i.e. an argument that is a point, a place, a seat (*sthāna*) of defeat, there is no defeat, there is not the possibility that defeat be *in it* in the sense that it be the object of a defeat, in the same way as for the place of enchainment (a prison for instance) there is no enchainment, there is not the possibility that enchainment be *in it* in the sense that it be the object of enchainment. As it is seen, an analogy based on the literal meaning of the words *tshar gcad paḥi gnas* (=Sk. *nigrahasthāna*) and *bciṅs paḥi gnas* (= Sk. *bandhanasthāna*) serves to demonstrate the inexistence of defeat in the category 'point of defeat'.

As a consequence of the inexistence of enchainment in the place of enchainment, there is no the possibility to ascertain the place of enchainment, since enchainment is an essential and characteristic attribute of the place of enchainment and it does not exist in this latter; and without its essential and characteristic attributes it is not possible to ascertain anything.

In the same way, applying this reasoning to the point of defeat, given the inexistence of the essential and characteristic attribute of 'defeat' in the point of defeat, it is not possible to ascertain the point of defeat, to know it with certainty, i.e. to be able to say in regard to it : this is a point of defeat. And we can add also that the point of defeat does not exist since nothing can exist without its essential and characteristic attributes.

Section LXXIII: **Nāgārjuna's conclusion: the only result reached by the previous discussion is that neither the *padārthas* nor their negation exist. And if things do not exist, names also do not exist.**

In the commentary before the Sūtra a possible objection is expressed: all the means of valid knowledge have been negated; in the same way negation also must be negated. In Section XIII the opponent has affirmed that the denial of the *padārthas* establishes the existence of the *padārthas*, because no negation is possible without the existence of the negated object. In the present Section his position is different and this Section does not mean a repetition of that previous one. In this Section the opponent maintains that the negation must be denied in the same way as the *padārthas* have been. After the negation of the *padarthas* it is not possible to maintain anymore the existence of the negation which presupposes the existence of the *padārthas*. The empirical reality is subsumed under the 16 *padārthas*. If they are negated, nothing remains and consequently Nāgārjuna's negation itself of the *padārthas* ceases to be, together with the *padārthas*.

Nāgārjuna in the first part of the Sūtra expresses which is the only reason which obliges us to affirm that the negation does not exist in the same way as it is the case with the Nyāya categories: owing merely to the abolishing reasoning of Nāgārjuna, the categories (in a direct and immediate way) and the negation (in an indirect and mediate way) have been declared to be logically impossible, and consequently cannot be accepted as existing. Nothing else must be adduced.

In the second part of the Sūtra Nāgārjuna indicates a consequence of the logical impossibility and of the non-acceptance of the existence of the categories and their negation, or (what is the same) a consequence of the non-establishing of the categories and the negation as existing: the only thing that can be said is that they are not established; nothing else can be affirmed in relation to the categories and the negation. This is the only result of the argumentation that precedes. In fact Nāgārjuna is right, since nothing can be speculated in regard to entities that do not exist.

Adopting these tenets (inexistence of the *padārthas*, inexistence of the negation, impossibility to affirm anything in regard to them) one is speaking according to what things really are: inexistent and mere creations of the mind and not according to what they seem to be: existent and true realities.

But, if we admit that the objects expressed by words (*padārthas*) are, from the point of view of absolute truth, inexisting and mere mental products (although from the point of view of relative truth they seem not so) we still may ask: which is the status of the words that express these objects? Are they really existing although what they express is not so?

Nāgārjuna answers saying that words also do not exist, because things do not exist and consequently words cannot exist without things to express. And why things do not exist? The reason given by Nāgārjuna as accepted by all is that things do not exist owing to the inexistence of relations of identity and difference. These relations do not really exist, because they are relative notions (as are unity and multiplicity, low-high, long-short) and as such cannot have a real own being, although they may appear as having such a being. In other words they have only a relative, conventional existence, what amounts to a false existence. This principle is stated in *Śū* 7 (see note 46 of our edition and cf. *MMK* 2, 21). Things cannot come into existence nor exist without possessing identity (with themselves) or difference (with others) as their characteristic attributes.

Nāgārjuna ends this Section expressing that, because of the inexistence of words, *nirvāṇa* and liberation are the same. Two interpretations are possible. (1) *Nirvāṇa* and liberation are the same, i.e. similar to all the categories whose existence has been denied. On one side *nirvāṇa* and liberation do not exist, and, on the other side, their negation and even their names do not exist either. And (2) *Nirvāṇa* and liberation are the same, i.e. similar the one to the other. In fact they are nothing else than *śūnyatā*, and the only statement that can be made, on using language that belongs to empirical reality, is that *śūnyatā* is the only 'entity' that 'exists'; and the only attitude that can be assumed, on facing it from the level of supreme reality, is silence, owing to the incapacity of human language and reason, as being products of the empirical reality, to reach transcendental entities.

NOTES

NOTES FOR THE INTRODUCTION

* National Council for Scientific Research (CONICET), Argentina.

1. i.e. the *lotsaba* Mdo-sde ḥbar (Sūtrajvāla) from Khu. Cf. *BTI* 18, p. 9 and *Cumulative Index* 14-18, p. 10a.

2. Cf. Naudou, *Les Bouddhistes Kaśmīriens*, pp. 188-89.

3. Cf. Naudou, *Les Bouddhistes Kaśmīriens*, pp. 171-74.

4. The *Madhyamakaśāstrastuti*, stanza 10, mentions '*Vidalā*' as the name of a work of Nāgārjuna.

5. Kajiyama, *Daijō Butten* 14, p. 186; Yamaguchi, *Chūgan Bukkyō Ronkō*, p. 114; Ui, *Indo Tetsugaku Kenkyū* V, p. 166; Mochizuki, *Bukkyō Dai Jiten* V, p. 4120 (*sub nyāya*). On the title of this treatise see Kajiyama, 'The Vaidalyaprakaraṇa of Nāgārjuna', pp. 131-33, *Daijō Butten* 14, p. 186 and Kajiyama and Uriūtsu, *Daijō Butten* 14 (Kaisetsu), pp. 424-25.

6. Yamaguchi (1929) translated it from Tibetan into French; Tucci (1929) edited the Tibetan text and translated it into English; Jayaswal and Sāṅkṛtyāyana (1937) edited for the first time the Sanskrit text; Johnston and Kunst (1951) published an improved Sanskrit edition; Bhattacharya (1978) reprinted the Johnston and Kunst's edition and translated the Sanskrit text into English.

Ruegg, *The Literature of the Madhyamaka School*, pp. 19-21 and Lindtner, *Nāgārjuniana*, p. 70 accept the authenticity of the *VV*. But perhaps some doubts may be raised against its authenticity on many of the same grounds that can be opposed to the authenticity of *V*.

7. Cf. Vācaspati Miśra, *Ṭīkā* ad *NSVārtt* 2, 1, 8 (p. 419 *infra*): *ayam atra pūrvapakṣiṇo mādhyamikasyābhisandhiḥ—yadyapi mama viśvavicārāsahatvavādinaḥ pramāṇaṃ nāma na kiñcid asti vicārasaham, tathā 'pi lokasiddhānyeva pramāṇāni tair eva pramāṇaiḥ paryālocyamānānivicāraṃ na sahante / so 'yaṃ pramāṇānām aparādho yāni svavirodhena vilīyante na mamāparādha iti.*

8. Cf. Tola, 'Tres concepciones del hombre en la Cultura de la India', with bibliography.

9. The *Tattvopaplavasiṃha* of Jayarāśi Bhaṭṭa has been edited by Pt. Sukhlalji Sanghavi and Prof. Rasiklal C. Parikh. There is a recent edition of this text, published in India, that we have not at hand now. Cf. Ruben, 'Über den Tattvopaplavasiṃha des Jayarāśi Bhaṭṭa, eine agnostizische Erkenntniskritik'; Franco, 'Studies in the Tattvopaplavasiṃha', 'Studies in the Tattvopaplavasiṃha II, The theory of Error', and *Perception, Knowledge and Disbelief: A Study of Jayarāśi's Scepticism.*

10. On Śrīharṣa see Dasgupta, *A History of Indian Philosophy* II, pp. 125-33, and Salomon, 'Scepticism or faith and Mysticism'; Ph. E. Granoff, *Philosophy and Argument in Late Vedānta: Śrī Harṣa's Khaṇḍanakhaṇḍakhādya.*

11. *The Carakasaṃhitā of Agniveśa*, edited by Vaidya Jādavaji Trikamji Ācārya, pp. 70-73 (*Sūtrasthāna* 11, 17-32) and pp. 264-72 (*Vimānasthāna* 8, 15-66). The sections

that interest more the *Vāda* (*ibid.*, pp. 266-72 = 8, 26-66) have been critically edited by Ui in *Indo Tetsugaku Kenkyū II*, pp. 1-12.

12. *Fang pien hsin lun, Taishō* Vol. XXXII, 1632. Edited and translated into Japanese and commented by Ui (1939) in *Indo Tetsugaku Kenkyū II*, pp. 473-585; translated into Sanskrit by Tucci (1929) in *Pre-Diṅnāga Buddhist Texts on Logic*, Part I. This treatise is known under the Sanskrit names of *Upāya(kauśalya)hṛdaya* or *Prayogasāra*. This treatise was translated into Chinese by Buddhabhadra. Afterwards another translation was made by Ki Kia Ye, who is to be located in the 5th century A.D. Cf. Tucci, 'Buddhist Logic before Diṅnāga', p. 452 notes 1 and 2.

13. *Ju shih lun, Taishō* XXXII, 1633. Translated into Sanskrit by Tucci (1929) in *Pre-Diṅnāga Buddhist Texts on Logic*, Part I. This treatise is known under the Sanskrit name of *Tarkaśāstra*. This treatise was translated into Chinese by Paramārtha between 546-69. As Tucci says, 'Buddhist Logic before Diṅnāga', p. 452, it is a 'fairly ancient work'.

14. For instance in the *Abhidharmasamuccaya* (pp. 104-06 Pradhan ed.) and in *Yogācārabhūmi*. On the *Vāda* teachings contained in these treatises see Vidyabhusana, *A History of Indian Logic*, pp. 263-65 (where the *Yogācārabhūmi* is called *Saptadaśabhūmiśāstrayogācārya*); Tucci, 'Buddhist Logic before Diṅnaga', pp. 455-67 (where the *Abhidharmasamuccaya* is called *Mahāyānābhidharmasaṅgītiśāstra*); Wayman, 'The Rules of Debate According to Asaṅga' and Oberhammer, 'Ein Beitrag zu den Vāda-Traditionen Indiens' (where the *Yogācārabhūmi* is referred to as a work of Maitreya). Some information also in Sugiura, *Hindu Logic as Preserved in China and Japan*, pp. 31-32.

15. But the *NS* cannot be looked upon as a mere *Vāda-śāstra*. Cf. Matilal, *Nyāya-Vaiśeṣika*, p. 78.

16. On the *tantrayuktis* see Randle, *Indian Logic in the Early Schools*, pp. 11-12; Ruben, 'Zur Frühgeschichte der indischen Philosophie'; Oberhammer, 'Notes on the Tantrayuktis', Renou, 'Sur la forme de quelques textes sanskrits', p. 184; and Hara, Review of Chakraborti, pp. 79-80.

17. *Carakasaṃhitā*, pp. 735-37 (= *Siddhisthāna* 12, 41-50) Vaidya Jādavaji ed.

18. *Suśrutasaṃhitā, Uttaratantra*, Chapter LXV.

19. Kautilya, *Arthaśāstra*, last chapter.

20. *Pai lun, Taishō* Vol. XXX, 1969. Translated into English by Tucci (1929) in *Pre-Diṅnāga Buddhist Texts on Logic*, Part I. This treatise is known under the Sanskrit name of *Śataśāstra*. This treatise was translated into Chinese by Kumārajīva (*circa* 350-410 A.D.) in the year 404. Cf. Gard, 'On the authenticity of the Pai lun and Shih-Erh-Mên-Lun'; Ruegg, *The Literature of the Madhyamaka School*, pp. 50-51; Vaidya, *Etudes sur Āryadeva*, p. 62. On the *Śata(ka)śāstra* in general see Lamotte, *Le Traite de la Grande Vertu de Sagesse* III, p. 1372.

21. Cf. Tucci, *Pre-Diṅnāga Buddhist Texts*, pp. IX and XI.

22. *Mūlamadhyamakakārikās (Madhyamakasūtras) de Nāgārjuna*, L. de la Vallée Poussin ed.

23. 'La Madhyamakaśāstrastuti de Candrakīrti, J.W. de Jong ed., in *Oriens Extremus* 9, 1, Februar, 1962, pp. 47-56.

24. We think that Bhavya, the author of the *Madhyamakaratnapradīpa*, belongs to a late period (7-8th centuries). Cf. Dragonetti 'On Śuddhamati's *Pratītyasamutpāda-hṛdayakārikā*', p. 119.

25. See note 20 of the Introduction.

26. See note 21 of the Introduction.

27. See note 6 of the Introduction.

28. Cf. Tucci, *Pre-Dinnāga Buddhist Texts*, pp. xxiii-xxx.

29. Hulin, *Sāṃkhya Literature*, p. 136.

30. Hulin, *Sāṃkhya Literature*, p. 139; Larson, *Classical Sāṃkhya*, pp. 148-49 and 281-82.

31. Hulin, *Sāṃkhya Literature*, p. 139.

32. Cf. Vogel, *Indian Lexicography*, pp. 309-10.

33. Cf. our forthcoming article 'Some remarks on Bhartṛhari's concept of Pratibhā', and Kunjunni Raja, *Indian Theories of Meaning*, p. 117.

34. Cf. Matilal, *Nyāya-Vaiśeṣika*, p. 54.

35. Cf. Keith, *Indian Logic and Atomism*, pp. 56-57, 126-27; Potter, *Encyclopedia of Indian Philosophies*, pp. 185-91.

NOTES FOR THE TEXT

Invocation

1. DD: phyug.

Section I

1. N: spoṅ.
2. P and C: sum.
3. N: byin.
4. P: tu.
5. P and N: bcad.
6. P and N: gtam.
7. P C and N: rnams; D: rnam.
8. P and N: śad *after* do.

Section II

1. P and N: tshad ma ni; D and C: *omitted.*
2. P and N: bltos.

Section III

1. N: ni.
2. P and N: śad *omitted.*
3. P and N: bltos.
4. P: pa *omitted.*
5. P and N: bskyed; C: skyod.
6. N: par.

Section IV

1. P and N: bltos.
2. P and N: paḥam; D and C: ḥam *omitted.*
3. P: na *omitted.*
4. P and N: gyi.

5. P: ra.
6. C: pa.
7. P: thal bar ḥgyur baḥi (*instead of* thal baḥi).

Section V

1. P: smras.
2. P: śad *after* na.
3. P and N: śad *after* te.
4. P and N: thal bar *omitted.*
5. P and N: śad *omitted.*
6. P: ñid *omitted.*
7. P and N: śad *after* no.
8. P N and C: tshad; D: chad.

Section VI

1. C: mad.
2. P and N: rab tu *omitted.*

Section VII

1. P: bar *omitted.*
2. P and N: yaṅ *omitted.*
3. P and N: na *omitted.*
4. P and N: śad *after* te.
5. P and N: yod pa *omitted.*
6. P and N: śad *omitted.*
7. P N and C: baḥi; D: paḥi.

Section VIII

1. P: śad *after* ro.
2. P: śad *after* na.
3. P: śad *after* te.
4. P and N: ḥdir.
5. P and N: lhas byin.
6. P and N: śad *omitted.*
7. P and N: na.
8. DD and N (?): sprul. Perhaps it should be: ḥphrul. Cf. *NSBh* 5, 1, 8 (*abhicārāt*).

9. P and N: śad *after* daṅ.
10. P and N: des na.
11. P and N: mar me; D and C: me.
12. P and N: rigs; D and C: sogs.

Section IX

1. P and N: dpyod.
2. P N and C: tshaṅs; D: chaṅs.
3. DD: ga gar.
4. P and N: ḥthun.
5. P and N: dper; D and C: dpe.
6. P and N: ltar.
7. P and N: pa *omitted.*
8. P: ni.
9. P and N: gsal.
10. P: ni *omitted.*
11. P and N: yin; D and C: ma yin.

Section X

1. P and N (?): byas te (*instead of* byed de).
2. P and N: śad *omitted.*

Section XI

1. P and N: śad *omitted.*
2. P and N: ḥthob.
3. P and N: gi.
4. P and N: pa.
5. P and N: bltos.
6. P and N: la *omitted.*

Section XII

1. P and N: śad *after* yaṅ.
2. C: tshod.
3. P and N: gi.
4. P and N: na.
5. C: śad *omitted.*
6. *Our correction*: ri boṅ gi rwa; D P N and C: ri bo.

7. DD: ra.
8. P and N: char.
9. P and N: dag.

Section XIII

1. P and N: dgag.
2. P and N: tshad ma daṅ; D and C *omitted.*
3. P and N: te.
4. P: pa.
5. P: ḥgog.
6. P and N: grub.
7. P and N: rtag.
8. *Our correction*: ḥam; D P N and C: ḥaṅ.
9. P and N: pa *omitted.*
10. N: pa *after* yin.
11. N: dgag.
12. P and N: śad after na.

Section XIV

1. P and N: pa; D and C: par.
2. P and N: źes *before* zer.
3. P and N: pa.
4. P and N: źe.
5. P and N: la.
6. P and N: śad *omitted.*
7. P and N: de yis.
8. P and N: ḥjigs.
9. P and N: dgag.
10. P and N: nam.

Section XV

1. P and N: smra.
2. P and N: dgag.

Section XVI

1. P and N: de *before* med.
2. P and N: śad *omitted.*

3. P and N: no.
4. P and N: ḥjig.
5. P and N: te.
6. P and N: bsal.
7. C: len na mtshuṅs paḥi skyon khas *omitted.*
8. C: źa ne ma (?).

Section XVII

1. P and N: yin; D and C: ma yin.
2. P and N: ḥdir; D and C: ḥdi.

Section XVIII

1. P and N: da.
2. P and N: nas.
3. P and N: dbaṅ po daṅ *before* dbaṅ.
4. N: mig gi *before* dbaṅ poḥi.
5. P and N: bltos.
6. P and N: deḥi.
7. P and N: mṅon.
8. P and N: des.
9. P and N: śad *omitted.*

Section XIX

1. P and N: śad *omitted.*
2. P and N: śad *after* no.
3. P and N: śad *after* na.
4. P and N: de *omitted.*
5. P and N: phyir; D and C: phyir *omitted.*
6. P and N: ma; D and C: *omitted.*

Section XX

1. P and N: gźan; D and C: gźal bya.
2. P N and C: brjod.
3. P and N: ltar.
4. P and N: śad *omitted.*

Section XXI

1. P and N: śad *omitted.*

2. P and N: śad *after* no.
3. P and N: mi.
4. P and N: pa *after* yod.
5. P and N: śad *after* na.
6. P and N: pa *omitted.*
7. P: pa *after* dmigs.

Section XXII

1. P and N: ma *omitted.*
2. P and N: bltos.
3. P and N: ni *after* pa.
4. P and N: śad *omitted.*
5. P and N: ḥphrug.
6. P and N: yin *instead of* ñid do.
7. P and N: śad *after* na.

Section XXIII

1. P and N: bltos.
2. P and N: ltar.
3. P and N: la *after* pa.
4. P and N: ni.
5. C: par.
6. N: pa ñid (*instead of* paḥi).
7. P and N: śad *omitted.*
8. P and N: śad *after* te.
9. P and N: gcig.

Section XXIV

1. P and N: bo *omitted.*
2. N: pa.
3. P: ṅes pa don (*instead of* ṅes par ma skyes paḥi dgos pa don).
4. P and N: śad *after* no.
5. P and N: śad *after* na.
6. P and N: na *after* kyis.

Section XXV

1. P and N: snal ma; D and C: snam bu.
2. P and N: ḥjag ma; D and C: ḥjug pa.

3. P and N: śad *after* no.
4. P and N: śad *after* na.

Section XXVII

1. P and N: śad *after* yaṅ.
2. P and N: gis; D and C: gi.
3. P and N: mthaḥ.

Section XXVIII

1. P and N: dpyod.
2. *Our correction*: gaṅ la (cf. Section IX, commentary); D P N and C: gaṅ.
3. P and N: śad *omitted.*
4. P and N: ñid *omitted.*
5. P and N: śad *after* no.
6. P and N: śad *after* na.
7. P and N: sgrub.

Section XXIX

1. P and N: ro *after* phyir.
2. P and N: śad *omitted.*
3. P and N: śad *after* no.

Section XXX

1. P and N: śad *after* na.
2. P and N: śad *after* no.
3. P and N: śad *after* ro.
4. P and N: źe.
5. C: śad *omitted.*
6. P and N: sgra.
7. *This last sentence beginning with gźan yaṅ is considered by Kajiyama as the first sentence of the next Section. It seems to us that it is related to the idea developed in Section XXX*

Section XXXI

1. P and N: las; D and C: la.
2. P and N: śad *after* ro.

3. P and N: śad *after* na.
4. P and N: pas; D and C: par.
5. P and N: las *after* ba.
6. P and N: kyaṅ.
7. P and N: ma *omitted.*
8. P and N: śad *omitted.*
9. P and N: las.

Section XXXII

1. P: grab mthaḥ; N: grub mthaḥ (*instead of* grub pa).
2. P and N: śad *after* na.
3. P and N: *from* gal te *up to* grub po *omitted.*

Section XXXIII

1. P and N: tu *omitted.*
2. P and N: ni *omitted.*
3. P and N: ma *omitted.*
4. C: ḥgog ba ba.
5. P and N: bzuṅ.
6. P and N: śad *after* na.
7. P: ḥjug.
8. P and N: rnams kyaṅ (*instead of* rnam pa).

Section XXXIV

1. P and N: can; D and C: can *omitted.*
2. P and N: grub; D and C: ma grub.
3. P and N: śad *after* na.

Section XXXV

1. P and N: pa *omitted.*
2. P and N: ma; D and C: yaṅ.
3. P and N: źig.

Section XXXVI

1. P and N: can *after* lag.
2. P and N: śad *omitted.*
3. P and N: rnams la; D and C: rnam pa las.

Section XXXVII

1. C: rtsa.
2. P and N: ltar *omitted.*
3. P and N: na *omitted.*
4. P and N: sogs pa; D and C: la *after* pa.
5. P and N: tshogs pa la; D and C: *omitted.*
6. *Our correction:* yod pa yin; D and C: yod pa ma yin; P and N: yod pa bźin.
7. P and N: śad *after* no.
8. P and N: śad *after* na.

Section XXXVIII

1. P: śad *after* ste.
2. P and N: cig.
3. P and N: skyed.
4. P and N: mar (*instead of* ma la).
5. P and N: ḥbyin pa *after* mar.
6. P and N: śad *omitted.*

Section XXXIX

1. DD: phyi; P: phye *or* phyi (?).
2. P and N: cig.
3. P: ma *before* yin.
4. P and N: śad *omitted.*
5. P and N: ga.
6. P and N: źe; C: śa.
7. P and N: śad *after* na.
8. P and N: laḥam; D and C: lam.
9. P and N: khaḥi.
10. P and N: śad *after* do.

Section XL

1. N: lag *omitted.*
2. P and N: śad *omitted.*
3. P and N: ba; D and C: baḥi.

Section XLI

1. P and N: *For the first part of the commentary up to* ḥon te, *we adopt the* P and N *text;* D *and* C: *have only*: dam bcaḥ ba ni sgrub byed na gaṅ pos mi ḥgrub paḥi phyir ro /.
2. *Our correction*: ma yin (*instead of*: P and N yin). *This part of the text is omitted in* D *and* C. *See the previous note.*
3. P and N: gźan *after* dag.
4. P and N: poḥo; D and C: poḥi.
5. P and N: śad *after* poḥo; D and C: śad *omitted.*

Section XLIII

1. P and N: la sogs pa (*instead of* daṅ gtan tshigs).
2. P and N: sdud.
3. P and N: bcaḥ.
4. P and N: med pa yin (*instead of* yod pa ma yin).

Section XLIV

1. P and N: śad *after* yaṅ.

Section XLV

1. P and N: śad *after* yaṅ.
2. P and N: na; D and C: can.
3. P and N: nas; D and C: naḥi.

Section XLVI

1. P and N: pa.

Section XLVII

1. P and N: śad *omitted.*
2. P and N: śad *after* no.
3. DD: baḥa.
4. P and N: bdag ni (*instead of* gtan tshigs kyis ḥgrub par).
5. P and N: gtan tshigs daṅ dpe la yaṅ bźin no; D and C: *omitted.*

Section XLVIII

1. P and N: *from* gźan yaṅ *up to* brjod pa; D and C: *omitted.*

2. P and N: la sogs pa med la gtan tshigs; D and C: *omitted.*
3. C: par (*instead of* pa na).

Section XLIX

1. P and N: kyis.
2. P and N: bcas.
3. P and N: śad *after* na.
4. P and N: bya ste (*instead of* byed de).
5. P and N: śad *omitted.*
6. P and N: tiḥi yi ge daṅ *omitted.*
7. P and N: braḥi.
8. P: la *omitted.*
9. P and N: praḥi *before* yi.
10. P: ruṅ (?).
11. P and N: mchu.
12. P and N: cig.

Section L

1. P and N: śad *omitted.*
2. N: brtag.
3. P and N: deḥi.
4. P and N: la *after* don.
5. P and N: śad *after* no.
6. P and N: śad *after* na.
7. P and N: ltar.
8. P and N: la *omitted.*

Section LI

1. C: dpyod.
2. P and N: pas; D and C: pa.
3. P and N rgyu; D and C: rluṅ.
4. P: na *and after it* śad. N: no (*as* D and C) *and after it* śad.
5. P and N: śad *after* na.
6. P: śad *omitted.*
7. P and N: gñi ga (*instead of* gñis ka).
8. P and N: cig.
9. P and N: pa *omitted.*

10. P and N: po *after* dbaṅ.
11. P and N: śad *after* ro.
12. P: te.

Section LII

1. P and N: śad *omitted.*
2. D P N and C: dmigs pa; *our correction*: klan ka. The Tibetan translator made a confusion: he understood *upālamba* ('criticism', cf. *NS* 1, 2, 1) as *upalambha* ('perception', *dmigs pa* in Tibetan). Kajiyama maintains the text indicating in note the translator's mistake and in note 59 of his Japanese translation (in *Daijō Butten*) expresses that instead of *dmigs pa* there should be *klan ka tsol ba.*
3. P and N: daṅ *after* khyod.
4. P and N: śad *after* no.
5. P and N: brjod.
6. P and N: du *after* bźin.
7. P and N: śad *omitted before* bum.
8. P and N: cig.
9. P and N: bltos.
10. P and N: brjod par *before* rtogs.

Section LIII

1. P and N: śad *after* no.
2. P and N: śad *after* na.
3. P: ba.
4. C: tshigs.
5. P: rig.
6. P and N: kyi.
7. P: byas byas.
8. P and N: lhas byin.
9. P and N: śad *omitted.*

Section LIV

1. P and N: śad *after* yaṅ.
2. P and N: śad *omitted.*
3. P and N: stiṅ.
4. P and N: tshig.

5. P and N: ḥjigs.
6. P and N: paṇ ḍi (*instead of* piṇ ḍa).
7. P and N: sgyur (?).
8. P and N: la *omitted.*

Section LV

1. P and N: brjod.
2. P and N: daṅ *after* ṅag.
3. P and N: ni *omitted.*
4. P: śad *omitted.*
5. P: mgu.
6. P and N: rluṅ.
7. P and N: bzuṅ.
8. P and N: śig.
9. P and N: śad *omitted.*
10. P: pa *after* ḥjig.
11. P and N: cig.
12. P and N: mdog.
13. P and N: ba.
14. P: brjod.
15. N: ḥdris (?).
16. N: ṅes par (*instead of* ma ṅes pas).

Section LVI

1. P and N: brjod.
2. DD: rtsoṅ.

Section LVII

1. P and N: te.

Section LVIII

1. P and N: śad *omitted.*
2. P and N: śad *after* no.
3. P and N: kyis.
4. P and N: ste.
5. P and N: phyir *omitted.*
6. P and N: su *omitted.*

7. P and N: ni.

Section LIX

1. P: khrul.
2. P and N: źe.
3. P and N: ltar.
4. P and N: *after* ḥgyur ro: ḥon te raṅ gi ṅo bo ḥdor bar byed pa de lta na yaṅ ḥkhrul pa daṅ bcas par mi ḥgyur ro (*which appears to be the repetition of the next sentence, which begins also with* ḥon te *and is also included in* P *and* N).
5. P and N: śad *omitted.*

Section LX

1. P and N: śad *omitted.*
2. N: khaḥ.
3. P and N: śad *after* buḥo.

Section LXI

1. P: śad *after* na.
2. *Our correction (cf. Sūtra and Commentary* D *and* P *editions)*; D P N and C: las.
3. P and N: ma; D and C: ma *omitted.*
4. P and N: ga.
5. P and N: źe.
6. N: khaḥ.
7. C: de *before* ni.
8. *Our correction*: mkhaḥi; D P and C: mkhaḥ ni; N: khaḥ ni.
9. N: khaḥi.
10. P N and C: de.
11. P and N: las; D and C: de *before* las.

Section LXII

1. P and N: śad *omitted.*

Section LXIII

1. P and N: kyis.
2. P and N: gtan tshigs *omitted.*

3. P and N: śad *after* na.

Section LXIV

1. P: de *omitted.*
2. P and N: gtan *omitted.*
3. P and N: ni.
4. P and N: cig.
5. P and N: da; D and C: *omitted.*

Section LXV

1. P and N: śad *after* na.
2. P and N: kyis.
3. P and N: phyir *omitted.*
4. P and N: śad *omitted.*
5. P and N: śad *after* daṅ.

Section LXVI

1. P and N: brjod.
2. P and N: du *omitted.*
3. *Our correction*: ma ṅes; D P and C: mṅas *or* mdas; N: (?); *Kajiyama reads in* D *and* P: ma ṅes.

Section LXVII

1. P and N: źe.
2. P and N: śad *after* na.
3. P and N: pa; D and C: pas.
4. P and N: gyis.
5. P and N: ni *after* pa.
6. P and N: śad *omitted.*

Section LXVIII

1. P and N: śad *after* na.
2. P and N: lan *omitted.*
3. P: de *omitted.*
4. N: ñid (?) *interlined.*
5. P and N: ga.

6. P and N: źe.
7. P and N: ma *before* yin.

Section LXIX

1. P and N: śad *omitted.*
2. P and N: śad *after* na.
3. P and N: źe.

Section LXX

1. P and N: bzlos.
2. P and N: bcad.
3. P and N: śad *after* na.
4. DD: se.
5. P and N: kyis.
6. P and N: ñid *omitted.*

Section LXXI

1. P and N: bcad.

Section LXXII

1. P and N: śad *omitted.*
2. P and N: bcad.
3. P and N: bciṅ.
4. P and N: ni; D and C: ḥdi.

Section LXXIII

1. P and N: śad *omitted.*
2. P: pa *omitted.*
3. P and N: dgag.
4. P and N: śad *after* no.

Colophon

1. P and N: gi; D and C: gis.
2. P and N: śad *after* po.
3. P and N: Jayāntata.

NOTES FOR THE TRANSLATION

Section I

1. The whole treatise is directed against the Naiyāyikas. The Naiyāyikas think that the *padārthas* or logical categories, which embrace the whole reality, have a real existence, that they exist *paramārthataḥ*. Accordingly the *pramāṇas* are absolutely valid, they give us a true knowledge of things. The position of the Śūnyatāvādins is completely opposite. For them the *padārthas* have only a relative existence, they belong to the realm of empirical reality, they exist only *saṃvṛtitaḥ*. But it is not the metaphysical status of the *padārthas* that interest the author of this treatise. On the contrary he does not want to examine and to analyze the *padārthas* from this metaphysical point of view, in the metaphysical level, in order to reach the conclusion that they are *śūnya*, that they do not exist *paramārthataḥ*. This is made clear from the Commentary of Sūtra LXVIII referred to *chala*. In this Section Nāgārjuna expresses that he has treated the *padārthas* in the same way as his Naiyāyika opponent has treated them: as *padārthas*, as logical categories, without entering to establish which is their metaphysical status. And on doing so he shows that the *padārthas* are affected by manifold logical defects: the *pramāṇas* cannot give us a valid knowledge of things; several of them (like the *jāti* for instance) are to be declared impossible or absurd from the logical point of view, etc. The criticism to which Nāgārjuna submits the Nyāya categories reveals the conception that the Śūnyatāvāda had of the traditional logic from the point of view of the empirical reality, although not from a metaphysical point of view.

2. The Nyāya in its earliest phase was '*mainly concerned with the study of reasoning and the art of philosophical debate*' Matilal, *Nyāya Vaiśeṣika*, p. 76. Matilal also expresses that '*in the Pāli canons and the early epic literature some materialistic philosophers were described as specialists indulging in idle and futile logic*', ibid. Not only materialistic philosophers. In *Dīgha Nikāya* (*Brahmajālasutta*) I, p. 26, there is a reference to those *sāmaṇas* and *brāhmaṇas* expert in dialectical subtleties (*vālavedhin*).

3. The enumeration of these 16 categories (*padārtha*) contained in the commentary of this Sūtra is nothing else than part of *NS* 1, 1, 1: *pramāṇaprameyasaṃśayaprayojanadṛṣṭāntasiddhāntāvayavatarkanirṇayavādajalpavitaṇḍāhetvā-bhāsacchala-jātinigrahasthānānāṃ tattvajñānān niḥśreyasādhigamaḥ*. The order of the categories is the same in the original Sanskrit text (of *NS*) and in the Tibetan translation (of *V*).

4. In Tibetan *stoṅ pa ñid du smra ba rnams* – Sk. *śūnyatāvādinaḥ*.

5. The Śūnyatāvādins, as they do not adhere to anything, have no thesis of their own to sustain and defend. Cf. Candrakīrti, *Prasannapadā ad* 1, 3, p. 23; Nāgārjuna, *Yuktiṣaṣṭikā* 50.

Section II

1. i.e. undistinguishably mixed, being the same thing, not being different. It is the *sahopalambha* argument that serves to prove the identity of the percipient and the percept. Cf. Mādhava, *Sarvadarśanasaṃgraha* (*Bauddhadarśana*), p. 16 ed. Bibliotheca Indica: *grāhyagrāhakayor abhedaścānumātavyaḥ yad vedyate yena vedanena tat tato na bhidyate... sahopalambhaniyamād abhedo nīlataddhiyoḥ.* Cf. Chatterjee, *The Yogācāra Idealism*, pp. 59-66.

2. In the world, according to the common world experience.

3. Tib. : *bdag ñid thob pa* = Sk. *ātmalābha* : 'coming to existence'.

4. Cf. *NS* 2, 1, 16: *prameyā ca tulā prāmāṇyavat*, and *Bh*: *gurutvaparimāṇajñānasādhanaṃ tulā pramāṇam, jñānaviṣayo guru dravyaṃ suvarṇādi prameyam. Yadā suvarṇādinā tulāntaraṃ vyavasthāpyate tadā tulāntarapratipattau suvarṇādi pramāṇaṃ tulāntaraṃ prameyam iti.*

Bh ad NS 2, 1, 19: *yathā pradīpaprakāśaḥ pratyakṣāṅgatvād dṛśyadarśane pramāṇaṃ, sa ca pratyakṣāntareṇa cakṣuṣaḥ sannikarṣeṇa gṛhyate /... evaṃ pratyakṣādīnāṃ yathādarśanaṃ pratyakṣādibhir evopalabdhiḥ.*

It is necessary to observe that for *NS* and its *Bh* anything can be according to circumstances sometimes a *pramāṇa* and sometimes a *prameya*, but for *V* which goes farther the same thing is *pramāṇa* and *prameya* of that same *prameya* which on its turn is *pramāṇa* of that same *pramāṇa*. This same idea is expressed in *VV* 49 and 50: *pitrā yadyutpādyaḥ putro, yadi tena caiva putreṇa / utpādyaḥ sa yadi pitā, vada tatrotpādayati kaḥ kam* (49) and *kaśca pitā, kaḥ putras tatra tvaṃ brūhi tāvubhāvapi ca/ pitṛputralakṣaṇadharau yato bhavati no 'tra saṃdehaḥ* (50) and Com. on 50: *tayośca pūrvopadiṣṭayoḥ pitṛputrayoḥ kataraḥ putraḥ kataraḥ pitā / ubhāvapi tāvutpādakatvāt pitṛlakṣaṇadharāvutpādyatvācca putralakṣaṇadharau / ...evam eva yānyetāni bhavataḥ pramāṇaprameyāṇi tatra katarāṇi pramāṇāni katarāṇi prameyāṇi / ubhayānyapi hyetāni sādhakatvāt pramāṇāni sādhyatvāt prameyāṇi/.*

Section IV

1. Cf. *MMK* 10, 8-10: 8. *yadīndhanam apekṣyāgnir apekṣyāgniṃ yadīndhanam/ katarat pūrvaniṣpannaṃ yad apekṣyāgnir indhanam// 9. yadīndhanam apekṣyāgnir agneḥ siddhasya sādhanam/ evaṃ satīndhanaṃ cāpi bhaviṣyati niragnikam// 10. yo'pekṣya sidhyate bhāvas tam evāpekṣya sidhyati/ yadi yo'pekṣitavyaḥ sa sidhyatāṃ kam apekṣya kaḥ //*

VV 40-48: 40. *yadi svataśca pramāṇasiddhir anapekṣya tava prameyāṇi / bhavati pramāṇasiddhir na parāpekṣā svataḥ siddhiḥ//* 41. *anapekṣya hi prameyān arthān yadi te pramāṇasiddhir iti / na bhavanti kasyacid evam imāni tāni pramāṇāni//* 42. *atha matam apekṣya siddhis teṣām ityatra bhavati ko doṣaḥ / siddhasya sādhanaṃ syān nāsiddho 'pekṣate hyanyat//* 43. *sidhyanti hi prameyāṇyapekṣya yadi sarvathā pramāṇāni / bhavati prameyasiddhir nāpekṣyaiva pramāṇāni//* 44. *yadi ca prameya siddhir nāpekṣyaiva bhavati pramāṇāni / kiṃ te pramāṇasiddhyā tāni yadarthaṃ prasiddhaṃ tat //* 45. *atha tu pramāṇasiddhir bhavatyapekṣyaiva te prameyāṇi / vyatyaya evaṃ sati te dhruvaṃ pramāṇaprameyāṇām //* 46. *atha te pramāṇasiddhyā prameyasiddhiḥ prameyasiddhyā ca / bhavati pramāṇasiddhir nāstyubhayasyāpi te siddhiḥ //* 47. *sidhyanti hi pramāṇair yadi prameyāṇi tāni tair eva / sādhyāni ca prameyais tāni kathaṃ sādhayiṣyanti //* 48. *sidhyanti ca prameyair yadi pramāṇāni tāni tair eva / sādhyāni ca pramāṇais tāni kathaṃ sādhayiṣyanti//*

It must be noted that there is a difference in the argumentation of the three texts: *V* affirms that something existing, non-existing or existing and non-existing cannot be dependent; *MMK* and *VV* maintain that neither fire and fuel nor *pramāṇa* and *prameya* can exist either as mutually dependent or not.

Section V

1. Cf. *NSBh* Introduction (beginning): *pramāṇam antareṇa nārthapratipattiḥ.* The comparison of this paragraph between a balance and the *pramāṇa* is better understood if one takes into account that the Sk. root *pra MĀ*, from which *pramāṇa* and *prameya* derive, means (1) to measure and (2) to know. Also the Sk. root *TUL*, from which *tulā* ('balance') is derived, means (1) to weigh and (2) to ponder, to examine. *NS* 2, 1, 16 and its *Bh* (both quoted in note 4 of Section II) have also recourse to the same comparison of *pramāṇa* and *tulā*.

2. On the first alternative contemplated by *V* (= if the *pramāṇas* need other *pramāṇas* to be established, *anavasthā* occurs) cf. *NS* 2, 1, 17: (*pūrvapakṣa*): *pramāṇataḥ siddheḥ pramāṇānāṃ pramāṇāntarasiddhiprasaṅgaḥ* and *Bh*: *yadi pratyakṣādīni pramāṇenopalabhyante, yena pramāṇenopalabhyante tatpramāṇāntaram astīti pramāṇāntarasadbhāvaḥ prasajyata iti anavasthām āha tasyāpyanyena tasyāpyanyeneti. Na cānavasthā śakyā 'nujñatum anupapatter iti.*

VV. 32*a-b*. *anyair yadi pramāṇaiḥ pramāṇasiddhir bhavet, tadanavasthā* and Com.: *yadi punar manyase pramāṇaiḥ prameyāṇāṃ prasiddhis, teṣāṃ pramāṇānām anyaiḥ pramāṇaiḥ prasiddhir evam anavasthāprasaṅgaḥ/.*

3. According to the reasoning of *VV* 2 and 33 and Com. *ad locum*, we would expect here the following idea. (1) if the *pramāṇas* were not established through other *pramāṇas*, there would be a difference (*vaiṣamikatva*): some objects would be proved through *pramāṇas* and some other, the *pramāṇas*, would not need that proof, and (2) if this difference is accepted, then it would be necessary to indicate which is the special *probans* that establishes these other objects, the *pramāṇas*, as existing. But the Tibetan text of *V* expresses that, in case the *pramāṇas* were not established by *pramāṇas*, the special proof *or* the difference has to be indicated. We would expect in *V* also either 'the difference and the special proof' or 'the special proof for the difference'.

4. This absurd consequence is the *regressus ad infinitum* already referred to in the Sūtra. See note 2 of this Section.

5. On the second alternative contemplated by *V* (= if the *pramāṇas* do not need other *pramāṇas*, absurd consequences will occur) cf. *NS* 2, 1, 18: (*pūrvapakṣa*): *tadvinivṛtter vā pramāṇasiddhivat prameyasiddhiḥ*, *Bh*: *yadi pratyakṣādyupalabdhau pramāṇāntaraṃ nivarttate, ātmādyupalabdhāv api pramāṇāntaraṃ nivartsyatyaviśeṣāt, Vārttika : yathā pramāṇāni svopalabdhau nivartante evaṃ prameyasiddhāvapi, Vṛtti : yadi ca pramāṇavinivṛttitaḥ pramāṇavyatirekāt pramāṇasiddhiḥ svīkriyate tadā tadvad eva tatsiddhiḥ* (*tatsiddheḥ* ?) *prameyasiddhiḥ svīkriyatāṃ, kiṃ pramaṇāṅgīkāreṇa.*

VV 33: *teṣām atha pramāṇair vinā prasiddhir vihīyate vādaḥ / vaiṣamikatvaṃ tasmin viśeṣahetuśca vaktavy aḥ / /* and Com.: *atha manyase teṣāṃ pramāṇānāṃ vinā pramāṇaiḥ prasiddhiḥ, prameyāṇāṃ punar arthānāṃ pramāṇaiḥ prasiddhir iti, evaṃ sati yas te vādaḥ pramāṇaiḥ prasiddhir arthānām iti sa hīyate / vaiṣamikatvaṃ ca bhavati keṣām cid arthānāṃ pramāṇaiḥ prasiddhiḥ, keṣāṃ cin neti / viśeṣahetuśca vaktavyo yena hetunā keṣāṃ cid arthānāṃ pramāṇaiḥ prasiddhiḥ keṣāṃ cin neti / sa ca nopadiṣṭaḥ / tasmād iyam api kalpanā nopapanneti.*

The order of the two alternatives (see note 2 of this Section) is the same in *NS* and in *V*.

In *VV* 1-2 (in the opponent's words) we find a similar reasoning applied to another subject, to the lack of an own self (*niḥsvabhāvatva*): *sarveṣāṃ bhāvānāṃ sarvatra na vidyate svabhāvaś cet / tvadvacanam asvabhāvaṃ na nivartayituṃ svabhāvam alam /* and: *atha sasvabhāvam etad vākyaṃ pūrvā hatā pratijñā te / vaiṣamikatvaṃ tasmin viśeṣahetuśca vaktavyaḥ //* and Com. *ad* 1: *yadyevaṃ, tavāpi vacanaṃ yad etac chūnyāḥ sarvabhāvā iti tad api śūnyam . . . tasmād anena sarvabhāvasva bhāvavyāvartanam aśakyaṃ kartum . . . evam asatā vacanena na śakyaḥ sarvabhāvasva bhāvapratiṣedhaḥ kartum,* and Com. *ad* 2: *athāpi manyase mā bhūd eṣa doṣa iti sasvabhāvam etad vākyaṃ sasvabhāvatvāc cāśūnyaṃ tasmād anena sarvabhāvasvabhāvaḥ pratiṣiddha iti atra brūmaḥ / yadyevaṃ, yā te pūrvā pratijñā śūnyāḥ sarvabhāvā iti hatā sā / . . . sarvabhāvāntargataṃ ca tvadvacanam.*

Section VI

1. *Mar me* in Tib., which corresponds to Sk. *dīpa* : 'light', 'lamp'. Because of the context we translate it by 'lamplight'. Cf. *NS* 2, 1, 19 and *Bh* which employ the word *pradīpaprakāśa* in a similar context.

2. Cf. *NS* 2, 1, 19 (denying the *anavasthā* defect): *na, pradīpaprakāśasiddhivat tatsiddheḥ.* The *prima facie* meaning of this Sūtra seems to be the affirmation of the *svayaṃsiddhi* of the *pramāṇas* (compared with the lamplight which can illuminate itself and others) as a means of avoiding the *anvasthā* defect of reasoning, adduced by the opponent in *NS* 2, 1, 17 (quoted in our note 2 of the translation of Section V). Nevertheless Vātsyāyana does not interpret the Sūtra 2, 1, 19 in this way and gives a different interpretation of it. Anyhow in the beginning of his commentary to 2, 1, 20 he presents the opinion of other authors (*kecit tu*) regarding the lamplight *dṛṣṭānta*: *kecit tu dṛṣṭāntam aparigṛhītaṃ hetunā viśeṣahetum antareṇa sādhyasādhanāyopādadate yathā pradīpaprakāśaḥ pradīpāntaraprakāśam antareṇa gṛhyatetathā pramāṇāni pramāṇāntaram antareṇa gṛhyanta iti.* These authors who have the same opinion as the opponent in *V* must certainly be also Naiyāyikas.

NS 5, 1, 10: (in order to show that the *dṛṣṭānta* does not need another *dṛṣṭānta* as the lamp does not need another lamp): *pradīpopādānaprasaṅgavinivṛttivat tadvinivṛttiḥ* and *Bh*: *antareṇāpi pradīpātantaraṃ dṛśyate pradīpaḥ tatra pradīpadarśanārthaṃ pradīpopādānaṃ nirarthakam /.* On *NS* 2, 1, 19 and 5, 1, 10 see Oberhammer, 'Ein Beitrag zu den Vāda-Traditionen Indiens', pp. 64-68, and Bhattacharya, 'On the Relationship Between *Vigrahavyāvartanī* and the *Nyāyasūtras*'.

VV 33 Com.: *atrāha* (the opponent in order to defend the validity of the *pramāṇas*:) *pramāṇānyeva svātmānaṃ parātmānam ca prasādhayanti/ yathoktam* :

> *dyotayati svātmanaṃ yathā hutāśas tathā parātmānam /*
> *svaparātmānāv evaṃ prasādhayanti pramāṇānīti //*

MMK 7, 8: (the opponent, in order to defend the *utpāda*, origination): *pradīpaḥ svaparātmānau saṃprakāśayitā yathā / utpādaḥ svaparātmānāv ubhāv utpādayet tathā,* and Candrakīrti *ad locum: yathā pradīpaḥ prakāśasvabhāvatvād ātmānaṃ prakāśayati ghaṭādīṃśca evam utpādo 'pyutpādasvabhāvatvād ātmānam utpādayiṣyati paraṃ ceti.* It is noteworthy to compare the similar progress of thought in both texts *NS* and *V*:

NS 2, 1, 16 and *Bh*: Analogy *pramāṇa-tulā*	*V* Section V, com. before Sūtra Analogy *pramāṇa*-balance
NS 2, 1, 17 and *Bh*: *anavasthāprasaṅga*	*V* Sūtra 5: *anavasthāprasaṅga*
NS 2, 1, 18 and *Bh*: If the *anavasthā* is not accepted, the *prameyas* would be ascertained without *pramāṇas*.	*V* Section V, com. last paragraph: If the *anavasthā* is not accepted then all the objects would not be ascertained by *pramāṇas*.
NS 2, 1, 19 and *Bh*: *svayaṃsiddhi* of the *pramāṇas*	*V* Sūtra 5 and com. : *svayaṃsiddhi* of the *pramāṇas*

This parallelism between *NS* and *V* could induce to think that *NS* 2, 1, 19 maintained the *svayaṃsiddhi* of *pramāṇa*. The defence of the *svayaṃsiddhi* of the *pramāṇas* by the Naiyāyika opponent in *V* as well as the possible acceptance of that *svayaṃsiddhi* in *NS* 2, 1, 19 are contrary to the general trend in the Nyāya regarding this matter. See note 1 of the translation Section XVII.

On the lamp *dṛṣṭānta* in general see My, *Candrakirti*, p. 113 note 284.

Section VII

1. Cf. *MMK* 7, 9: *pradīpe nāndhakāro 'sti yatra cāsau pratiṣṭhitaḥ / kiṃ prakāśayati dīpaḥ prakāśo hi tamovadhaḥ* and Candrakirti *ad locum* : *iha prakāśo nāma tamaso vadhaḥ / tamaśca pradīpasvātmani tāvan na saṃbhavati, virodhāt, yat tamo nighnataḥ svātmaprakāśatvaṃ syāt / na cāpi pradīpo yatra deśe tiṣṭhati tatra tamo 'sti, yat tamo nighnataḥ pradīpasya paraprakāśakatvaṃ syāt / ato 'pi nāsti pradīpasya svaparātmaprakāśakatvam.*

VV 37: *nāsti tamaśca jvalane yatra ca tiṣṭhati parātmani jvalanaḥ / kurute kathaṃ prakāśaṃ sa hi prakāśo 'ndhakāravadhah //* and Com.: *iha cāgnau nāsti tamo nāpi ca yatrāgnis tatrāsti tamaḥ / prakāśaśca nāma tamasaḥ pratighātaḥ / yasmāccāgnau nāsti tamo nāpi ca yatrāgnis tatrāsti tamaḥ, tatra kasya tamasaḥ pratighātam agniḥ karoti yasya pratighātād agniḥ svaparātmānau prakāśayatīti /.*

Śaṅkara, *Brahmasūtrabhāṣya ad* 1, 1, 1 (p. 6) refers also to the opposition between *tamas* and *prakāśa*. Padmapāda, *Pancapādikā ad locum*.

2. On the *prāpya* and *aprāpya* alternatives cf. *NS* 5, 1, 7: (describing the futile rejoinders called *prāptisama* and *aprāptisama*) : *prāpya sādhyam aprāpya vā hetoḥ prāptyā 'viśiṣṭatvād aprāptyā 'sādhakatvāc ca prāptyaprāptisamau* and *Bh*: *hetuḥ prāpya vā sādhyaṃ sādhayet aprāpya vā? na tāvat prāpya prāptyām aviśiṣṭatvād asādhakaḥ / dvayor vidyamānayoḥ prāptau satyāṃ kiṃ kasya sādhakaṃ sādhyaṃ vā / aprāpya sādhakaṃ na*

bhavati, nāprāptaḥ pradīpaḥ prakāśayatīti.

MMK 7, 10: *katham utpadyamānena pradīpena tamo hatam / notpadyamāno hi tamaḥ pradīpaḥ prāpnute yadā* and Candrakīrti *ad locum: ihālokāndhakārayor yaugapadyābhāvāt prāpter abhāvaḥ / yadā caivaṃ prāpter abhāvaḥ tadā kathaṃ kena prakāreṇedānīm utpadyamānena pradīpena tamo hatam iti yuktaṃ parikalpayitum / yamācca evam utpadyamānaḥ pradīpaḥ tamo na prāpnoti / tasmān naivāprāptatvāt pradīpaḥ kiṃcid api prakāśayatītyavasīyatām.*

VV 38: *utpadyamāna eva prakāśayatyagnir ityasad vādaḥ / utpadyamāna eva prāpnoti tamo na hi hutāśaḥ//* and Com. : *ayam agnir utpadyamāna eva prakāśayati svātmānaṃ parātmānaṃ ceti nāyam upapadyate vādaḥ / kasmāt / na hyutpadyamāna evāgnis tamaḥ prāpnoti, aprāptatvān naivopahanti tamasaś cānupaghātān nāsti prakāśaḥ.*

ŚS, p. 169*a*, lines 7-8 (Tucci's translation p. 8): The lamp, whether it is already born or not yet born, in both cases, is not co-present with (litt. cannot reach) darkness. Because this is contradictory to its nature. If the lamp cannot reach darkness, how can it destroy darkness?

U, p. 28 *a-b*, lines 27-1 (Tucci's Sanskrit translation p. 29 par. 11-12): *anyac ca / ātmā nityo 'naindriyakatvād iti bhavatsthāpanā / atha prāpyāprāpya va heturiti / aprāpya ced asiddho hetuḥ / yathāgnir aprāpya dahanāsamarthaḥ, asiścāprāpya chedanāsamarthaḥ / ātmānam aprāpya kathaṃ hetur bhavet / ityaprāpti[samam] / anyac ca / prāpya iti cet, prāpter ahetutvam.*

TŚ, p. 31 *c*, lines 4-7 (Tucci's Sanskrit translation p. 17 par. 5): *prāptyaprāptikhaṇḍanam / hetuḥ sādhyaṃ prāpnoti na vā? yadi tāvat sādhyaṃ prāpnoti tadāsādhakaḥ / atha hetuḥ sādhyaṃ na prāpnoti tadāpyasādhakaḥ / etat prāptyaprāptikhaṇḍanam ucyate / prativādī prāha / yadi hetuḥ sādhyaṃ prāpnoti tadā sādhyena saṃsargāt sādhyaṃ na sādhayati / yathā nadīvāri samudravāripraviṣṭaṃ na punar nadīvāri, hetus tadvad asādhakaḥ / yadi sādhyam asiddhaṃ, tadā hetur aprāpakaḥ / yadi tu prāpakas tadā kiṃ siddhasy [ārthasya] hetunā / tasmād hetur asiddhaḥ / atha na prāpnoti tadā so 'nyavastuvad asādhakaṃ, tasmād hetur asiddhaḥ / yadi hetur aprāpakas tadā 'samarthaḥ / yathāgnir aprāpya dahanāsamartho 'siś cāprāpya chedanāsamarthaḥ.*

U, p. 28*a*, line 29 (Tucci's Sanskrit translation p. 29 par. 11) and *TŚ*, p. 31*c*, lines 12-13 (Tucci's Sanskrit translation p. 18 line 5) already quoted employ also the comparison of the sword that without coming into contact cannot cut.

Section VIII

1. *i.e.* the fact that the lamplight be able to illuminate or remove darkness without coming into contact with it.

2. The belief that the stars have good or evil influence on men has been always current in India.

Cf. *NS* 5. 1, 8 which adduces magic as a case of influence without contact in order to show that the two futile rejoinders of *prāptisama* and *aprāptisama* are not justified (cf. note 2 of the translation Section VII): *ghaṭādiniṣpattidarśanāt pīḍane cābhicārād apratiṣedhaḥ* and *Bh*: *ubhayathā khalvayuktaḥ pratiṣedhaḥ kartṛkaraṇādhikaraṇāni prāpya mṛdaṃ ghaṭādikāryaṃ niṣpādayanti, abhicārāc ca pīḍane sati dṛṣṭam aprāpya sādhakatvam iti.*

ŚS, p. 169*a*, lines 9-11 (Tucci's translation p. 9 *supra*): (The unbeliever:) The magic formulae can bring from afar, evil to distant men, and the change of stars which takes place in the sky, can bring unhappiness to men. The same happens as regards the lamp. Although it does not reach darkness it can destroy darkness.

3. There is lack of correspondence between both.

4. On the absurd consequence that occurs with the *aprāpya* alternative cf. *MMK* 7, 11: *aprāpyaiva pradīpena yadi vā nihataṃ tamaḥ / ihasthaḥ sarvalokasthaṃ sa tamo nihaniṣyati.*

VV 39: *aprāpto 'pi jvalano yadi vā punar andhakāram upahanyāt/ sarveṣu lokadhātuṣu tamo 'yam iha saṃsthito hanyāt//.*

ŚŚ, p. 169*a*, lines 11-13 (Tucci's translation p. 9): If the lamp has a force which does not reach darkness, and yet can destroy darkness, then why a lamp—in India cannot destroy the darkness in China?

Section IX

1. We have been unable to locate a Nyāya text where investigators are compared to lions. But perhaps such analogy does not exist at all, if one admits that the Tibetan translation of this Sūtra may not render the meaning of the Sanskrit original as explained in the following note. If the hypothesis of the next note is accepted, then we have here another direct reference to Gautama's *Nyāyasūtras.*

2. The translation of this Sūtra offers serious difficulties. It is why Kajiyama prefers not to translate it, giving instead the translation of *NS* 1, 1, 25 (for the text of this Sūtra see note 5 of the translation of this Section). Probably the original Sanskrit Sūtra contained an idea that had to do with the Nyāya's definition of *dṛṣṭānta* included in the commentary, as for instance: 'according to your treatise (*bstan bcos; śāstra*) ordinary people and investigators (*hjig rten pa, spyod pa po; laukika, parīkṣaka*) like Hari etc. (*seṅ ge la sogs pa; hari-ādi*) in relation to this point (*de yaṅ; atra*) think (*mṅon par ḥdod pa; abhi MAN*) in a similar way (*mtshuṅs par; samam*)'. Perhaps the confusion in the translation was produced by a misunderstanding of the Sanskrit word '*hari*' which was taken with the meaning of '*lion*' instead of 'Viṣṇu', which is in the commentary at the first place in a series of names of 'investigators'. 'Lions etc.' in the Sūtra would be a wrong translation of 'Hari and others' which appear in the commentary.

3. Among the names that are enumerated here some belong to Hindu gods (Viṣṇu, Śiva, Brahmā), some to real or legendary authors and sages. Kapila is the founder of the Sāṃkhya system of philosophy; Ulūka is another name for Kaṇāda, the founder of the Vaiśeṣika system; Vyāsa is regarded as the compiler of several works of Hindu literature (*Veda, Mahābhārata* etc.) and also as the author of *Yogasutrabhaṣya*; Vaśiṣṭha is regarded as the author of several works, among which a law-book; Vyāghra is the name of various authors; Māṭhara is the name of an old Sāṃkhya teacher. No author named Samṛddha is known. Gagar (DD) and Gagara may perhaps be a wrong reading for Garga, the name of an old sage.

In the beginning of the *ŚŚ*, Viṣṇu, Mahesvara, Kapila, Ulūka and others are mentioned as beings who have been believed to be the Blessed One (cf. p. 168*a*, line 3).

4. They: the ordinary men and the investigators.

5. This is the Nyāya definition of *dṛṣṭānta* as given in *NS* 1, 1, 25: *laukikaparīkṣakāṇāṃ yasminn arthe buddhisāmyaṃ sa dṛṣṭāntaḥ* and *Bh: lokasāmānyam*

anatītāḥ laukikā naisargikaṃ vainayikaṃ buddhyatiśayam aprāptāḥ / tadviparītāḥ parīkṣakāḥ / tarkeṇa pramāṇair arthaṃ parīkṣitum arhantīti / yathā yam arthaṃ laukikā budhyante tathā parīkṣakā api so 'rtha dṛṣṭāntaḥ. The order of ideas is the same in *Bh* and in *V*: (1) who are the *laukikas,* (2) who are the *parīkṣakas* and (3) the definition of *dṛṣṭānta.*

6. The Vaiśeṣika school of philosophy maintained that darkness is only non-existence (*abhāva*), absence of light (*prakāśābhāva*). Cf. *Vaiśeṣikasūtra* 5, 2, 19-20: *dravyaguṇakarmaniṣpattivaidharmyād abhāvas tamaḥ* (19) and: *tejaso dravyāntareṇāvaraṇāc ca* (20). The Nyāya school maintained the same opinion. Cf. Potter, *Encyclopedia of Indian Philosophies,* pp. 110-11, 297 (Praśastapāda), 340 (Śaṅkara), 524 and 589 (Udayana), 614 ([Śri]Vallabha). The Prābhākara school of Mīmāṃsā maintained also that darkness is not a substance, that it is the mere absence of light (cf. Keith, The *Karma-Mīmāṃsā,* p. 53; Gaṅgānātha Jha, *The Prābhākara School of Pūrva Mīmāṃsā,* p. 92; *TŚ,* has also a reference to this opinion: p. 41*b,* line 25 (Tucci's Sanskrit translation p. 22): *andhakāre jyotiṣo 'bhāvaḥ tasmād andhakāraḥ /*).

7. 'Other investigators' in Tib.: *dpyod pa po* in the text. *Dpyod pa* = Sk. *mīmāṃsā, vicāra, vicāraṇa. Dpyod pa po* may mean (1) the *Mīmāṃsakas* and (2) *investigators* in general.

8. What does not exist cannot be removed.

9. i.e. an example that demonstrates or supports it.

Section X

1. Cf. note 1 of the translation Section VII.

2. On the opposition light-darkness see note 1 of the translation Section VII.

Section XI

1. i.e.: what will be the (absurd) consequence that could be deduced from the example?

2. Cf. *MMK* 7, 12: *pradīpaḥ svaparātmānau saṃprakāśayate yadi/ tamo 'pi svaparātmānau chādayiṣyatyasaṃśayam.*

VV 36: *yadi ca svaparātmānau tvadvacanena prakāśayatyagniḥ/ pracchādayiṣyati tamaḥ svaparātmānau hutāśa iva //.*

Section XII

1. Cf. *NS* 2, 1, 8 (*pūrvapakṣa*) : *pratyakṣādīnām aprāmāṇyaṃ traikālyāsiddheḥ.*

2. Cf. *NS* 2, 1, 9 (*pūrvapakṣa*) : *pūrvaṃ hi pramāṇasiddhau nendriyārthasannikarṣāt pratyakṣotpattiḥ.*

3. The horns of the hare are a common example in Indian Philosophy to indicate a non-existing thing, as well as the city of the Gandharvas, the flower in the sky, the son of the barren woman.

4. Cf *NS* 2, 1, 10 (*pūrvapakṣa*): *paścāt siddhau na pramāṇebhyaḥ prameyasiddhiḥ.*

5. 'That', i.e. the relation of *pramāṇa-prameya.* This relation is not possible in the alternative of simultaneity, as it is not possible in the first and second alternatives.

6. Cf. *NS* 2, 1, 11 (*pūrvapakṣa*): *yugapat siddhau pratyarthaniyatatvāt kramavṛttitvābhāvo buddhīnām.*

7. Cf. for a similar reasoning *NS* 2, 1, 12 and its *Bh* where the three alternatives dealt with in Section XII of our text are presented together in relation to *pratiṣedha* and *pratiṣedhya* and in order to refute the opponent's argument against *pramāṇa: Sūtra : traikālyāsiddheḥ pratiṣedhānupapattiḥ; Bh : asya tu vibhāgaḥ / pūrvaṃ hi pratiṣedhasiddhāv asati pratiṣedhye kim anena pratiṣidhyate / paścāt siddhau pratiṣedhyāsiddhiḥ pratiṣedhābhāvād iti / yugapat siddhau pratiṣedhyasidhyabhyanujñānād anarthakaḥ pratiṣedha iti / pratiṣedhalakṣaṇe ca vākye 'nupapadyamāne siddhaṃ pratyakṣādīnāṃ pramāṇatvam iti.*

Also *NS* 5, 1, 18 and its *Bh* (in relation to *sādhana* and *sādhya* and in order to illustrate what is the rejoinder called '*ahetusama*'): *Sūtra: traikālyāsiddher hetor ahetusamaḥ; Bh: hetuḥ sādhanam, tat sādhyāt pūrvaṃ paścāt saha vā bhavet / yadi pūrvaṃ sādhanam asati sādhye kasya sādhanam? atha pāścāt, asati sādhane kasyedaṃ sādhyam? atha yugapat sādhyasādhane, dvayor vidyamānayoḥ kiṃ kasya sādhanaṃ kiṃ kasya sādhyam iti hetur ahetunā na viśiṣyate / ahetunā sādharmyāt pratyavas-thānam ahetusamaḥ.*

VV 20 (the opponent in relation to negation and what is denied and in order to discard the negation of an own being): *pūrvaṃ cet pratiṣedhaḥ paścāt pratiṣedhyam ity anupapannam / paścāccānupapanno yugapacca yataḥ svabhāvaḥ san //* and Com.: *iha pūrvaṃ cet pratiṣedhaḥ paścācca pratiṣedhyam iti nopapannam / asati hi pratiṣedhye kasya pratiṣedhaḥ / atha paścāt pratiṣedhaḥ pūrvaṃ pratiṣedhyam iti ca nopapannam / siddhe hi pratiṣedhye kiṃ pratiṣedhaḥ karoti / atha yugapat pratiṣedhapratiṣedhya iti tathāpi na pratiṣedhaḥ pratiṣedhyasyārthasya kāraṇam, pratiṣedhyo na pratiṣedhasya ca, yathā yugapad utpannayoḥ śaśaviṣāṇayor naiva dakṣiṇaṃ savyasya kāraṇaṃ savyaṃ vā dakṣiṇasya kāraṇaṃ bhavatīti /.*

ŚŚ, p. 175*c*, lines 14-28 (Tucci's translation pp. 50-51) (in order to demonstrate the impossibility of knowledge): The follower says: 'If knowledge arises after having seen *rūpa*, what will be its use?' (S.) If, first, the eye sees the *rūpa* and then the knowledge arises, what will be the use of knowledge? If knowledge arises before and afterwards the eye sees the *rūpa*, then, this [assumption] also is not valid. Why? 'If (the eye) does not see the *rūpa*, on account of the non-existence of the cause, the birth (of the knowledge) also is not existent.' (S.) If the eye does not see the *rūpa* first, then, there is no union with the cause [of vision]. Because there is no union, knowledge must not arise. You say that owing to the union of the perception by the senses, of objects and of *manas* the knowledge arises. So if (one says that) knowledge arises, when there is no union, such a statement is not valid. The unbeliever says: 'What is the mistake if it arises at the same time?' The follower: If it arises at the same time, then, the thesis is not valid, because birth and non-birth cannot be born at the same time together, on account of the existence (of the one), on account of the non-existence of the other, and on account of the refutation mentioned before. (S.) If vision and knowledge arise at the same time either, being already existent as reciprocally interdependent, or being before not-existent or being before half-existent and half not existent, in all these three cases, the birth at the same time is not valid; and why? If vision and knowledge are existent before, then, they must not arise, because they are existent. If they are before non-existent, they also must not arise, because they are not existent. If they are non-existent, then, they are not interdependent and also there is no birth. If they are half-existent and half non-existent each one (of the two hypotheses) has been already refuted in the two preceding *sūtras*. Moreover, how can one *dharma* be existent and also non-existent? And again, if they arise at the same time, knowledge is not dependent on vision, and vision is not dependent on knowledge.

TŚ, p. 31*c*, lines 21-26 (Tucci's Sanskrit translation p. 18 par. 6): (the opponent in relation to *hetu* and *sādhya* and in order to reject the *hetu*): *prativādī prāha / kiṃ hetuḥ sādhyāt pūrvaṃ paścād yugapad vā / yadi tāvad hetuḥ prāk sādhyañca paścāt tadāsati sādhye, hetuḥ kasya sādhakaḥ ? / atha paścāt, sādhyañca prāk, tadā siddhe sādhye kiṃ hetunā ? / atha yugapat tadāhetuḥ / yathā yugapatsadbhāvādgoḥ śṛṅge dakṣiṇaṃ vāmaṃ vā parasparotpādake ityayuktam / tasmād yaugapadyañ cet tadā hetutvāsambhavaḥ.*

TŚ, p. 34*a*, lines 18-26 (Tucci's Sanskrit translation p. 30 par. 3): (the *prativādin* against the *hetu*): *yadi hetuḥ pūrvaṃ pratijñā tu paścāt, tadā pratijñā 'bhāve sa kasya hetuḥ / atha pratijñā pūrvaṃ hetus tu paścāt tadā, siddhāyāṃ pratijñāyāṃ kiṃ hetunetyeṣo 'pyasiddho hetuḥ /* (and refutation of the previous argument through a similar reasoning applied to *pratijñā* and its refutation): *yadi bhavatkhaṇḍhanaṃ pūrvam asmatpratijñā tu paścād asmadarthābhāve kiṃ bhavatā khaṇḍyate / yadyasmatpratijñā pūrvaṃ bhavatkhaṇḍanaṃ tu paścāt tadāsmatpratijñāyāṃ sthāpitāyāṃ kiṃ bhavatkhaṇḍanena / bhavān asmatkhaṇḍanānujñānād asmatkhaṇḍanopādānena māṃ khaṇḍayatīti cet tad ayuktam / kasmād iti cet / mayā prakaṭitaṃ yad bhavatkhaṇḍanaṃ bhavadartham eva pratiṣedhati na tu bhavatkhaṇḍanam avalambyāsmadartho pratiṣṭhāpitaḥ /.*

TŚ, p. 29 *a*, lines 6-13 (Tucci's Sanskrit translation p. 3): *bhavatkhaṇḍanavacanam asmadvacanasya samakālīnam asamakālīnaṃ vā ? samakālīnaṃ ced asmadvacana-khaṇḍane 'samarthaṃ, yathā gośṛṅge 'śvakarṇau vā parasparaṃ khaṇḍayituṃ na śaknuvataḥ / samakālīnatvāt / asamakālīnañ ced, bhavataḥ khaṇḍanaṃ pūrvam asmadvacanaṃ paścāt / athāsmadvacanānuccāraṇāt, kiṃ bhavatā khaṇḍyate ? / tasmād bhavataḥ khaṇḍanam asiddham / athāsmadvacanaṃ pūrvaṃ, bhavataḥ khaṇḍanaṃ tu paścād, evaṃ tarhyasmadvacanasiddhatvāt kasya khaṇḍanaṃ bhaviṣyati ? / samakālīnañ cet, tato 'smadvacanaṃ bhavataśca khaṇḍanam ityetayor etat khaṇḍanam etacca khaṇḍanīyam iti viśeṣo na syāt / yathā nadīsamudravārisaṃyogakāle viśeṣāsambhavaḥ.*

U, p. 28*a*, lines 24-27 (Tucci's Sanskrit translation pp. 28-29 par. 10) (describing the *kālasama* rejoinder, applied to the opponent's thesis of the eternality of the soul): *anyac ca / ātmā nityo 'naindriyakatvād iti bhavatsthāpanā / so 'yaṃ [hetur] vartamāne 'tīte 'nāgate vā / atīta iti ced atītatvān naṣṭaḥ / anāgata iti ced abhāvaḥ / vartamāna iti cet tadā 'hetuḥ / yathā śṛṅge yugapad eva jātatvān nānyonyahetuke / iti kālasamam.*

Nāgārjuna's *Śū* 6 (in relation to cause and effect in order to demonstrate the logical impossibility of the cause) (Our translation p. 25): If the effect existed, (there would be) a cause provided (already) with its effect; if that effect does not exist, the cause is similar to (something) inexistent; and it is contradictory that (the effect) be not existent and be not inexistent (at the same time as the cause). (Therefore) the cause is not logically possible in any of the three times.

Section XIII

1. On the Nyāya principle that the negation implies the existence of the denied thing and that there is no possible negation of something inexistent, see *VV* 11 (the opponent): *sata eva pratiṣedho nāsti ghaṭo geha ityayaṃ yasmāt / dṛṣṭaḥ pratiṣedho 'yaṃ sataḥ svabhāvasya te tasmāt //* and Com.: *pratiṣedhaḥ kriyate nāsataḥ; VV* 20 Com. (the

opponent): *asati hi pratiṣedhye kasya pratiṣedhaḥ.*

Cf. also Matilal, *The Navya-Nyāya Doctrine of Negation*, p. 53.

2. Cf. *NS* 2, 1, 12 and *Bh*; and *VV* 20 quoted in note 7 of the translation of Section XII.

The opponent, acting as the *siddhāntin* in *NS* 2, 1, 12, applies to Nāgārjuna the same reasoning Nāgārjuna has applied to the *pramāṇa* and *prameya* in relation to the three times. The implicit conclusion of the opponent's reasoning (= not being possible the negation of the *pramāṇa* and *prameya*, the *pramāṇa* and *prameya* stand unrefuted) is a case of the logical principle contained in *NS* 5, 1, 20: *pratiṣedhānupapatteśca pratiṣeddhavyāpratiṣedhaḥ.*

3. If the object to be negated does not exist, its negation is not logical, according to the principle stated in note 1 of the translation of this Section. Cf. *VV* 15: *atha naivāsti grāho naiva grāhyaṃ na ca grahītāraḥ / pratiṣedhaḥ pratiṣedhyaṃ pratiṣeddhāro nanu na santi //.*

4. On the idea that the negation of something inexistent is possible only without words, cf. *VV* 12 (the opponent); *atha nāsti sa svabhāvaḥ kiṃ nu pratiṣidhyate tvayānena / vacanenarte vacanāt pratiṣedhaḥ sidhyate hyasataḥ //* and Com.: *atha nāstyeva sa svabhāvo 'nena vacanena niḥsvabhāvāḥ sarvabhāvā iti kiṃ bhavatā pratiṣidhyate / asato hi vacanād vinā siddhaḥ pratiṣedhaḥ tadyathāgneḥ śaityasya, apāmauṣṇyasya/.*

5. In this Section we have an example of the *matānujñā* defect of reasoning on the part of the opponent. Cf. *NS* 5, 2, 20: *svapakse doṣābhyupagamāt parapakṣe doṣaprasaṅgo matānujñā* and *Bh*: *yaḥ pareṇa coditaṃ doṣaṃ svapakṣe 'bhyupagamyānuddhṛtya vadati-bhavatpakṣe 'pi samāno doṣa iti, sa svapakṣe doṣābhyupagamāt parapakṣe doṣaṃ prasañjayan paramatam anujānātīti matānujñāṃ nāma nigrahasthānam āpadyata iti.*

Section XIV

1. i.e. the previous acceptance of the negation of *pramāṇa* and *prameya* put forward by Nāgārjuna at the beginning of the present argumentation.

Section XV

1. Tib.: *lha mams dgaḥ ba* = Sk. *devānāṃpriya*: 'dear to the gods', and also: 'foolish', 'stupid', 'silly'. On the word '*devānāṃpriya*' see Scharfe, 'The Maurya dynasty and the Seleucids', pp. 211-19. According to the context in this Section and in Section LIII it must be taken in the second pejorative meaning.

Section XVI

1. We have understood *dgag par byed pa med na* as *pratiṣeddhum abhāve sati.* Kajiyama suggests the reading *dgar par bya ba* instead of *dgag par byed pa.*

2. Cf. *VV* quoted in our commentary of this Section.

3. Cf. *VV* 13 (exposition of Nāgārjuna's opinion): *bālānām iva mithyā mṛgatṛṣṇāyāṃ yathājalagrāhaḥ / evam mithyāgrāhaḥ syāt te pratiṣedhyato hyasataḥ //* and Com.: *syāt te buddhiḥ, yatha balānāṃ mṛgatṛṣṇāyāṃ mithyā jalam iti grāho bhavati, nanu nirjalā sā mṛgatṛṣṇeti tatra paṇḍitajātīyena puruṣeṇocyate tasya grāhasya vinivartanārtham, evaṃ niḥsvabhāveṣu yaḥ svabhāve grāhaḥ sattvānāṃ tasya vyāvartanārthaṃ niḥsvabhāvāḥ sarvabhāvā ityucyata iti.*

Section XVII

1. On efficiency as the criterion of validity of knowledge see D'Almeida, *Nyāya Philosophy, Nature and Validity of Knowledge,* pp. 46-62; Bijalwan, *Indian Theory of Knowledge,* pp. 53-60. The Nyāya thought that the confirmation of the knowledge was extrinsic to knowledge. It is the so-called: *parataḥprāmāṇya.*

2. This Section reveals the confidence of the Nyāya in the real existence of the empirical world and in the capacity of our senses and reason to give us a knowledge of that world.

Section XVIII

1. Vasubandhu, *Viṃśatikā* and Dignāga, *Dmigs pa brtag paḥi ḥgrel pa* (= *Ālamabanaparīkṣā*) analyze the atoms and reaches the conclusion that, either as separated entities or as aggregates, they cannot become object of knowledge (*prameya*). The *V* reaches the same conclusion, but on the ground that a cognitive process (as the perception or the inference), which is of a mental nature, can have as its correspondent object only an equally *mental* object.

2. According to the oldest Buddhist teaching the cognition's act comes forth depending on several factors. So *Śālistambasūtra* says: In this way the eye-consciousness (*cakṣurvijñāna*) comes forth through five causes, which five? Through the eye, the form, the light, the space and the attention produced by the former ones the eye-consciousness comes forth (p. 15 N. Aiyaswami Sastri edition).

ŚŚ, p. 171*b,* lines 19-20 (Tucci's translation p. 24): Out of the union of the perception by the senses, the *manas* and the objects, knowledge arises.

NS 2, 1, 21-23 (the *pūrvapakṣa* criticizing the Nyāya definition of *pratyakṣa* as not mentioning all the conditions that make it possible): *pratyakṣalakṣaṇānupapattir asamagravacanāt* (21), *na "tmamanasoḥ sannikarṣābhāve pratyakṣotpattiḥ* (22), and *digdeśakālākaśeṣvapyevaṃ prasaṅgaḥ* (23).

3. *NS* 1, 1, 5: *atha tatpūrvakaṃ trividham anumānaṃ pūrvavaccheṣavat sāmānyatodṛṣṭaṃ ca.* The *Vṛtti* has *tatpūrvakaṃ pratyakṣapūrvakam.*

Section XIX

1. Cf. note 2 of the translation of the previous Section.

Section XX

1. In the *NS* 1, 1, 9, quoted in the following note.

2. The Tibetan text presents a translation of *NS* 1, 1, 9: *ātmaśarīrendriyārthabuddhimanaḥpravṛttidoṣapretyabhāvaphaladuḥkhāpavargās tu prameyam.*

It must be taken into account that for the Nyāya a *prameya* can also in some circumstances become a *pramāṇa* according to *NS* 2, 1, 16 (quoted in note 4 of the translation of Section II) and *Bh ad locum:* . . . *ātmā tāvad upalabdhiviṣayatvāt prameye paripaṭhitaḥ, upalabdhau svātantryāt pramātā / buddhir upalabdhisādhanatvāt pramāṇam, upalabdhiviṣayatvāt prameyam; ubhayābhāvāt tu pramitiḥ / evam arthaviśeṣe samākhyā samāveśo yojyaḥ.*

Section XXI

1. This sentence connects the subject-matter of the previous Sections (II-XX) (*pramāṇa-prameya*) with that of Sections XXI-XXIII (*saṃśaya*). This reminds the way in which Candrakīrti connects the subject-matter of each chapter of the *MMK* with the preceding one.

2. The commentary does not comment the last sentence of the Sūtra.

3. *Saṃśaya* is dealt with *NS* 1, 1, 23.

Section XXII

1. A literal translation of the Sūtra would be: The doubt does not exist because of the non-reference to peculiarities: *nāstyeva saṃśayo viśeṣānapekṣāt,* being the meaning that whenever there is not reference to peculiarities, doubt does not occur and *contrario sensu* that whenever there is reference to peculiarities doubt does occur. We have given to Tibetan *phyir* the conditional value with which many times in Sanskrit it is necessary to translate causal constructions in ablative.

2. Cf. *NS* 1, 1, 23: *samānanekadharmopapatter vipratipatter upalabdhyanupalabdhyavyavasthātaśca viśeṣāpekṣo vimarśaḥ saṃśayaḥ* and *Bh: samānadharmopapatter viśeṣāpekṣo vimarśaḥ saṃśaya iti / sthāṇupuruṣayoḥ samānaṃ dharmam ārohapariṇāhau paśyan pūrvadṛṣṭaṃ ca tayor viśeṣaṃ bubhutsamānaḥ kiṃsvid ityanyataraṃ nāvadharayati, tadanavadhāraṇaṃ jñānaṃ saṃśayaḥ / samānam anayor dharmam upalabhe viśeṣam anyatārasyá nopalabha ityeṣā buddhiḥ apekṣā-saṃśayasya pravarttikā varttate, tena viśeṣāpekṣo vimarśaḥ saṃśayaḥ.*

Section XXIII

1. Cf. *NSBh,* Introduction: *kiṃ punas tattvam ? sataśca sadbhāvo 'sataśca 'sadbhāvaḥ / sat sad iti gṛhyamānaṃ yathābhūtam aviparītaṃ tattvaṃ bhavati / asaccā 'sad iti gṛhyamānaṃ yathābhūtam aviparītaṃ tattvaṃ bhavati.*

Section XXIV

1. As in the case of doubt and *pramāṇa-prameya* there is also here a sentence that connects *prayojana* with doubt.

2. Cf. *NS* 1, 1, 24: This is the Nyāya definition of *prayojana* quoted in our commentary to this Section.

3. Another direct reference to Gautama as the author who has given the definition of *prayojana.*

4. Reference to the *sikatātailanyāya.* See our commentary on this Section. On this *nyāya* see Jacob, *A Handful of Popular Maxims,* p. 147.

5. For a similar scheme of argumentation see the texts quoted in note 7 of Section XII.

Section XXV

1. We find here again a connection between the new category submitted to analysis (*dṛṣṭānta*) and the previous one (*prayojana*). Cf. notes 1 of Sections XXI and XXIV.

Section XXVIII

1. Cf. *NS* 1, 1, 25 (definition of *dṛṣṭānta*) whose text is given in note 5 of Section IX.

2. Cf. *NS* 1, 1, 34-35 : *udāharaṇasādharmyāt sādhyasādhanaṃ hetuḥ* (34) and *tathā vaidharmyāt* (35) and *Bh ad* 34: *udāharareṇa sāmānyāt sādhyasya dharmasya sādhanaṃ prajñāpanaṃ hetuḥ, sādhye pratisandāya dharmam udāharaṇe ca pratisandhāya tasya sādhanatāvacanaṃ hetuḥ* and *ad* 35 : *udāharaṇavaidharmyācca sādhyasādhanaṃ hetuḥ*.

NS 2, 1, 44 (where Gautama and Vātsyāyana refer to three kinds of *upamāna* which they do not accept): *atyantaprāyaikadeśasādharmyād upamānāsiddhiḥ* and *Bh: atyantasādharmyād upamānaṃ na sidhyati / na caivaṃ bhavati yathā gaur evaṃ gaur iti / prāyaḥsādharmyād upamānaṃ na sidhyati, na hi bhavati yathā 'naḍvān evaṃ mahiṣa iti / ekadeśasādharmyād upamānaṃ na siddhyati, na hi sarveṇa sarvam upamīyata iti.*

NS 2, 1, 45: *prasiddhasādharmyād upamānasiddher yathoktadoṣānupapattiḥ* and *Bh: na sādharmyasya kṛtsnaprāyālpabhāvam āśrityopamānaṃ pravarttate / kiṃ tarhi? prasiddhasādharmyāt sādhyasādhanabhāvam āśritya pravarttate / yatra caitad asti na tatropamānaṃ pratiṣeddhuṃ śakyam / tasmād yathoktadoṣo nopapadyata iti /.*

3. Cf. *NS* 2, 1, 44 quoted in the previous note.

Section XXIX

1. The following is the text of the *Vaiśeṣikasūtra* 2, 2, 5 referred to in our commentary to this Section: *apsu śītatā.*

Section XXX

1. Cf. *NS* 2, 1, 44-45 quoted in note 2 of the translation of Section XXVIII.

2. The reference to a comparison between Mount Sumeru and a hair of the head seems odd. *Vārttikatātparyaṭīkā ad NS* 2, 1, 44 explains that the resemblance through slight similarity cannot be admitted, because all could be compared with all and being so even Mount Sumeru could be compared with a mustard seed (*tathā sati sumeror api sarṣapeṇopamānaprasaṅgāt*). Viśvanātha's *Vṛtti, ibid.*, develops the same idea and has the same comparison (*merur iva sarṣapa iti*). The comparison between Mount Meru and a mustard seed (Sk. *sarṣapa* = *skye tshe* or *ske thse* in Tibetan) seems more appropriate.

3. The *TŚ*, p. 31*b*, line 7 (Tucci's Sanskrit translation p. 16), treating the *aviśeṣasama* rejoinder, mentions also the existence, the unity and the cognizableness as general characteristics on the basis of which no similarity between two things can be established.

Section XXXI

1. This kind of *dṛṣṭānta* is not mentioned by *NS* and its *Bh.*

Section XXXII

1. We have understood *grub pa* as referring to the *dṛṣṭānta*, whose refutation has been concluded in the previous Sūtra, which ends just with the words *ma grub pa yin.*

2. The *NS* defines the *siddhānta* category in 1, 1, 26: *tantrādhikaraṇābhyupagamasaṃsthitiḥ siddhāntaḥ* and mentions, *ibid.* 28-31, different classes of *siddhānta*.

We find here again a connection made by the commentary of our treatise between the new category to be analyzed and the preceding one. Cf. note 1 of Sections XXI, XXIV and XXV.

Section XXXIII

1. The discussion on the whole and the parts is contained in Sections XXXIII-XL. The 'whole' is here the *nyāya* or syllogism and the 'parts' are the parts of the syllogism. Nāgārjuna applies to the *nyāya* and to the *avayavas* of the *nyāya* the argumentation employed against the whole and the parts in general.

On the connection of the category '*avayava*' dealt with in this Section and the category '*siddhānta*' dealt with in the previous Section see our commentary of this Section.

2. *i.e.* the parts of the syllogism enumerated in the same order at the end of the commentary and in *NS* 1, 1, 32: *pratijñāhetūdāharaṇopanayanigamanānyavayavāḥ*.

3. On the problem of the whole and the parts in Indian Philosophy see Tola and Dragonetti, 'Dignāga's Ālambanaparikṣāvṛtti', p. 129 note 6, where we have quoted texts and included bibliography referring to this question.

4. Cf. *NS* 4, 2, 8 (*pūrvapakṣa*): *teṣu cāvṛtter avayavyabhāvaḥ* and *Bh* (which gives arguments against the thesis of the existence of the whole in the parts): *na tāvat pratyavayavaṃ varttate, tayoḥ parimāṇabhedād dravyasya caikadravyatvaprasaṅgāt / nāpyekadeśaiḥ* (or *ekadeśena*) *sarveṣu anyāvayavābhāvāt.*

ŚŚ, p. 175*b*, lines 6-13 and *b*, lines 29-*c*, line 2) (Tucci's translation pp. 47-49): The believer says: 'If the whole is in the part, how is it that the head is not in the foot?' (S). If there is a *dharma* which is the body, then in the parts such as the foot and so on, does it exist as a totality or (does it exist) as a part? Now if it exists as a totality, the foot must exist in the head, on account of the unity of that *dharma* which is the body. If it exists as a part, this also is not possible; and why? 'The whole is like the part' (S). If (one says that) in the foot the whole is similar to that part which is the foot etc., and the same is the case as regards the other parts, then, the whole must be one with the parts. And therefore, that whole which is called the body must be non-existent. In the same way, the existence by itself of the parts like the foot and so on, is equally refuted as the whole. Because the whole does not exist, the parts also are not existent . . . and again because the whole is not existent, therefore, parts also are not existent. If, the parts cannot be demonstrated, when the whole does not yet exist, how can they have the power of the cause? If the whole already exists, what use will the power of the parts have?

5. Cf. Sections XXXIV, XXXVI and XXXIX and *ŚŚ*, p. 175*b*, lines, 6-13. (Tucci's translation pp. 48-49) where a similar conclusion is reached without any reason.

Section XXXV

1. For our translation of *phyir* by 'if' see note 1 of the translation of Section XXII.
2. Cf. *ŚŚ*, p. 174 *a*, lines 12-16 (Tucci's translation pp. 40-41) : If the head, the feet

and the other parts are not different from the body, the foot must be the head, since both are not different from the body, just as Indra is Śakra, because Indra and Śakra are not different . . . If the foot and the head are different, and the head is different from the foot and the other parts, then, only the parts would be existent, but not the whole.

Section XXXVII

1. *Bal ba dsa,* in Tibetan, which is transliterated by *balbaja,* is the *Eleusine Indica,* a kind of grass with which ropes are made.

2. Cf. *ŚŚ,* p. 175*b,* lines 20-22 (Tucci's translation p. 48) (the opponent): As each one of the threads cannot restrain an elephant and one drop of water cannot fill a pot, but a collection of many can produce (an effect) like this, so the atoms, when collected together, have the force to produce a pot.

Section XXXVIII

1. Cf. *NS* 1, 2, 8 quoted in our commentary to this Section.

2. Cf. *ŚŚ,* p. 175*b,* lines 22-25 (Tucci's translation p. 48) (this text comes immediately after the *Śataśāstra*'s text quoted in note 2 of the translation of previous Section): As no barren woman can have a son and none of the blind men can see *rūpa,* and no grain of sand can produce oil they cannot do it, even if they are collected together; also the same is the case with regard to the atoms; because each one [of them] cannot [produce that effect], then, many also cannot (do it). On the sand and oil simile see our commentary of Section XXIV.

Section XXXIX

1. Cf. *ŚŚ,* p. 175*b,* lines 26-28 (Tucci's translation p. 49) (this text comes immediately after the text quoted in note 2 of the translation of the previous Section): The thread and the drop have separately the power of restraining an elephant and filling the pot; but because a barren woman, the blind, a grain of sand, have not any power separately, when they are many, also they have no power.

It is to be noted that the development of reasoning in *V* and in *ŚŚ* is the same.

2. *i.e.* the Balbaja grass *dṛṣṭānta.*

3. The syllogistic reasoning with its parts: *pratijñā* etc. and the word with its parts: the letters.

4. The idea of the gradual coming forth of words and sentences appears also in Bhartṛhari's *Vākyapadīya* II, 19. Cf. our article on *Pratibhā* and Kunjunni Raja, *Indian Theories of Meaning,* p. 117.

5. Nāgārjuna's denial of the whole has been demonstrated in this way.

Section XL

1. The definition of *pratijñā* (proposition to be proved, thesis) is given in *NS* 1, 1, 33, quoted in our commentary.

Section XLI

1. *Hetu* is dealt with in *NS* in 1, 1, 34-35 : *udāharaṇasādharmyāt sādhyasādhanaṃ hetuḥ* and *tathā vaidharmyāt.*

Section XLII

1. For another case of *anavasthā-prasaṅga* in this treatise see Sections V, VI.

Section XLIII

1. For the definition of *upanaya* and *nigamana* cf. *NS* 1, 1, 38 and 39 quoted in our commentary to this Section.

Section XLVII

1. Cf. *NS* 3, 1, 1-30 and *Bh,* where Gautama and Vātsyāyana defend the existence and eternity of the soul.

Section XLVIII

1. Cf. Bhartṛhari's doctrine of the gradual and successive forthcoming of the words and sentences. In *kārikā* II, 19 of *Vākyapadīya, śabda* is described as being perceived with sequence (*kramavant*), although really it is without sequence. We have here the expression of the idea that words and sentences have two faces: (1) the external phonetic one, which is submitted to time and as such has sequence, (2) the internal semantic face which is timeless and as such has no sequence (cf. our article on Bhartṛhari's *pratibhā* and Kunjunni Raja's *Indian Theories of Meaning,* p. 117). Moreover, sentences and words as soon as they are uttered they perish. This fact, entirely in agreement with the Buddhist idea of momentariness, is also expressed in the *TŚ,* p. 30a, lines 2-3 (Tucci's Sanskrit translation p. 8, line 16): *sarve śabdā yadā mukhān nirgatās tadā nāṣṭā(h).* These graduality and successiveness and momentariness have as an effect that the sentences which constitute the syllogism cannot coexist. This same reasoning is employed by Nāgārjuna in Sections XLIX and LXII.

Section XLIX

1. Cf. note 1 of the previous Section.

2. Reference to the *śabdotpatti,* one of the themes dealt with in the *Śikṣās* attached to the *Vedas.* On the *Śikṣās* see Winternitz, *A History of Indian Literature I,* pp. 282-85 and Scharfe, *Grammatical Literature,* pp. 78 and 176-77. In the *Pāṇinīya Śikṣā* (edited by Weber in *Indische Studien* IV, pp. 345-71) par. 2, 13, we find the following verse: *aṣṭau sthānāni varṇānām uraḥ kaṇṭhaḥ śiras tathā / jihvāmūlaṃ ca dantāś ca nāsikauṣṭhau ca tālu ca //*; and in the commentary of the *Vājasaneyi-Prātiśākhya* (edited also by Weber, *ibid.*, pp. 65-160 and 177-331) *ad* I, 9, we find a reference to *puruṣasya prayatnaḥ* as one of the factors that produce the transformation of breath into voice. There are several references to the *sthānāni* in Bhartṛhari, *Vyākyapadīya* as for instance in I, 109 (117) and I, 114 (122).

Section L

1. When there is the state of hesitation in the mind one reasons in order to reach the truth and to put an end to that hesitation and 'reason' requires to employ the members of syllogism. This is the connection between the new category '*tarka*' and the previous category '*avayavas*'. See notes 1 of Sections XXI, XXIV, and XXV and note 2 of Section XXXII.

2. For the definition of *tarka* cf. *NS* 1, 1, 40 and *Bh*, quoted in our commentary.

Section LI

1. Cf. *NS* 1, 1, 41: *vimṛśya pakṣapratipakṣābhyām arthāvadhāraṇaṃ nirṇayaḥ* and *Bh: sthāpanā sādhanam, pratiṣedha upālambhaḥ / tau sādhanopālambhau pakṣapratipakṣāśrayau vyatiṣaktāv anubandhena pravartlamānau pakṣapratipakṣāv ityucyete / tayor anyatarasya nivṛttir ekatarasyāvasthānam avaśyambhāvi, yasyāvasthānaṃ tasyārthāvadhāraṇaṃ nirṇayaḥ.*

2. As in the case of the previous categories a connection is established in the commentary between the new category '*nirṇaya*' and the last category dealt with, '*tarka*': the latter is the cause of the former. Cf. Sections XXI, XXIV, XXV, XXXII, and L.

3. Cf. *ŚŚ*, p. 173*b*, line 29-*c* line 3 (Tucci's translation p. 37): If existence, unity and pot are a unity, then, as *Indra*, *Śakra* and *Kauśika* are identical, and in the place where *Indra* is, there *Śakra* and *Kauśika* must also be, in the same way, in the place of existence there will then be unity and pot. In the place of unity there will be existence and pot. In the place of pot there will be existence and unity. Cf. also Section XXX (text/translation and commentary) and note 3 of the translation.

Section LII

1. *NS* 1, 2, 1, in its definition of *vāda* (see the text in our commentary to this Section), has the word '*upālambha*' which means 'criticism' ('*pratiṣedha*' in *Bh*). Its Tibetan translation is *klan ka*. The Tibetan translator wrongly understood *upālambha* as *upalambha* (perception) and consequently translated it by '*dmigs pa*' ('perception' in Tibetan).

2. Cf. *NS* 1, 2, 1 and *Bh* quoted in our commentary.

3. Nāgārjuna's intention to deny the possibility of determining any object means the rejection of the *nirṇaya* category of logic.

4. Let us remark also in the case of *vāda* the connection that the commentary establishes between *vāda* and *nirṇaya*: on rejecting the possibility of *nirṇaya* (= the ascertainment of the pot etc.) Nāgārjuna is taking part in a debate (*vāda*) and consequently *at least* he has to admit that the debate exists. Cf. Sections XXI, XXIV, XXV, XXXII, L, and LI.

5. Cf. Nāgārjuna's *Lokātīta* 7: *saṃjñārthayor ananyatve mukhaṃ dahyeta vahninā / anyatve 'dhigamābhāvas tvayoktaṃ bhūtavādinā //.*

NS 2, 1, 53: *pūraṇapradāhapāṭanānupalabdheś ca sambandhābhāvaḥ* and *Vṛtti: śabdena sahārthasya sambandhābhāvaḥ vyāptyabhāvaḥ / hetum āha-pūraṇeti / yadi śabdasyārthena vyāptiḥ syāt tadā annāgnyasiśabdair mukhapūraṇamukhadāha-*

mukhapāṭanāni syuḥ, śabdasya vyāpyasya sattvenānnāder arthasyāpi sattvāt. This Sūtra is located in the Section of the *NS* comprising Sūtras 50-57, where Gautama and Vātsyāyana reject their opponent's thesis of the natural relation of the word and its object, and maintain that the relation is a conventional one. It is this conception of that relation that Nāgārjuna criticizes in the Section related to *vāda.* Sūtras 2, 1', 55 and 56 belonging to this Section of the *NS* are quoted in note 1 of Section LIV.

Section LIII

1. The nature of the relation between the word and the object it designates was a subject very much discussed in Indian philosophy. See our '*Anāditva* or Beginninglessness in Indian Philosophy', pp. 14-15, Steinkellner, *Pramāṇaviniścaya*'s edition note 208, Bijalwan, *Indian Theory of Knowledge,* pp. 227-32. The Naiyāyikas (as the opponent in this treatise and also the authors of *NS* and its *Bh*) consider that the relation word-object is established by convention. Cf. *NS* 2, 1, 55: *na sāmayikatvācchabdārthasampratyayasya* and *Bh* : *na sambandhakāritaṃ śabdārthavyavasthānam / kiṃ tarhi ? samayakāritam / . . . kaḥ punar ayaṃ samayaḥ? asya śabdasyedam arthajātam abhidheyam iti abhidhānābhidheyaniyamaniyogaḥ / tasminn upayukte śabdād arthasampratyayo bhavati /*.

2. The fact that the opponent has adduced the theory of the conventional nature of the words gives opportunity for examining the consequences that theory will have for the *padārthas.* This examination will show that the *padārthas* designate unreal entities and that consequently liberation cannot be obtained through their knowledge, as the Nyāya maintains.

3. Cf. *NS* 1, 1, 1 (quoted in note 1 of Section 1) where it is said that liberation is attained by means of a correct knowledge of the Nyāya *padārthas.*

4. Cf. note 1 of Section XV.

5. For Nāgārjuna it is an absurdity to put together the great metaphysical aim of liberation and the mean quibbles taught by logicians.

6. On this thesis of the Nyāya cf. Bhaduri, *Studies in Nyāya-vaiśeṣika Metaphysics,* pp. 1-5.

7. The 'wise men' are the Buddhist Masters who, starting from the idea, maintained also by the Naiyāyikas, that words are a product of convention, reached the conclusion that the objects designated by words (as 'Devadatta', 'Indragupta' etc.) are unreal. This conclusion is expressed in the sentence that follows.

8. For similar arguments see Vasubandhu's *Trisvabhāva* 35 (*mokṣāpatter ayatnataḥ*) and Sthiramati's *Ṭīkā* of Maitreya's *Madhyāntavibhāga ad* 1, 2, *aprayatnena mokṣaprasaṅgaḥ*).

Section LIV

1. Owing to the presence in the commentary of some unintelligible words it is not possible to give a translation of it, although its general meaning and the aim of the examples given in it are clear. Kajiyama prefers not to translate this Section.

2. Cf. *NS* 2, 1, 56 : *jātiviśeṣe cāniyamāt* and *Bh* : *sāmayikaḥ śabdād arthasampratyayaḥ, na svābhāvikaḥ / ṛṣyāryamlecchānāṃ yathākāmaṃ śabdaviniyogo 'rthapratyāyanāya pravarttate / svābhāvike hi śabdasyārthapratyāyakatve yathākāmaṃ na syāt, yathā taijasasya*

prakāśasya rūpapratyayahetutvaṃ na jātiviśeṣe vyabhicaratīti and *Vārttika: na svābhāvikaḥ śabdārthayoḥ sambandhaḥ / yadi svābhāvikaḥ sabdārthasambandho 'bhaviṣyan na jātiviśeṣe śabdārthavyavasthā 'bhaviṣyat / asti tu yathākāmaṃ prayogaḥ—jātiviśeṣe yathākāmaṃ prayogo dṛṣṭaḥ na tu svābhāvikena sambandhena sambaddhānāṃ jātiviśeṣe vyabhicāro dṛṣṭaḥ / na hi pradīpo 'smākam anyathā prakāśayaty anyathā jātiviśeṣa iti / jātiviśeṣaśabdena punar deśo 'bhidhīyata iti/* and *Ṭīkā : svābhāviko hi sambandhaḥ kasyacicchabdasya kenacid arthenāsti na sarvasya sarveṇa, tathā sati śabdārthavyavasthā na syāt / evaṃ ca tarhi na ṛṣyāryamlecchānāṃ niyamaḥ syāt.*

Section LV

1. The words '*go*' and '*hari*' are quoted in Sanskrit in the Tibetan version.
2. Cf. *Amarakośa* III, 3 (*nānārthavarga*), 25: *svargeṣupaśuvāgvajradiṅnetraghṛṇibhūtale / lakṣyadṛṣṭyā striyāṃ puṃsi gauḥ.* But the Tibetan text is a faithful translation of a *śloka* quoted in *Abhidharmakośa ad* II, 47 (p. 81 Pradhan ed.): *vāgdigbhūraśmivajreṣu paśvakṣisvargavāriṣu / navasvartheṣu medhāvī gośabdam upadhārayet //.*
3. *Ne tsho* in the original Tibetan text = *ne tso*: 'parrot'.
4. Cf. *Amarakośa* III, 3, 175 (*c-d*) and 176 (*a-b*): *yamānilendracandrārkaviṣṇusiṃhāṃśuvājiṣu / śukāhikapibhekeṣu harir nā kapile tṛṣu //.*
5. The stanza enumerates names of Viṣṇu/Nārāyaṇa in his diverse manifestations in different beings.
6. *ŚŚ*, p. 173*b*, line 29-*c*, line 3 (Tucci's translation p. 37) mentions the words *Indra, Śakra* and *Kauśika* as indicating the same person.
7. What is not known is considered not to exist.

Section LVII

1. For the definitions of *jalpa* and *vitaṇḍā* and also for the analogy between both categories and *vāda* see our commentary, where the pertinent texts are transcribed.

The connection between *jalpa* and *vitaṇḍā* on one side and *vāda* on the other side consists in their being considered all of them similar. Cf. Sections XXI, XXIV, XXV, XXXII, L, LI and LII.

Section LVIII

1. *Hetvābhāsa* category is dealt with in NS 1, 2, 4-9. Gautama and Vātsyāyana do not define what, in general terms, is *hetvābhāsa*, fallacious, pseudo- or false reason or *probans*, lit. '(mere) appearance of a reason'. Uddyotakara in his *Vārttika ad locum* explains what are the *hetvābhāsas: hetulakṣaṇābhāvād ahetavo hetusāmānyād hetuvadābhāsamānāḥ* and then indicates the differences and similitudes between both categories.

This sentence expresses the connection between *hetvābhāsa* and *jalpa* ('discussion'): if Nāgārjuna has been discussing in order to prove that every *hetu* is *hetvābhāsa*, he has been implicitly admitting the existence of both categories, the *jalpa* and the *hetvābhāsa*. Cf. Sections XXI, XXIV, XXV, XXXII, L, LI, LII and LVII.

Section LIX

1. The Tibetan word *ḥkhrul ba* corresponds to the Sanskrit words *anaikāntika, savyabhicārin*. These words can be added, as epithets to *hetu*, 'reason' and in this case transform the *hetu* into a *hetvābhāsa*, a 'mere appearance of a reason', a fallacy, a false *probans*. An *anaikāntika* or *savyabhicārin hetu* is an 'inconclusive, indecisive reason', 'a reason affected by indecision', which is one of the kinds of *hetvābhāsa*. This kind of *hetvābhāsa* is dealt with in *NS* 1, 2, 5: *anaikāntikaḥ savyabhicāraḥ* and *Bh: vyabhicāra ekatrāvyavasthitiḥ/ saha vyabhicāreṇa vartlate iti savyabhicāraḥ / nidarśanam—nityaḥ śabdo 'sparśatvāt, sparśavān kumbho 'nityo dṛṣṭaḥ na ca tathā sparśavān śabdas tasmād asparśatvān nityaḥ śabda iti / dṛṣṭānte sparśavattvam anityatvaṃ ca dharmau na sādhyasādhanabhūtau gṛhyete sparśavāṃścānur nityaśceti / ātmādau ca dṛṣṭānte 'udāharaṇasādharmyāt sādhyasādhanaṃ hetuḥ'* (1, 1, 34) *iti asparśatvād iti hetur nityatvaṃ vyabhicarati, asparśā buddhir anityā ceti / evaṃ dvividhe 'pi dṛṣṭānte vyabhicārāt sādhyasādhanabhāvo nāstīti lakṣaṇābhāvād ahetur iti / nityatvam apyeko 'ntaḥ anityatvam apyeko 'ntaḥ ekasminn ante vidyata iti ekāntikaḥ viparyayād anaikāntikaḥ ubhayāntavyāpakatvād iti.*

Section LXII

1. Cf. note 1 of the translation of Section XLVIII.

Section LXIII

1. This opinion of Nāgārjuna has been expressed at the end of the last paragraph of Section LXI.

The two kinds of *hetvābhāsa* (inconclusive and contradictory) are connected in the refutation.

2. This opinion of Nāgārjuna has been expressed in Section LXI (in the beginning of the last paragraph of our translation).

Section LXIV

1. *NS* 1, 2, 6, which contains a definition of a contradictory reason, is quoted in our commentary of this Section.
2. Cf. the texts of *TŚ* quoted in note 7 of the translation of Section XV.

Section LXV

1. *NS* 1, 2, 9 defines this kind of *hetvābhāsa: kalatyayāpadiṣṭaḥ kālātītaḥ* and *Bh: kālātyayena yukto yasyārthaikadeśo 'padiśyamānasya sa kālātyayāpadiṣṭaḥ kālātīta ityucyate.*

The *kālātīta* ('whose time has passed away') *hetvābhāsa* is also connected with the *viruddha* ('contradictory') *hetvābhāsa*.

2. Has ceased to be; is not anymore; does not exist. The meaning of this Sūtra is not very clear on account of the use of the word '*ḥdas pa*' (*atīta*) four times. We have understood it in this sense : the past has ceased to be, does not exist; a reason whose time has passed away belongs to the past; consequently, it does not exist anymore.
3. Cf. *ŚŚ*, p. 174*b*, lines 16-18 (Tucci's translation p. 42) (against the cause and effect being one): The time, when (the pot) is a rounded clod of earth, is present; the

time when it is not yet a pot is future; the time when it is earth is past. If cause and effect are one, then, in the round clod there must be the pot and the earth, and therefore the three times would be one.

Cf. also Nāgārjuna's *Śū* 29 and note 116 of our edition: Because they do not remain, because they are admitted one in relation to the other, because they are inferred, because they cannot be admitted as a substance, because things do not exist, the three times do not exist, they are only an idea.

4. Cf. *MMK* 19, 1-3: *pratyutpanno 'nāgataśca yadyatītam apekṣya hi / pratyutpanno 'nāgataśca kāle 'tīte bhaviṣyataḥ // pratyutpanno 'nāgataśca na stas tatra punar yadi / pratyutpanno 'nāgataśca syātāṃ katham apekṣya tam // anapekṣya punaḥ siddhir nātītaṃ vidyate tayoḥ / pratyutpanno 'nāgataśca tasmāt kālo na vidyate //* and 6 : *bhāvaṃ pratītya kālaścet kālo bhāvād ṛte kutaḥ / na ca kaścana bhāvo 'sti kutaḥ kālo bhaviṣyati //*

Section LXVII

1. Has ceased to be, does not exist anymore.

Cf. *TŚ*, p. 30*a*, lines 2-3 (Tucci's Sanskrit translation p. 8, line 16): *sarve śabdā yadā mukhān nirgatās tadā nāṣṭā(ḥ)*, already quoted in note 1 of our translation of Section XLVIII.

2. Cf. MMK 19, 1-3, quoted in note 4 of our translation of Section LXV; and Nāgārjuna's *Śū* 29, quoted in notes 4 and 3 of our translation of Section LXV.

Section LXVIII

1. The new category '*chala*', 'sophism' is connected with all the categories refuted till now.

2. *i.e.* Nāgārjuna has maintained his refutation in the level of *padārthas.*

Section LXIX

1. About *jāti*, 'irrelevant rejoinder', in *NS*, see our commentary where the pertinent texts are transcribed.

2. Nāgārjuna has adduced numerous refutations (which the opponent considers irrelevant) against the opponent's ascertained thesis. So the opponent can affirm that the behaviour of Nāgārjuna authorizes him to say that, through Nāgārjuna's refutations, the arising of irrelevant objections has taken place. In this way the category '*jāti*', that is now examined, is connected with the previous ones.

3. Cf. Nāgārjuna's *Śū* 4: (Something) existent cannot be born, since it is (already) existent; (something) inexistent (can)not (be born), since it is inexistent; (something) existent and inexistent (at the same time) (can)not (be born), since (both concepts) are contradictory between themselves. Because birth does not exist, neither permanence nor destruction exist.

MMK 7, 20: *sataśca tāvad utpattir asataśca na yujyate / na sataścāsataśceti pūrvam evopapāditam //* ; cf. *MMK* 1, 3 and Buddhapālita's text quoted by Candrakīrti *ad locum.*

ŚŚ, text quoted in note 7 of our translation of Section XII.

Section LXX

1. This sentence connects the new category, that comes into discussion, the reiterative argumentation (*punarukta* or *punarvacana,* one of the *nigrahasthānas*) with all the previous categories already refuted by Nāgārjuna.

2. For the *nigrahasthānas* in the *NS* see our commentary, where the pertinent texts are quoted.

3. Cf. texts quoted in note 3 of our translation of Section LXIX.

4. On the momentariness argument see note 1 of the translation of Section XLVIII.

Section LXXI

1. The similarity of the *jāti* with the *nigrahasthānas* constitutes the link between the two categories.

ABBREVIATIONS AND REFERENCES

Abhidharmakośa of Vasubandhu, ed. P. Pradhan, Patna, Jayaswal Research Institute, 1967.

Amarasiṃha, *Amarakośa*, ed. A.R. Ramanathan, Vol. II, Adyar, The Adyar Library, 1978.

Annambhaṭṭa, *Tarkasaṃgraha*, Bombay, Bombay Sanskrit Series, 1930.

Āryadeva, *Pai lun = Śataśāstra in Taishō* XXXII, 1569.

Asaṅga, *Abhidharmasamuccaya*, ed. P. Pradhan, Santiniketan, Viśvabharati Studies, 1950.

Bh = Vātsyāyana's *Bhāṣya* of *NS* See *Nyāyadarśanam.*

Bhaduri, S., *Studies in Nyāya-Vaisesika Metaphysics*, Poona, Bhandarkar Oriental Research Institute, 1975.

Bhartṛhari, *Vākyapadīya*, (*Khaṇḍa I*), ed. K.A. Subramania Iyer, Poona, Deccan College, 1966.

Bhattacharya, K., 'On the Relationship Between the Vigrahavyāvartanī and the Nyāyasūtra-s', in *The Journal of Indo-European Studies*, Vol. 5, No. 3, Fall 1977, pp. 265-73.

——— *The Dialectical Method of Nāgārjuna* (*Vigrahavyāvartanī*), Delhi, Motilal Banarsidass, 1978.

Bhavya (?), *Madhyamakaratnapradīpa*, in *Sde-dge* edition; *Tōhoku* 3854.

Bijalwan, C.D., *Indian Theory of Knowledge, Based upon Jayanta's Nyāyamañjarī*, New Delhi, Heritage Publishers, 1977.

Böhtlingk, O. and Roth, R., *Sanskrit-Wörterbuch*. Tokyo, Meicho-Fukyū-Kai, 1976.

Bronkhorst, J., 'Nāgārjuna and the Naiyāyikas' in *JIP*, Vol. 13, No. 2, June, 1985, pp. 107-32.

BTI = *Buddhist Text Information*, ed. by R.A. Gard, quarterly, Stony Brook, The Institute for Advanced Studies of World Religions, 1974.

Buston, *History of Buddhism (Chos ḥbyung), I. Part, The Jewelry of Scripture*, translated by E. Obermiller, Heidelberg, O. Harrassowitz, 1931 (Reprint: Suzuki Research Foundation).

Candrakīrti, *Madhyamakaśāstrastuti*, 'La Madhyamakaśāstrastuti, de Candrakīrti', ed. J.W. de Jong, in *Oriens Extremus*, 9, 1, Februar, 1962, pp. 47-56.

——— *Prasannapadā*, in Nāgārjuna's *Mūlamadhyamakakārikās*, ed. L. de la Vallée Poussin.

Carakasaṃhitā of Agniveśa, ed. by Vaidya Jādavaji Trikamji Āchārya, Delhi, Munshiram Manoharlal, 1981.

Catalogue = *A Catalogue and Index of the Tibetan Tripiṭaka*, Peking Edition, ed. D.T. Suzuki, Tokyo, Suzuki Research Foundation, 1962.

C = Cone edition of the Tibetan Buddhist Canon: Microfiches of the Institute for Advanced Studies of World Religions, State University of New York at Stony Brook, U.S.A.

Chatterjee, A.K., *The Yogācāra Idealism*, Varanasi, Banaras Hindu University, 1962.

Comparative List = *A Comparative List of the Tibetan Tripitaka of Narthang Edition (Bstan Ḥgyur Division) with the Sde-Dge Edition*, Compiled by Taishun Mibu, Tokyo, 1967.

D = Sde-dge edition of the Tibetan Buddhist Canon. See Sde dge.

DD = Sde-dge edition from Delhi. See Sde-dge.

D'Almeida, A., *Nyāya Philosophy, Nature and Validity of Knowledge*, Alwaye, (Kerala, India), Pontificial Institute of Theology and Philosophy, 1973.

Dasgupta, S., *A History of Indian Philosophy*, Vol. II, Cambridge, The University Press, 1932.

Dīgha Nikāya, ed. J. Kashyap, Nālandā, Nālandā Devanāgarī-Pāli-Series.

Dignāga, Ālambanaparīkṣā, see Tola, F. and Dragonetti, C.

Dragonetti, C., 'On Śuddhamati's Pratītyasamutpādahṛdayakārikā and on Bodhicittavivaraṇa', in *WZKS*, Band XXX, 1986, pp. 109-22.

Fang pien hsin lun (= *Upāyahṛdaya, Prayogasāra*) in *Taishō* Vol. XXXIII, 1632, and in H. Ui's *Indo Tetsugaku Kenkyū II*, pp. 473-585. Cf. note 12 of our Introduction.

Franco, E. 'Studies in the Tattvopaplavasiṃha', in *JIP* Vol. 11, No. 2, June, 1983, pp. 147-66.

——— 'Studies in the Tattvopaplavasiṃha II, The Theory of Error', in *JIP* Vol. 12, No. 2, June 1984, pp. 105-38.

——— Perception, Knowledge and Disbelief: A Study of Jayarāśi's

Scepticism, Stuttgart, F. Steiner, 1987.

Gard, R.A., 'On the Authenticity of the Pai-Lun and Shih-Erh-Men-Lun', in *Indogaku Bukkyōgaku Kenkyū* Vol. 2, No. 2, March, 1954, pp. 751-42.

Gautama. See *Nyāyadarśana.*

Granoff, Ph. E., *Philosophy and Argument in Late Vedānta: Śrī Harṣa's Khaṇḍanakhaṇḍakhādya,* Dordrecht, Reidel, 1978.

Hara, M., Review of *Pāśupata Sūtram with Pañchārtha-Bhāṣya of Kauṇḍinya* by Haripada Chakraborti, Calcutta, Academic Publishers, 1970, in *Indo-Iranian Journal* XVI, 1, 1974, pp. 57-80.

Hulin, M., *Sāṃkhya Literature,* Wiesbaden, O. Harrassowitz, 1978.

Iyer, S., *Bhartṛhari,* Poona, Deccan College, 1969.

Jacob, G.A., *A Handful of Popular Maxims,* Delhi, Nīrājanā, 1983.

Jayarāśi, *Tattvopaplavasiṃha* of Jayarāśi Bhaṭṭa, ed. Sukhlalji Sanghavi and Rasiklal C. Parikh, Baroda, Gaekwad's Oriental Series, 1940.

Jhā, G., *The Prābhākara School of Pūrva Mīmāṃsā,* Delhi, Motilal Banarsidass, 1978.

JIP = *Journal of Indian Philosophy.*

Johnston, E. H., and Kunst, A., 'The Vigrahavyāvartanī of Nāgārjuna', in *Melanges Chinois et Bouddhiques* IX, 1948-51, pp. 99-152.

Ju shih lun (= *Tarkaśāstra*) in *Taishō* Vol. XXXIII, 1633. Cf. note 13 of our Introduction.

Kajiyama, Y., 'Kōha Ron to Seirikyō', in *Indogaku Bukkyōgaku Kenkyū* Vol. V, No. 1, January 1957, pp. 192-95.

——— Japanese translation of the *Vaidalya,* in *Daijō Butten* 14, pp. 185-229.

——— 'The Vaidalyaprakaraṇa of Nāgārjuna', in *Indogaku Shiron Shū,* 1965, 6-7, pp. 129-55.

Kangle, R.P., ed. *Kauṭilīya Arthaśāstra,* Bombay, University of Bombay, 1960-65.

Keith, A.B., *The Karma-Mīmāṃsā,* Delhi, Oriental Books Reprint Corporation, 1978.

——— *Indian Logic and Atomism,* Delhi, Oriental Books Reprint Corporation, 1977.

Kunjunni Raja, K., *Indian Theories of Meaning*, Madras, The Adyar Library, 1969.

Lamotte, E., *Le Traité de la Grande Vertu de Sagesse*, Tome III, Louvain, Institut Orientaliste, 1970.

Larson, G.J., *Classical Sāṃkhya*, Delhi, Motilal Banarsidass, Second Edition, 1979.

Lindtner, Ch., *Nagarjuniana*, Copenhagen, Akademisk Forlag, 1982.

Mādhava, *Sarvadarśanasaṃgraha*, ed. by Isvarachandra, Calcutta, Bibliotheca Indica, 1958.

Maitreya, *Madhyāntavibhāga-bhāṣya*, Tokyo, Suzuki Research Foundation, 1964.

Matilal, B.K., *Nyāya-Vaiśeṣika*, Wiesbaden, O. Harrassowitz, 1977.

——— *The Navya-Nyāya Doctrine of Negation*, Cambridge Mass., Harvard University Press, 1968.

MMK= Nāgārjuna, *Mūlamadhyamakakārikās*, ed. L. de la Vallée Poussin, Osnabrück, Biblio-Verlag, 1970.

Mochizuki, Shinko, *Bukkyō Dai Jiten*, Tokyo, Sekai Seiten Kankō Kyōkai, 1960-1963.

N = Snar thaṅ edition of the Tibetan Buddhist Canon, in Tōyō Bunko, Tokyo. (Quite blurred).

Naudou, J., *Les Bouddhistes Kaśmīriens au Moyen Age*, Paris, Presses Universitaires de France, 1968.

NS= Gautama, *Nyāyasūtras.* See *Nyāyadarśanam.*

Nyāyadarśanam [Sūtras of Gautama] with Vātsyāyana's Bhāṣya, Uddyotakara's Vārttika, Vācaspati Miśra's Tātparyaṭīkā and Viśvanātha's Vṛtti, ed. by Taranatha Nyaya-Tarkatirtha and Amarendramohan Tarkatirtha, Delhi, Munshiram Manoharlal, 1985.

NSBh = *Nyāyasūtra's Bhāṣya.* See *Nyāyadarśanam.*

NSVārtt = Uddyotkara's *Vārttika* of *NS.* See *Nyāyadarśanam.*

Nyāyapraveśa, ed. A.B. Dhruva, Baroda, Oriental Institute, 1968.

Oberhammer, G., 'Ein Beitrag zu den Vāda-Traditionen Indiens', in *WZKSOA*, Vol. VII, 1963, pp. 63-103.

———'Notes on the Tantrayuktis', in *The Adyar Library Bulletin (Dr. V. Raghavan Felicitation Volume)*, Vols. 31-32, 1967-68, pp. 600-16.

P = Peking edition of the Tibetan Buddhist Canon: *The Tibetan Tripiṭaka Peking Edition*, ed. D.T. Suzuki, Tokyo, Suzuki Research Foundation, 1955-61.

Pai lun (= *Śataśāstra*) in *Taishō* Vol. XXX, 1569. Cf. note 20 of our Introduction.

Potter, K.H., *Encyclopedia of Indian Philosophies, Indian Metaphysics and Epistemology: The Tradition of Nyāya-Vaiśeṣika up to Gaṅgeśa*, Princeton, Princeton University Press, 1977.

Randle, H.N., *Indian Logic in the Early Schools*, New Delhi, Oriental Books Reprint Corporation.

Renou, L., 'Sur la Forme de quelques Textes Sanskrits', in *Journal Asiatique*, Tome CCXLIX, 1961, 2, pp. 163-211.

Ruben, W., 'Über den Tattvopaplavasiṃha des Jayarāśi Bhaṭṭa, eine agnostizistische Erkenntniskritik', in *WZKSOA*, Band II, 1958, pp. 140-53.

——— " 'Zur Frühgeschichte der indischen Philosophie', in *Beiträge zur Literaturwissenschaft und Geistesgeschichte Indiens*, Festgabe Hermann Jacobi, Bonn, 1926, pp. 346-57.

Ruegg, D.S., *The Literature of the Madhyamaka School of Philosophy in India*, Wiesbaden, O. Harrassovitz, 1981.

Śālistambasūtra = *Ārya Śālistamba Sūtra* etc., ed. by N. Aiyaswami Sastri, Adyar, Adyar Library, 1950.

Salomon, E.A., 'Scepticism or faith and Mysticism: A Comparative Study of Tattvopaplavasiṃha and Khaṇḍanakhaṇḍakhādya', in *Journal of the Oriental Institute* (Baroda), 8, 1959, pp. 219-33 and 349-68.

Scharfe, H., 'The Maurya Dynasty and the Seleucids', in *Zeitschrift für Vergleichende Sprachforschung*, 85 Band, 1971, pp. 211-25.

——— *Grammatical Literature*, Wiesbaden, O. Harrassowitz, 1977.

Sde dge edition; *Sde Dge Tibetan Tripiṭaka Bstan Ḥgyur*, preserved at the Faculty of Letters of the University of Tokyo, Tokyo, 1977 ff. and *Dbu ma' i skor: The Collected Commentaries and exegetic works concerned with the elucidation of the Madhyamika literature, translated from Sanskrit into Tibetan*, Vol. I, Delhi, Karmapae Choedhey, Gyalwae Sungrab Partun Khang, 1985.

Sempā Dorje, *Vaidalyasūtram*, Vārāṇasī, Tibbatī-Himdī Keṃdra, 1974.

Śrīharṣa, *Khaṇḍanakhaṇḍakhādya*, ed. L.S. Dravida, Vārāṇasī,

Chowkhamba, 1904-14.

Steinkellner, E., *Dharmakīrti's Pramāṇaviniścayaḥ*, Teil II, Wien, Der österreichische Akademie der Wissenschaften, 1979.

ŚŚ = *Pai lun or Śataśāstra.* See *Pai lun.*

Śū = *Śūnyatāsaptati.* See Tola, F. and Dragonetti, C.

Sugiura, S., *Hindu Logic as preserved in China and Japan*, Philadelphia, 1900.

Suśrutasaṃhitā, ed. Vaidya Jādavji Trikamji, Bombay, Pāndurang, Jāwajī, 1931.

Taishō = *Taishō Shinshū Daizokyō* (The Tripiṭaka in Chinese). Ed. by J. Takakusu, K. Watanabe, Tokyo, The Taishō Shinshu Daizokyo Kanko Kai, 1960 ff.

Tāranātha = *Tāranāthae de Doctrinae buddhicae in India propagatione narratio* (Tibetan text), ed. A. Schiefner, Petropoli, 1868 (Reprint: Suzuki Research Foundation).

Tōhoku = *A Complete Catalogue of the Tibetan Buddhist Canons*, ed. H. Ui and others, Sendai, Tōhoku Imperial University, 1934.

TŚ = *Ju shih lun* (= *Tarkaśāstra*). See *Ju shih lun.*

Tola, F. and Dragonetti, C., 'Dignāga's Ālambanaparīkṣāvṛtti', in *JIP* 10, 1982, pp. 105-34.

Tola, F., 'Tres concepciones del hombre en la filosofia de la India', in *Pensamiento*, Vol. 42, Madrid, 1986.

Tola, F. and Dragonetti, C., 'Some Remarks on Bhartṛhari's Concept of *Pratibhā*, in *JIP* (forthcoming).

——— "*Anāditva* or Beginninglessness in Indian Philosophy", in *ABORI*, Vol. LXI, 1980, pp. 1-20.

——— '*Śūnyatāsaptati*, The Seventy Kārikās on Voidness (according to the *Svavṛtti*) of Nāgārjuna', in *JIP*, 15, 1987, pp. 1-55.

———, 'The *Yuktiṣaṣṭikākārikā* of Nāgārjuna', in *The Journal of the International Association of Buddhist Studies*, Vol. 6 No. 2, 1983, pp. 94-123.

——— 'The *Trisvabhāvakārikā* of Vasubandhu', in *JIP*, 11 (1983), pp. 225-66.

Tucci, G., *Pre-Diṅnāga Buddhist Texts on Logic from Chinese Sources*, Baroda, Oriental Institute, Gaekwad's Oriental Series, 1929.

——— 'Buddhist Logic Before Diṅnāga', in *Journal of the Royal Asiatic Society*, July, 1929.

Uddyotakara's *Vārttika*. See *Nyāyadarśanam*.

Ui, H., *Indo Tetsugaku Kenkyu*, II, Tokyo, 1939.

——— *Indo Tetsugaku Kenkyu*, V, Tokyo, 1929.

U = Fang pien hsin lun (= *Upāyahṛdayaśāstra or Prayogasāra*).

V = Vaidalyaprakaraṇa.

Vācaspati Miśra's *Tātparyaṭīkā*. See *Nyāyadarśanam*.

Vaidya, P.L., *Etudes sur Āryadeva et son Catuḥśataka*, Paris, P. Geuthner, 1923.

Vaiśeṣikasūtra = The Vaiśeṣikadarśana of Maharṣi Kaṇāda, ed. Nārāyaṇa Miśra, Varanasi, The Chowkhamba Sanskrit Series Office, 1969.

Vasubandhu, *Vijñaptimātratāsiddhi. Viṃśatikā et Triṃśikā*, ed. S. Levi, Paris, H. Champion, 1925.

Vātsyāyana's *Bhāṣya*. See *Nyāyadarśanam*.

Vidyabhusana, S. Ch., *A History of Indian Logic*, Delhi, Motilal Banarsidass, 1971.

Viśvanātha's *Vṛtti*. See *Nyāyadarśanam*.

Vogel, C., *Indian Lexicography*, Wiesbaden, O. Harrassowitz, 1979.

VV = Vigrahavyāvartanī. See Bhattacharya, K., and Johnston, E.H. and Kunst, A. Cf. note 6 of our Introduction.

Wayman, A., 'The Rules of Debate According to Asaṅga', in *Journal of the American Oriental Society*, Vol. 78, 1958, pp. 29-40.

Weber, A., *Indische Studien* IV, Hildesheim, Olms, 1973.

Williams, P.M., Review of Karl H. Potter's (ed.), *Indian Metaphysics and Epistemology. The Tradition of Nyāya-Vaiśeṣika up to Gaṅgeśa*, in *JIP*, Vol. 6, No. 3, November, 1978, pp. 277-98.

Winternitz, M., *A History of Indian Literature I*, New Delhi, Oriental Books Reprint Corporation, 1977.

WZKSOA = Wiener Zeitschrift für die Kunde Süd-und Ost-Asiens.

Yamaguchi, S., Japanese translation of the *Vaidalya*, in *Chugan Bukkyō Ronkō*, Kyoto, 1944, pp. 113-66.

——— 'Pour écarter les vaines discussions (Vigraha-vyāvartanī)', in *Journal Asiatique*, Juillet-Septembre 1929, pp. 1-86.

Yu = Yuktiṣaṣṭikākārikā. See Tola, F. and Dragonetti, C.